MUSIC IN MEXICO

A Historical Survey

Music in Mexico

A HISTORICAL SURVEY

ROBERT STEVENSON

New York
THOMAS Y. CROWELL COMPANY

PREFACE

This book is the first in English devoted to the history of music in Mexico. Several excellent manuals in English dealing with the history of the various other fine arts in Mexico—painting, architecture, and sculpture—are now available. The absence of a historical survey of music in Mexico is therefore a conspicuous example of neglect, especially when it is remembered how important music has always been in the total culture of our southern neighbor.

The basic research which was a necessary preliminary to the writing of the present book was made possible by a grant from the Mexican Government during 1950 under terms of the Buenos Aires Convention for the Promotion of Inter-American Cultural Relations. My cordial thanks are due the many officials in Mexico who made the traversing of the road over Mexico's musical past a richly rewarding experience. Without attempting an exhaustive list, I should like to remember here Dr. Silvio Zavala, Director of the Chapultepec Museum, Maestro Carlos Chávez, Director of the Instituto Nacional de Bellas Artes, Luis Sandi, Chief of the Music Section in the Instituto, Jesús Bal y Gay of the Music Section, Blas Galindo, Director of the Conservatorio Nacional, Dr. Jesús Romero, Professor of Music History in the Conservatorio, Dr. Gabriel Saldívar, eminent music historian, Julián Carrillo, veteran composer and former head of the conservatory, Jesús Estrada, organist of the Mexico City Cathedral, Julián Zuñiga, organist of the Guadalupe Basilica, Gerónimo Baqueiro Fóster, music critic, José F. Vásquez, composer, Miguel Bernal Jiménez, director of the Escuela Superior de Música Sagrada at Morelia, Mr. George T. Smisor, formerly of the Biblioteca Benjamín Franklin in Mexico City, Mr. Dorsey Gassaway Fisher of the American Embassy,

v

and Miss Dorothy Jester of the American Embassy. A mere listing of names is, of course, but a token. In the text and footnotes I have indicated more precisely the extent of my indebtednesses, which are everywhere extensive.

Among those in this country whose aid has proved invaluable have been Dr. Lota Spell, pioneer researcher in Mexican music history, Dr. Ethelyn Davis, sociologist and expert in Mexican antiquities, Dr. Steven Barwick, author of an authoritative Harvard dissertation on colonial music in Mexico, Miss Alice Ray, researcher in Puebla music history, Eduardo Guerra, formerly of Mexico City Union Seminary, Mrs. Hallett Johnson, El Paso, Texas, concert manager with extensive Mexican connections, Mr. Charles Seeger, Music Division Chief of the Pan American Union, Dr. Carleton Sprague Smith, Music Division Chief at the New York Public Library, Dr. Edmund King of Princeton University, Mr. Arthur Cohn of the Philadelphia Free Public Library, and Dr. Thomas E. Cotner of the United States Office of Education at Washington.

My thanks are also due staff members of several libraries both in Mexico and in the United States specializing in Mexican imprints: notably the Biblioteca Nacional and Conservatorio Nacional Library at Mexico City; and The Huntington and Bancroft Libraries at San Marino and Berkeley respectively in California.

CONTENTS

CONTENTS

Chávez. Chávez's Musical Style. Silvestre Revueltas. Candelario
Huízar. Blas Galindo. El Grupo de los Cuatro. Luis Sandi. Miguel
Bernal Jiménez. *Schola Cantorum; Nuestra Música; México en
el Arte*. Other Composers. Popular Music in Mexico Today. Foreign Contributors to Mexican Musical Life. Outlook for the Future.

MEXICAN CHRONOLOGY

Mexican history divides itself into three principal epochs: (1) the Pre-Spanish, ending at 1521, (2) the Colonial, extending from 1521 until 1810, (3) the Independence, lasting from 1810 until the present time. Many present-day Mexican historians add a fourth division to the above three, the Reform epoch which began in 1910 with the revolt against Porfirio Díaz.

A table of dates is supplied below; this table is an abridgment of a longer one found in Alfonso Teja Zabre's *Historia de México* (México: Imp. de la Secretaría de Relaciones Exteriores, 1935). All dates are in the Christian era.

200–400	Rise of Southern Maya culture in Guatemala and Honduras
500–600	Southern Maya culture reaches its zenith in such cities as Copan, Tikal, and Palenque
1000–1200	Northern Maya culture flourishes in Yucatan, a principal center being Chichen-Itza
1325	Tenochtitlán, principal city of the Aztecs, founded
1418–72	Nezahualcoyotl, poet-king of Texcuco
1440–69	Montezuma I ruler in Tenochtitlán
1482	Work begins on the construction of a great new temple at Tenochtitlán
1487	At consecration ceremonies for new great temple 20,000 captives are sacrificed
1503–20	Montezuma II succeeds as ruler of the Aztec "empire"
1519, April 21	Cortés arrives at San Juan de Uloa

1519, August 16	He leaves the coast and marches toward Tenochtitlán with a force of 400 infantry, 16 horses, 6 cannon, and 1500 Indian allies
1519, November 7	He arrives at Tenochtitlán; a week later he seizes the person of Montezuma, overthrows idols in the great temple, and sets up a cross in it
1520, June 29	Montezuma, after vainly trying to quiet his people, is slain
1520, June 30	Cortés flees the city in disastrous defeat: "Noche triste"
1521, August 13	Tenochtitlán surrenders; Cuauhtemoc, last ruler of the Aztecs, is taken prisoner
1523, August 30	First Franciscan friars land at Veracruz
1525, February	Cuauhtemoc executed during Cortés's expedition to Honduras because of his part in a conspiracy
1535	Don Antonio de Mendoza, first viceroy, arrives
1536, January 7	College of Santa Cruz de Tlatelolco for Indians opens with 60 students who are taught reading, writing, Latin grammar, rhetoric, philosophy, and music
1553, January 25	Luis de Velasco (I), 2nd viceroy, opens University of Mexico
1573	Work begins on Cathedral of Mexico (present structure)
1608	Luis de Velasco (II) inaugurates a large system of drainage works in order to reclaim Mexico City from marshland
1642	Juan de Palafox y Mendoza, Bishop of Puebla, named 18th viceroy
1692, June 8	Riot on account of corn shortage in the capital
1693	*Mercurio Volante*, first newspaper in New Spain, founded by Don Carlos de Sigüenza y Góngora
1711	Fernando de Alencastre, Duque de Linares, 34th viceroy
1742	3,900,000 inhabitants in Mexico
1767, June 27	Expulsion of the Jesuits
1789	2nd Conde de Revillagigedo, 51st viceroy
1792	Opening of School of Mines at Mexico City
1793	4,500,000 inhabitants in Mexico
1793–94	Mexico City has an approximate population of 135,000
1805, October 1	First issue of *Diario de México*, a daily newspaper
1808	6,500,000 inhabitants (Humboldt's estimate)
1809, September 9	Abortive conspiracy at Valladolid (now Morelia)

1810, September 15 and 16	Cry for independence at the village of Dolores where Miguel Hidalgo is parish priest: "Grito de Dolores"
1810, November 26	Hidalgo enters Guadalajara
1811, March 21	Hidalgo captured
1811, July 30	Hidalgo executed at Chihuahua
1815, December 22	Morelos, the other principal insurrectionary leader, executed
1821, July 30	Juan O'Donojú, 62nd and last viceroy, arrives
1822, May 18	Agustín Iturbide proclaimed emperor
1822, December 2	Santa Anna starts a revolt against Iturbide
1823, March 19	Iturbide abdicates
1824, October 4	Constitution of the Republic of Mexico proclaimed
1833, October 21	Univerity of Mexico suppressed
1834	7,734,292 population
1835, November 7	Texas Convention moves separation from Mexico
1836, April 21	Santa Anna, captured by the Texans at San Jacinto, promises Texas independence
1846, March 25	General Zachary Taylor advances on Matamoros
1846, May 13	United States Congress declares war on Mexico
1847, September 14	American troops occupy Mexico City
1848, February 2	Treaty of Guadalupe Hidalgo, ceding territory to the United States
1853, November 5	First electric telegraph operated in Mexico
1853, December 16	Santa Anna proclaims himself a dictator with the title of "Most Serene Highness"
1855, August 9	He is forced to leave Mexico
1856, June 24	Secularization of church property decreed
1860, December 28	Laws of reform closing monasteries, convents, secularizing church property, establishing civil marriage
1863, May 31	President Benito Juárez forced to leave Mexico City
1863, June 7	French army enters Mexico City
1864, May 28	Maximilian and Carlotta arrive at Veracruz
1866, December 18	French troops begin to leave Mexico
1867, June 19	Maximilian, Miramón, and Mejia, shot at Querétaro
1867, July 21	Benito Juárez reestablishes his government at Mexico City
1869, September 16	Opening of railroad from Mexico City to Puebla
1869	8,743,614 population
1871, November 8	Revolt led by Porfirio Díaz
1872, July 18	Juárez dies
1876, November 26	Díaz president of Mexico

1910, November 20	Revolt at Chihuahua and Puebla
1911, May 25	Díaz leaves Mexico City
1911, July 7	Francisco I. Madero enters Mexico City in triumph
1913, February 22	Madero killed
1917, May 1	Venustiano Carranza president
1920, May 21	Carranza killed
1921	14,234,780 population
1924, December 1	General Plutarco Calles president
1934, November 30	General Lázaro Cárdenas president
1938, March 18	Expropriation of American and British oil properties
1940, December 1	General Avila Camacho president
1942, May 28	War declared against Germany, Italy, and Japan
1946, December 1	Miguel Alemán president
1950	25,706,458 population
1952, December 1	Adolfo Ruiz Cortines president

A GUIDE TO PRONUNCIATION

Spanish words

a: as in "father"

c: as a *k* before *a, o, u;* as an *s* before *e, i*

ch: as in "*ch*in"

e: as in "v*e*in"

g: hard as in "*g*as" before *a, o, u;* as an *h* before *e, i*

h: always silent

i: as in "mach*i*ne"

j: as in "Nava*j*o" (like a strong *h*)

ll: like *y* in "*y*ou"

ñ: like *ny* in "ca*ny*on"

qu: like *k*

u: as in "r*u*de"

Indian words are all transliterations and are therefore to be pronounced according to the rules for the pronunciation of Spanish words.

MUSIC IN MEXICO

A Historical Survey

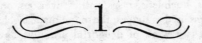

EARLY ABORIGINAL MUSIC
IN MEXICO

"ANCIENT" MEXICAN MUSIC AT THE MUSEUM OF MODERN ART

The first attempt to present an organized historical survey of Mexican music to the American public occurred as recently as 1940. During May of that year the Museum of Modern Art in New York city sponsored a series of programs containing representative works from each of the principal epochs in Mexican history. During the same month the Columbia Corporation recorded an album of selected orchestral pieces from the series. The concerts for those who heard them, and later the recordings for the wider public, were important not only because they proved Mexican achievements in music could match Mexican achievements in the other arts. They were significant also because they showed that Mexican music, like painting and sculpture in that country, had spoken most powerfully when inspired by the aboriginal, rather than the Hispanic, forces in Mexican cultural tradition.

The selections presented in the museum concerts which were felt most aptly to express Mexico's own indigenous spirit were Luis Sandi's *Yaqui Music*, Carlos Chávez's *Danza á Centeotl* from the Aztec ballet *Los Cuatro Soles*, and Chávez's Aztec evocation, *Xochipilli-Macuilxochitl*. In this last piece Chávez, by using instruments constructed in facsimile of those known to have been used by the pre-Conquest Mexicans, sought to recapture the sonorities that characterized pre-Spanish music. Howard Taubman in describing *Xochipilli-Macuilxochitl* for the *New York Times* wrote:

1

Mr. Chavez scored the work for copies of archaeological instruments: flutes, teponaztlis, huehuetls, rasps, rattles, whistles, and trombone. The last instrument was used to suggest the sound made by blowing into a conch shell. The result is a work of delightful primitive flavor, employing its strange instrumental resources with rare effect.

The music editor of *Time* magazine spoke in similar terms: "Flutes and pipes shrilled and wailed, a trombone (substituting for the snail shell) neighed an angular melody, to the spine-tingling thrump-and-throb of drums, gourds, rattles. . . . *Xochipilli-Macuilxochitl* sounded almost as primitive as Stravinsky."

Much music of a more conventionalized type was, of course, presented during the Museum of Modern Art Mexican series. In order to show the kind of music popular in Mexico during the nineteenth century two medleys were played, and in addition a Mass for four voices with orchestra by the colonial composer, Don José Aldana, was sung. But this Aldana *Mass,* because it was thought to sound altogether too much like some such joyous Haydn Mass as the *Mariazellermesse,* was passed over with only a perfunctory gesture in the press reviews and was not released in the Columbia album of recordings.

A study of the press comments along with a survey of the numbers actually recorded proves conclusively that none of the colonial or nineteenth century music was most favored. Rather the music chosen by critics and public with considerable unanimity was that which was thought to show the least traces of European influence. *Xochipilli-Macuilxochitl* with its teponaztlis and huehuetls, the *Danza á Centeotl* with its orchestrally-accompanied chorus chanting Mazahua melodies in Nahuatl (the language of the Aztecs), and *Yaqui Music* from the Sonora tribe which longer than any other resisted mission influences, were the compositions that created the most lasting impressions.

Simultaneously with the historic programs of Mexican music the Museum displayed an exhibit of the other arts in Mexico. "What really held the Manhattan gallery-goers spellbound was the enormous collection of gaunt, contorted monumental stone sculpture by long-forgotten Maya, Toltec, and Olmec craftsmen representing the first 1,500 of Mexico's 2,000 years of art," reported *Time* magazine. And the art critic, Edward Jewell, wrote in the *New York Times:* "In both the pre-Spanish and the modern periods Mexican art reached a cultural apogee."

As with the visual arts, so with music. The Museum concerts proved that Mexican music constructed along its most "ancient" lines was that which most strongly appealed to moderns.

CHANGING ATTITUDES TOWARDS ANCIENT ABORIGINAL MUSIC

If our new interest in "Aztec" music after these 1940 concerts seems a somewhat belated tribute to the culture of the aboriginal races who lived in Mexico, the reason for our tardiness is easily enough explained. In the United States we have necessarily awaited the lead of Mexican scholars, most of whom have themselves until comparatively recent times shown no marked interest in the music of the Aztecs, Mayas, or other ancient tribes who inhabited Mexico during the pre-Conquest era.

Mexican music historians can only be said to have begun the sympathetic study of ancient indigenous music during the 1920's. Before 1920 most Mexican writers on music were either content to repeat the strictures against Aztec music uttered by early conquistadores such as Bernal Díaz del Castillo, or were willing to follow the authority of later historians such as the eighteenth century Jesuit, Francisco Clavijero, who called Aztec music the poorest art of the pre-Conquest natives.

Bernal Díaz, because his astonishingly vivid accounts of the music played and sung by the Aztecs during their ritual sacrifices of Spanish prisoners-of-war were picturesque, was a favorite authority. Quite naturally Aztec music could have seemed to Díaz only dismal and horrible. He associated it always with the memory of his comrades-in-arms sacrificed on the altar-stone of their war-god, Huitzilopochtli. Even their battle music, exciting though he admitted it to have been, could not have won any tributes of praise from Bernal Díaz, the "true historian" of all that befell the conquerors. Locked in a life-and-death struggle with the Aztecs the conquistadores could not easily have discerned the higher elements in the opposing culture, even had they wished to be fair.

A modern historian comfortably remote from the scene can describe Aztec civilization in terms of their "well-planned cities with towering pyramids and impressive temples," of their "vast and brilliantly colored palaces with extensive apartments and terraces," of their "huge market squares and continually moving caravans of traders," of their "monetary system using gold and copper for currency," of their "highly developed system of picture writing," and of their "elaborate patronage of the arts"; [1] but what Díaz, who was closer to the scene, could see of their patronage of the arts afforded him less cause for rejoicing. He was a soldier; and the references in his *Historia verdadera* occur oftenest in the midst of his battle descriptions. His musical references include mention of the large Aztec war-drum (tlapanhuehuetl), of their instruments made of animal and human bone (tzicahuastli and omitzicahuastli), of their conch shell trumpets (tepuzquiquiztli), of their flutes (tlapitzalli), and of certain other instruments that are now less easily identifiable.

The following extracts, which are given in Maudslay's translation, show the kind of contact Bernal Díaz had with Aztec music:

> As we were retreating we heard the sound of the trumpets from the great Cue, which from its height dominates the whole city [the great Cue was the principal sacrificial temple, and stood on the exact spot where now rises the Cathedral of Mexico City]. We heard also a drum, a most dismal sound indeed it was . . . as it resounded so that one could hear it two leagues off, and with it many small tambourines and shell trumpets, horns and whistles. At that moment . . . they were offering the hearts of ten of our comrades and much blood to the idols that I have mentioned. . . .
>
> Again there was sounded the dismal drum of Huichilobos [Huitzilo-pochtli]. There sounded also many other shells and horns and things like trumpets and the sound of them all was terrifying. We all looked towards the lofty Cue where they were being sounded, and saw our comrades whom they had captured when they defeated Cortés being carried by force up the steps, and they were taking them to be sacrificed. When they got them up to a small square where their accursed idols were kept, we saw them place plumes on the heads of many of them . . . and they forced them to dance. After they had danced they immediately placed them on their backs on some narrow stones, and with stone knives they sawed open their chests and drew out their palpitating hearts and offered them to the idols. . . .
>
> The Mexicans offered great sacrifice and celebrated festivals every night and sounded their cursed drum, trumpets, kettle drums and shells, and uttered yells and howls. Then they sacrificed our comrades. . . .[2]

It is too much to expect that the conquerors who fought with Cortés should have been able dispassionately to have evaluated Aztec music. The memory of their own battles must surely have been too immediate and overwhelming. On the other hand certain sixteenth-century missionaries —the learned Franciscan, Bernardino de Sahagún, for instance, or the laborious Dominican, Diego Durán—heard Aztec music with different ears, and were therefore able to render a more favorable account of it. But the unfavorable comments of Bernal Díaz, rather than these favorable accounts, created the climate of opinion in which the older generation of Mexican music historians lived up until about 1920.

As late as 1917 a member of the National Conservatory of Music faculty, Alba Herrera y Ogazón, published under the official auspices of the Dirección General de las Bellas Artes a treatise on Mexican music entitled *El Arte Musical en México* in which she vigorously condemned Aztec music. In her way of thinking, Aztec music, since it exactly expressed the soul of a cruel and barbarous people, was a degenerate expression, and therefore unsuited to the refined tastes of civilized Europeans. The following two sentences carried the main drift of her argument against Aztec music:

> From the remaining exemplars of Aztec instruments preserved in the National Museum of Mexico, we may infer that the music of the people during the pre-Conquest era was as barbarous and harsh as were the ceremonies at which their music was heard. . . .
>
> The conch-shell, the Mixtecan tún, the teponaztli, the chicahuaztli, the sonaja, the Zapotec chirimía, and the Yaqui tambor, are not instruments capable of producing either alone, or in conjunction with each other, a grateful harmony: nor can the sound of any of them induce a spiritual response that is in harmony with presently accepted standards of behavior. . . .[3]

The only indigenous music she could praise, on the other hand, was a Tarascan melody which fortuitously resembled a theme from the third movement of Beethoven's *Symphony No. 7*. Her mentor, Gustavo E. Campa, a former head of the National Conservatory, had already discovered the note-for-note resemblance of the Tarascan melody in question, and since it exactly duplicated a theme already admired by cultivated musicians she too selected it for conspicuous praise. But this tendency to admire nothing in indigenous art unless some chance resemblance to a recognized European masterpiece could be discovered prevented her, as it prevented others in Mexico, from seeing the idiomatic virtues of aboriginal art.

After 1920, however, a change occurred. At a time when Stravinsky's "primitive" *Le Sacre du Printemps* and Prokofieff's "barbaric" *Suite Scythe* were revolutionizing art concepts in Europe, the much more

authentic primitivism and barbarism of native art in Mexico began to
win praise instead of censure. Within a decade after the publication of
Herrera y Ogazón's text, *El Arte Musical en México,* so complete a
reversal of opinion on the merits of indigenous expression had taken
place that Aztec music rather than being decried was being held up for
the first time as the worthiest music for Mexican composers to imitate.
Qualities in indigenous music which only a few years before had been
looked upon as basic defects suddenly began to be spoken of as merits.
Carlos Chávez spoke for the newer generation when he said Mexicans
must now learn to "reconstruct musically the atmosphere of primitive
purity." [4]

THE "AZTEC RENAISSANCE"

In a lecture delivered under the auspices of the National University
of Mexico in October, 1928, Chávez summarized the newer ideas on
aboriginal music which were soon to become regnant. In this lecture, entitled *La Música Azteca,* he advocated a return to pre-Conquest musical
ideals because pre-Spanish music "expressed what is profoundest and
deepest in the Mexican soul." As he saw it "the musical life of the
aborigines constitutes [not a regrettable but rather] the most important
stage in the history of Mexican music." Concerning the melodic system
of the Aztecs he said:

> The Aztecs showed a predilection for those intervals which we call the
> minor third and the perfect fifth; their use of other intervals was
> rare. . . .
> This type of interval preference, which must undoubtedly be taken to
> indicate a deep-seated and intuitive yearning for the minor, found ap-
> propriate expression in modal melodies which entirely lacked the semitone.
> [The pentatonic series which lacks the semitone was the type of five-note
> scale used by most aboriginal American tribes.] Aztec melodies might
> begin or end on any degree of the five-note series. In discussing their music
> one might therefore appropriately speak of five different melodic modes,
> each of them founded on a different tonic in the pentatonic series.
> Since the fourth and seventh degrees of the major diatonic scale (as we
> know it) were completely absent from this music, all the harmonic implica-
> tions of our all-important leading tone were banished from Aztec melody.
> If it should seem that their particular pentatonic system excluded any

possibility of "modulating"—which some feel to be a psychological necessity even in monody—we reply that these aborigines avoided modulation (in our sense of the word) primarily because modulation was alien to the simple and straightforward spirit of the Indian. . . .

For those whose ears have become conditioned by long familiarity with the European diatonic system, the "polymodality" of indigenous music inevitably sounds as if it were "polytonality." (Polytonality in music we might say is analogous to the absence of perspective which we encounter in aboriginal painting. The paintings of the pre-Conquest codices show us what this absence of perspective means.)

It seems evident that either the aborigines possessed an aural predisposition, or that an ingrained habit of listening was developed among them, which we today do not possess. They were thus enabled to integrate into meaningful wholes the disparate planes of sound that (in the European way of thinking) clashed in their music.[5]

These excerpts are of value because they summarize the findings of enlightened musical ethnology, but more especially because they show how completely Mexican musical opinion had reversed itself during the 1920's. Characteristics that previously had been looked upon as basic faults in the indigenous music of Mexico—its "minor quality," its "monotony," its "simultaneous sounding of different pentatonic melodies" which are out of tune with each other in our way of thinking, its fondness for "two or more rhythms the beats of which never coincide"—all these qualities previously thought of as crude distortions came now in the 1920's to be regarded not as defects but as virtues.

Thus it happened that at the very hour Diego Rivera was praising what the pre-Conquest natives had done in the visual arts and calling it an achievement actually superior to that of their conquerors,[6] Chávez was finding similar virtues in the music of the pre-Cortesian aborigines. If when he first began summoning Mexican musicians to heed the Aztec past his may have been a voice crying in the wilderness, it did not long remain so. He was so soon joined by others in his own generation, in fact, that to list their names would be to list nearly every well-known Mexican composer in our epoch. Such contemporaries as Daniel Ayala, Francisco Domínguez, Blas Galindo, Raúl Guerrero, Eduardo Hernández Moncada, Candelario Huízar, Vicente Mendoza, Pablo Moncayo, and Luis Sandi, have all followed Chávez's lead in extolling the virtues of indigenous music, and in copying indigenous models wherever possible.[7]

The three lines of investigation which have been most fruitfully pursued by Mexican scholars who during recent years have studied pre-Conquest music have been (1) the systematic study of the musical instruments which such peoples as the Aztecs, Mayas, and Tarascans are known to have used (2) the assembling of opinions on Aztec music from sixteenth-century authors who were friendly to Indian culture rather than opposed to it (3) the collection of melodies from certain out-of-the-way Indian groups which even today after the lapse of centuries may still preserve in their music some of the basic elements found in the pre-Cortesian system.

For more than a century the minute scrutiny of archaeological instruments has been a favorite method in the study of music from buried cultures. Among the pioneers in musical archaeology was the famous nineteenth-century encyclopedist and historian, F. J. Fétis, who based his conclusions concerning ancient Egyptian music on the results he obtained from the study of Egyptian flutes. Using Fétis's methods, such investigators as F. W. Galpin and Kathleen Schlesinger have in our own time conducted exhaustive studies in the music of the ancient Sumerians and Babylonians, and in the music of the ancient Greeks. The use such Mexican investigators as Daniel Castañeda and Vicente T. Mendoza have made of archaeological instruments is therefore no new idea.

After prolonged investigation of pre-Conquest instruments Castañeda and Mendoza gathered sufficient evidence to establish the following conclusions concerning the organography of the aborigines in Mexico:

I. *An essential sameness prevailed everywhere in the types of instruments used.* Obviously enough, the same instrument was given different names in the different languages spoken in pre-Conquest Mexico. But the Aztec teponaztli was the same instrument as the Maya tunkul and as the Zapotec tún. The Aztec tlapitzalli was the same instrument as the Tarascan cuiraxezaqua, and the Aztec huehuetl was the same instrument as the Maya zacatán. This sameness everywhere in the types of instruments used seems the more remarkable when we stop to consider the differences such ethnically distinct groups as the Aztecs, the Mayas, the Mixtecs, the Otomies, and the Zapotecs, showed in their handicrafts and plastic arts. Any archaeologist can readily discern the differences between Zapotec and Otomí pottery; but not between Aztec and Tarascan or Aztec and Maya musical instruments.

II. *The organography of pre-Conquest music was static.* On the walls of an eighth-century temple at Bonampak (located in what is now one of the most inaccessible jungles in the Chiapas) was found in 1947 a series of remarkably preserved Maya paintings from the Old Empire period. Interestingly enough, it was found that the same instruments were pictured on the walls of eighth century Bonampak that were still in use when Cortés arrived in the sixteenth century.[8] Examples of instruments that were pictured on the temple walls at Bonampak and that were still in use when the Spaniards arrived may be cited here (these instruments are listed not with their Maya names but with their Aztec names): the *ayotl* (a rasp made from the shell of a turtle; the player scraped the serrated shell with a two-pronged stag's antler); the *huehuetl* (an upright drum fashioned out of a hollowed tree trunk; stretched across the top of the drum was a jaguar skin which could be tightened or loosened to raise or lower the pitch; the player used his fingers rather than mallets); the *ayacachtli* (a rattle made from a gourd to which a handle was attached; the ayacachtli resembled the maracas used in modern Cuban bands).

III. *All pre-Conquest instruments were either idiophones, aerophones, or membranophones. Stringed instruments were entirely unknown in pre-Cortesian Mexico.* Among idiophonic instruments the following were characteristic:

The *teponaztli*

Best described perhaps as a two-keyed xylophone, this instrument in appearance resembled a wooden barrel enclosed at both ends. It was often covered with elaborate carvings representing birds, beasts, or grotesque human heads.

On top of it was cut an ⊥ shaped incision. The two tongues created by this incision each sounded different pitches—sometimes a major second apart, sometimes a minor or major third apart, or sometimes a perfect fourth or fifth apart. The hollow interior of the teponaztli acted as a resonator, and beneath the ⊥ shaped incision was cut on the bottom side a rectangular opening. This opening, like the opening of a piano lid, increased the volume.

As pictured for us in such codices as the Codex Florentinus, the teponaztli was usually placed on some kind of support so that the player could stand upright. The player used a pair of mallets tipped with rubber. These mallets were called *olmaitl*.

The Codex Florentinus and Durán's *Atlas* show teponaztlis not only with the conventional two keys, but also with as many as four or five keys.[9] Oviedo in his *Historia general de las Indias* (Seville, 1533) gives a picture of a three-keyed teponaztli of Central American provenience. Such an instrument may also have been known in Mexico even though no exemplar survives.[10]

Certain evidence concerning the use of multi-keyed teponaztlis can also be derived from the *Cantares en Idioma Mexicano*,[11] a collection of Nahuatl songs written down shortly after the Conquest. This evidence is, of course, literary and not strictly archaeological. Almost one hundred of the Nahuatl songs in this collection prescribed teponaztli accompaniment. The directions for accompaniment were written in the form of headings for each of the songs. Invariably in the songs prescribing teponaztli accompaniment, the directions called for more than two keys in the accompaniment. Sometimes three, sometimes four, and sometimes even five different keys are called for in the directions for teponaztli accompaniment which precede each song.

Either several two-keyed teponaztlis were used conjointly in the accompaniment of each song, or multi-keyed teponaztlis similar to those shown in the Codex Florentinus and in the *Atlas* of Durán were available for song-accompaniment.

The *omitzicahuastli*

A rasp made out of notched human or animal bone, the omitzicahuastli was the instrument most frequently used at commemorative ceremonies for the dead. The Spaniards considered its music to be "extremely doleful." Evidently the pitch was raised and lowered by scratching the notches faster or slower, just as a small boy nowadays scratching the teeth of his comb with a coin can make a species of music with varying pitches.

The *ayacachtli*

The head of this rattle was made either of a gourd filled with dry seeds, or was made of clay and filled with pebbles. In the codices the players of the ayacachtli are shown usually with a rattle in each hand.

Among aerophones the following types were notable:

The *tlapitzalli*

A four-hole flute made of either clay, reed, or bone, this instrument was capable of producing five different sounds. If recourse was had to overblowing or half-stopping, then the number of pitches that this recorder-type instrument was capable of producing exceeded five. Some investigators, such as H. T. Cresson [12] for instance, have assumed that Aztec flutists over-blew and half-stopped as a matter of course. If they did, it necessarily follows that they were able to play on their flutes a more elaborate type of melody than the mere pentatonic type.

An examination of ancient flutes now preserved in the National Museum of Mexico has produced several interesting results. The four holes were by no means so cut always that a pentatonic scale approximating our conventional d—e—g—a—b series was produced. For purposes of comparison the five-note series emitted by Flutes 129, 130, 131, 132, are shown.[13] Since the Aztecs had no inkling of our equal temperament system the pitches given here represent at best approximations. In the case of Flutes 130 and 131 it should be noted that only four different pitch-names were sounded.

Since the intervals emitted by stopping the successive holes depart from the ideals we have arrived at for the minor third and major third in Western music, it has been conjectured that the Aztecs were familiar with "in-between" intervals—that is to say, intervals larger than a minor third but smaller than a major third. Such in-between intervals occur, as is now generally known, in the slendro scale used in Javanese music, and also in other exotic scale-systems.

The *tepuzquiquiztli*

A conch shell trumpet, this instrument uttered with ease the third, fourth, fifth, sixth, and eighth tones in the harmonic series. Daniel Castañeda examined a conch shell trumpet in the National Museum and found that the tones easily emitted were a, d', f#', a', and d''.[14]

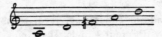

The Aztecs used in addition to their conch shell trumpets another type of trumpet. This second type of trumpet, made of clay or wood, was tubular in shape; trumpets of this second type often exceeded two feet in length. The Bonampak paintings show warriors in the thick of battle blowing on trumpets that were over a man's arm in length.[15]

To the membranophone class belonged the different varieties of:

The *huehuetl*

This instrument, a congener of the kettledrum, came in several sizes, each of which was designated by an appropriate prefix, such as *pan*huehuetl, or *tlapan*huehuetl. Since the huehuetls sounded a definite pitch, which like that of the modern kettledrum could be raised or lowered at will by adjusting the tightness of the drumskin, it would be incorrect to think of the huehuetls as simply a family of noisemakers.

The fact that the ancient Mexicans lacked stringed instruments need cause us no surprise if we constantly bear in mind that none of the aboriginal peoples of either North or South America possessed stringed instruments at the time of Columbus's discovery. Some investigators who have given considerable attention to Aztec and Maya achievements in mathematics, astronomy, picture-writing, and the various plastic arts, have thought it strange that the Aztecs and Mayas never stumbled upon so simple an idea as the use of the hunter's bow for a musical instrument. But for one reason or another, or for no reason at all, they did not. Just as the Nahuatl language may surprise a beginning student because it completely lacked such consonants as b, d, f, g, r, and v, so Nahuatl music may surprise a beginning student because it completely lacked string tone.

IV. *The Aztecs frequently inscribed their instruments with carvings which tell (symbolically) what purposes their instruments were intended to serve.* The significance of the hieratic carvings which Aztec instrument-makers inscribed on such instruments as the teponaztli and huehuetl can now be understood only by scholars who can decipher the hieroglyphs used by the Aztecs in their system of picture-writing.

Eduard Seler has undoubtedly contributed more to our present-day understanding of the hieratic carvings inscribed on Aztec instruments than has any other scholar of our time. In an article of his entitled "The Wooden Drum of Malinalco" [16] he explained the various carvings inscribed on a tlapanhuehuetl which he examined in the museum at Toluca. According to Seler, the carvings on this particular tlapanhuehuetl show a group of captured warriors who are being forced to dance to their own music, just prior to being sacrificed. These carvings on the Malinalco tlapanhuehuetl show the same type of scene which we find pictured in Durán's *Atlas* (Trat. I°, Lam. 19ª, Cap. 54).

Seler called attention to the drawing in Durán's *Atlas* because it can be readily understood (Durán's picture uses no glyphs). The Durán drawing shows several captured warriors who are being forced to dance to their own music before being dragged off to the sacrificial stone. Two captive warriors shake the ayacachtli while two others play the teponaztli and huehuetl. Standing over the captives and forcing them to dance and play are two of the victorious captors who carry clubs edged with obsidian knives.

After calling attention to the Durán drawing Seler went on in his article to show how the symbols and glyphs carved on the Malinalco tlapanhuehuetl tell exactly the same story of warriors awaiting sacrifice:

The carvings on the Malinalco drum run completely around the upper half of it. The upper half is divided from the lower half by a carved band running completely around the middle of the drum. The lower half is so cut that the drum stands on three legs, each of which is separately carved.

The upper half of the drum is on one side inscribed with a carved eagle and jaguar, representing warriors. The eagle and the jaguar carry sacrificial banners and face the sun. The upper half of the drum is on the other side inscribed with a figure representing Xochipilli-Macuilxochitl, god of music and dancing.

Xochipilli-Macuixochitl wears the feathers of the coxcoxtli bird. He holds in his left hand a flower and in his right hand a feather fan. Below his feet appears the glyph for music [*cuicatl*] in the shape of an ascending vapor. In close association with the glyph for music appears another glyph signifying "green jewel, costliness." He wears on his sandals the insignia of the god of dancing.

The raised band running around the middle of the drum shows the hieroglyph for war, *atl tlachinolli.* This raised band shows five separate stretches of rope. These five stretches signify the rope that binds the captive warriors to the sacrificial stone. Five shields appear also on the raised band around the middle of the drum.

The three legs of the drum show two jaguars and an eagle. The jaguars and eagle, like the jaguar and eagle on the upper half of the drum, are shown carrying sacrificial banners. Again, as on the upper half, these signify warriors who are about to be sacrificed.

Seler's explanation, which we have presented in abridged form, gives some idea of the complicated symbols Aztec instrument-makers inscribed on their huehuetls. Their teponaztlis were often inscribed with hieratic carvings of equal complexity.[17]

Another archaeologist whose contribution to our understanding of the symbology inscribed on Aztec musical instruments deserves mention is the renowned American ethnologist and archaeologist, Marshall H. Saville. In his monograph, *The Wood-Carver's Art in Ancient Mexico,* Saville cites at least a dozen instruments of the huehuetl or teponaztli class scattered in various museums which can today be profitably studied by those interested in the kinds of symbols ancient Mexican instrument-makers inscribed on their instruments. Over and over again in this particular monograph he repeats the statement that the carvings are like pages from the pre-Cortesian codices.

Depicting such things as "gods, houses, ceremonial objects, and dates," [18] any given set of carvings may reveal such important details of information as the following: the exact time and place the instrument was to have been used; the exact part it was to have played in the ceremonial functions at which it was heard; the length of time it was to have been sounded; the exact persons who were designated to play upon it.

TESTIMONY OF EARLY SPANISH HISTORIANS ON THE CHARACTER OF ABORIGINAL MUSIC

Earlier in our discussion of research techniques we listed three lines of investigation that have proved fruitful: the scrutiny of archaeological instruments, the re-evaluation of early Spanish opinion on indigenous music, and the gathering of melodic fragments from remote tribes. The more important conclusions reached by researchists working with museum instruments have now been listed, and we pass therefore to the second principal method of research, which involves a re-study of early Spanish opinion on aboriginal music.

The lengthiest excerpt dealing with Aztec music which has thus far been translated into English is an excerpt from Fray Juan de Torquemada's *Veinte i un libros rituales i Monarquía Indiana,* the original edition of which was published at Seville in 1615. The excerpt that has been chosen for translation is Chapter 11 of Book XIV, which bears the title, "Of the manner in which these Natives had Dances, and of the great dexterity and conformity they all had, in the Dance and in the Song." The English translation of this excerpt, which is well worth reading, can be found in *Renascent Mexico,*[19] a book published in 1935 under the auspices of the Committee on Cultural Relations with Latin America; the same excerpt can also be found in *Mexican Music,* a brochure edited by Herbert Weinstock and published in 1940 by the Museum of Modern Art at the time of the Chávez concerts.

In the opinion of Chávez Torquemada's description is of paramount value to the student of Aztec music. Of Torquemada's description Chávez said: "It will be helpful to transcribe the description . . . since nothing will be likely to give with better authority a clear general idea of the development of these arts [music and dancing] in Mexican antiquity."[20] And later Chávez said: "This narrative of Torquemada's is a very important document, illustrating our understanding of pre-Cortesian music."[21]

Torquemada (1565?–1624), who is not to be confused with his namesake who became a cardinal, wrote his narrative eighty years after the conquest; his description, because of its lateness, would have little or no value were it not for the fact that Torquemada, who was a Franciscan missionary, relied heavily upon unpublished descriptions of Indian life written by two predecessor Franciscan historians—Fray Toribio Motolinía (1490?–1569), who was among the first missionaries in Mexico, and Fray Gerónimo de Mendieta (1525?–1604), who if not a missionary of the first generation nevertheless wrote a uniquely valuable account of Indian life which he spent some twenty-five years in preparing. Since Torquemada relied upon these two, Motolinía and Mendieta, it therefore seems advisable to study not only the second-hand account in *Monarquía Indiana,* but also the unpublished accounts upon which he drew when compiling his book.

Despite the fact that "nothing will be more likely to give a clear general idea of the development of music and dancing in Mexican antiquity" than the accounts left us by such missionaries as Motolinía, Mendieta, and Torquemada, the missionaries as a group are often accused of having attacked everything Indian. Such missionary bishops as Zumárraga and Landa, first bishops of Mexico and Yucatán respectively, are often charged with having "wantonly destroyed every available record of Indian culture," and of having deliberately set out to "sow with Carthaginian salt" the prostrate Indian mind. This charge cannot be fully substantiated, however.

Our understanding of the Indian codices that do remain is, after all, founded entirely on the glosses the missionaries themselves wrote as marginal explanations of the pictographs. The marginal annotations of the missionaries really provide the "Rosetta stones" without which we could not even begin to read the codices. It is known that many codices collected in the eighteenth century by Boturini Benaduci perished simply through neglect, and the small number that now remain would be doubled or tripled if those that are known to have existed 250 years after the conquest were still extant. Where the missionaries themselves failed to provide marginal notations (as in the case of the Maya codices) we still today cannot read the picture-symbols.[22]

If a great many priceless records were burned it should be also at the same time remembered that missionaries such as José de Acosta (who was in Mexico in 1586) argued for the preservation of the Indian records. Acosta in his *Historia natural y moral de las Indias*, after complaining of the loss of Maya records, went on to say:

> The same has happened in other cases where our people, thinking that all is superstition, have lost many memories of ancient and hidden things which might have been used to no small advantage. This follows from a stupid zeal when without knowing or without wishing to know the things of the Indies, they say as in the sealed package, that everything is sorcery and that the peoples there are only a drunken lot and what can they know and understand. The ones who have wished earnestly to be informed of these have found many things worthy of consideration.[23]

The group of missionary pioneers who did "earnestly wish to be informed concerning the things of the Indies," and who did find "many things worthy of consideration," included not only Motolinía and Mendieta, but also Alonso de Molina, Bernardino de Sahagún, Diego Durán, Alonso Ponce, José de Acosta, and others too numerous for us to name here. Since the missionary evidence is in reality all that we have, if we wish to claim for Aztec music any cultural importance, it is well for us to give the missionaries their due. Certainly when such an account as Torquemada's is brought forward to support claims for Aztec musical achievement, it is only fair to give tribute where tribute is due by telling his identity, and also the identity of the missionaries from whom he compiled his account of Indian cultural achievements.

The missionaries came with the express idea of living and working with the Indians. They made it their business first to learn the Indian tongues. Insofar as they could possibly do so, they strove to understand the patterns of Indian life, and to accommodate their teachings to the Indian mentality. If not all as outspoken as Las Casas in denouncing the abuses of the encomienda system, nevertheless they all befriended the Indian in his struggle with the encomendero, and sought to alleviate the lot of the oppressed.

The conclusions which can be reached on the basis of missionary evidence concerning indigenous music are, because of their friendliness, generally of a favorable kind. Clarity will perhaps best be achieved if we list first the general conclusions their evidence enables us to reach, and then quote the passages upon which the conclusions rest. The passages documenting the general conclusions will each be prefaced by a short biographical account of the author who wrote the particular passage; with certain of the lengthier passages a short précis will be affixed defining its contents. Because our present study of music in Mexico is the first attempt at any account in English, we have chosen wherever possible to quote in entirety the passages upon which rest our conclusions, leaving the reader freedom to draw any other conclusions he chooses from the basic data here supplied.

CONCLUSIONS CONCERNING PRE-CONQUEST MUSIC DERIVED FROM EARLY SPANISH TESTIMONY

The following conclusions (some of which necessarily duplicate those already arrived at through the study of archaeological instruments) can be drawn from Spanish accounts of Aztec life:

I. Music had no independent life of its own apart from religious and cult observances; music as an art (in our sense of the word art) was a concept alien to their mentality.

II. All musical life was in the hands of a professionalized caste similar to the Levitical guild in ancient Hebrew times.

III. Training of an extremely rigid kind was prerequisite to a career in music; since music itself was always thought of as a necessary adjunct to ritual, absolutely perfect performances—such as only the most highly trained singers and players could give—were constantly demanded.

IV. Imperfectly executed rituals were thought to offend rather than to appease the gods, and therefore errors in the performance of the ritual music—such as missed drum beats—carried the death penalty.

V. Singers and players, because of the important part music played in Aztec life, enjoyed considerable social prestige.

VI. Despite this prestige, however, the names of musicians were not recorded, just as the names of poets—unless the poet were a royal personage such as King Nezahualcoyotl of Texcuco—were not preserved.

VII. Music was regarded as essentially a means of communal rather than of individual expression, and therefore concerted rather than solo music was the norm.

VIII. Instrumental performance was always conjoined to singing, insofar as we can judge from the descriptions of Aztec musical performance bequeathed us by the Spanish chroniclers.

IX. Certain instruments were thought to be of divine origin, and the teponaztli and huehuetl, for instance, were even held to be gods temporarily forced to endure earthly exile; the teponaztli and the huehuetl were therefore often treated as idols as well as musical instruments.

X. Not only were certain instruments thought to have "mana" in them—that is to say, mysterious supernatural powers—but also certain instruments were held to represent symbolically such emotional states as joy, delight, or sensual pleasure.

XI. Aztec music communicated states of feeling that even the Spaniards, habituated in alien patterns of musical expression, could grasp and appreciate; whereas much of the Indian music of tribes who lived in the territory now embraced by the United States meant nothing to European ears, Aztec music seems to have communicated in many instances the same emotions to Indian and European listener alike. Thus a sad song, as they conceived it, was sad not only in the opinion of the Indians who heard it and understood the words, but also in the opinion of the Spaniards who heard it and did not know the words.

XII. Every piece of music was composed for a certain time, a certain place, and a certain occasion; and therefore the musician needed a wide repertory if he were to satisfy the demands of the different days in the religious calendar. The religious cycle lasted 260 days, and just as the priests consulted the omens for each of the 260 days, so the players had to have appropriate songs ready for each of the different days.

XIII. The Aztecs possessed no system of music notation—or if they did, none that the Europeans knew anything about; therefore the Aztec musicians needed prodigious memories.

XIV. Musicians not only learned the old songs, but composed new ones. Creative ability was prized, especially in the households of those powerful caciques who were able to employ singers to compose ballads telling of their military successes.

XV. Though their music lacked string tone and was predominantly percussive, they had acute pitch sense and tuned their instruments (using their own system, of course) with considerable care.

FRAY TORIBIO DE MOTOLINÍA (1490?–1569)

Fray Toribio, a Franciscan who came with the pioneer missionary group of twelve, arrived in 1524. The Indians, seeing his miserable habit and noting that he walked barefoot, called him *motolinía*, meaning *poor*. This word was the first one that he learned and he henceforth adopted it as his own. Like Las Casas who lived to be ninety-two, Pedro de Gante who lived to be ninety, and Sahagún who also lived to be ninety, Motolinía lived to a great age. His two principal works still extant were written in middle life. The *Historia de los Indios* (finished in 1541) and the *Memoriales* (less easily dated, but presumably written about the same epoch in Motolinía's life) both remained unpublished until 1858 and 1903 respectively; both, however, circulated widely in manuscript. Nearly everything Torquemada said on aboriginal music was copied either directly from Motolinía, or from Mendieta (who copied Motolinía's description of pre-Conquest music); Motolinía's early arrival assures authenticity.

Motolinía hated the Spaniard overlords almost as much as did the crusading Las Casas; at one time Motolinía was even accused of petition-

ing for the recall of all Spaniards from Mexico (except the clergy) because the bad example and conduct of the laity impeded the work of
conversion. He undoubtedly favored the same exclusion of traders and
encomenderos that the Jesuits later favored (and successfully enforced)
in the famous Paraguay reductions.

In the following extract, which combines passages selected from Chapters 26 and 27 in Part II of the *Memoriales,* Motolinía offers his description of pre-Conquest music; he tells how music functioned in Aztec
life, what kinds of instruments they used, how the Aztecs rehearsed their
songs and dance music; how it was rendered in actual performance, how
musicians were evaled in Aztec society, and why composers enjoyed
special prestige.

One of the commonest occurrences in this country were the festivals of
song and dance, which were organized not only for the delight of the
inhabitants themselves, but more especially to honor their gods, whom
they thought well pleased by such service. Because they took their festivals
with extreme seriousness and set great store by them, it was the custom
in each town for the nobility to maintain in their own houses singing-
masters some of whom [not only sang the traditional songs, but] also
composed new songs and dances.

Composers skilled in fashioning songs and ballads were held in high
repute and were everywhere in great demand. Among singers those who
possessed deep bass voices were the ones most sought after because it was
customary to pitch the songs all extremely low at the frequent private
ritual observances held inside the houses of the principal nobility.

Singing and dancing were nearly always prominent features in the
public fiestas which occurred every twenty days. . . . The big fiestas
were held outdoors in the plazas, but the less important ones either in the
private patios of the nobility or indoors in the houses of the nobles.

When a battle victory was celebrated, or when a new member of the
nobility was created, or when a chieftain married, or when some other
striking event occurred, the singing-masters composed new songs especially
for the occasion. These singing-masters also sang, of course, the old songs
appropriate for the various observances in honor of their gods, or in celebration of historical exploits, or in praise of their deceased chieftains.

The singers always decided what they were going to sing several days
beforehand and practised diligently on their songs. In the large towns
(where there was always an abundance of good singers) those who were
to participate in a particular fiesta got together for rehearsal well in ad-

vance, especially if there were a new song or dance to be performed, so that on the day of the fiesta all might go off with smoothness and propriety.

The day of the fiesta a large mat was spread in the middle of the plaza, and on this mat they placed their drums [teponaztlis and huehuetls]. The musicians all gathered at the house of the chieftain and there dressed themselves for the fiesta. They came out of the lord's house singing and dancing. Sometimes they started their dances in the early morning and other times at the hour we celebrate high mass. At nightfall they re-entered the chieftain's house and there ended their singing either soon after dark, or occasionally at a much later hour, sometimes even at midnight [depending on the importance of the fiesta they were celebrating].

The two types of drum were: one, a tall round drum, bigger around than a man's body, and between three and four feet high. It was made of excellent wood, and carefully hollowed out inside. The exterior of the drum was painted; over the top of it was stretched a cured deerskin [or other animal skin]. By tightening or loosening a particular skin, the pitch could be raised or lowered within the limits of a fifth. The players changed its pitch with the changing pitch of the singers. The other drum cannot adequately be described in words without a picture at hand to show its appearance [teponaztli]. This other drum served as a deep counterbass; both had a fine sound which carried a great distance.

While the dancers were getting in position the players got ready to strike their drums. Two of the best singers acted as song leaders and gave the singers their pitch when they were ready to start. The large drum with the animal drumskin was played with the bare hands; but the other (like the drums in Spain) was played with sticks. The sticks had, however, a different shape from those used in Spain.

. . . . .

When they were ready to begin the dance three or four sounded some shrill music on their whistles, which was the signal to begin. Then the drumming began in a low, muffled tone, gradually increasing in volume. Hearing the sound of the drums at the beginning of the dance, the dancers [took the pitch of their song from the sound of the drums, and then] [24] started singing. The first songs were pitched low, sounding as if everything had been transposed down. Moreover the tempo was slow. The first song had to do with the particular occasion of the fiesta. Two leaders (as we already said) always began the singing, and the entire chorus following their lead then joined in singing and dancing. The whole crowd often united in a dance routine that would challenge the skill of the very best dancers in

Spain. More remarkable yet was the fact that not only their feet, but the entire body, head, arms, and hands, moved together in their dances. . . . Following their leaders in the singing and drumming, everyone changed position at the same instant, and with such precision that the best Spanish dancers marvelled upon seeing them in action, and greatly admired the dances of these people. . . . The dancers in the outside ring adopted a beat twice as fast as those who danced in the inside ring; this was done so that both outside and inside circles might stay together. . . . Those in the inner circle, perfectly coordinating their movements, shifted their feet and bodies more slowly than those in the outside circle, but it was marvellous to see with what graceful dignity they moved their arms.

Each verse or couplet was repeated three or four times. The whole ensemble of singing and playing not only was kept in tune, but the dancing rigorously followed the beat of the music. . . . Upon finishing one song, immediately the drum pitch was changed, and everyone stopped singing while several measures of rest intervened in the singing (although the dancing kept going). During this interval of time the drum tuning took place. Then the leaders began another song somewhat higher in pitch and in a faster tempo, thus ascending the musical scale as if a bass were to change by degrees into a soprano, and a dance into a scramble.

. . . . . .

At times they played their trumpets and also their flageolets; their flageolets often seemed not to be well tuned [according to our ideas]. . . . From the hour of vespers until nightfall their songs and dances became extremely lively, and the pitch of the songs ascended into a bright register so that the sound became extremely attractive, somewhat like that of our tuneful carols in fast tempo. . . . The crowds were [usually] immense, and the sound of the singing carried a tremendous distance.[25]

FRAY BERNARDINO DE SAHAGÚN (1500?-1590)

Fray Bernardino, also a Franciscan, pursued his studies at Salamanca University, where he early distinguished himself as a student of languages. He arrived in New Spain during 1529, five years after Motolinía, and immediately began studying Nahuatl, the language of the Aztecs. Although he lacked the advantages of boyhood association with the Indians which Fray Alonso de Molina possessed (Molina compiled the best Nahuatl dictionary of the century), nevertheless he made up for a late start with overwhelming industry. In time he became the most learned Aztecist of the century, and ethnology today owes him an incalculable debt. His *Historia General de las Cosas de Nueva España*, which he originally wrote in Nahuatl about the year 1547, and which he thirty years later translated into Spanish, provides an inestimable gold-mine of information concerning pre-Conquest life.

In order to compile this history he gathered together a group of sachems who still remembered pre-Conquest customs. With painstaking care he wrote down a compendious description of Indian life which so minutely set forth pre-Conquest customs that Sahagún's superiors refused permission for it to circulate; they feared the younger generation of Indians whom they were trying to wean away from idolatry would capture from it a vision of vanished glory, and become restive for the old ways. Because the *Historia General de las Cosas* was hidden away, it was finally forgotten, and not until 1829 was it brought to light and published.

Like most of the first generation missionaries, Sahagún was intensely interested in music, and even taught it to the Indians who attended the missionary college at Tlatelolco. His comments on Indian music therefore represent a more informed opinion than that of a mere dilettante. He appreciated Indian music sufficiently to prepare a collection of Christian hymns entitled *Psalmodia Christiana* (published at Mexico City in 1583), whose words in Nahuatl were fitted to already existing Indian tunes.

The first two excerpts presented here have to do with human sacrifices, and the part music played in the sacrificial system. One excerpt, which because of the interesting story it tells is frequently repeated in popularized accounts of Aztec life, concerns a handsome youth. After a year of perfect bliss he is taken to the sacrificial altar, and as he mounts the steps he breaks his flutes; each flute he breaks symbolizes some joy or happiness that has been his during the previous year of continuous festivity. The second excerpt offers a description of the sacrifice of a young maiden; the tecomopiloa, a musical instrument which must have been rare since archaeologists have unearthed no exemplars of it, is described in this second excerpt.

At the festival of the sixth month they sacrificed a handsome youth whose body was perfectly proportioned. . . . They selected for this purpose the best looking among their captives . . . and took great pains to choose the most intelligent . . . and one without the least physical defect. The youth chosen was carefully trained to play the flute well, and taught . . . how to walk about as do the nobles and people of the court. . . .

The one chosen for the sacrifice . . . was greatly venerated by all those who met him. . . . He who was thus chosen to die at the next great feast went through the streets playing the flute and carrying flowers. . . . On his legs he wore golden bells which rang at every step he took. . . . Twenty days before the feast . . . they married him to four beautiful maidens. . . . Five days before the sacrifice they worshipped the young man as one of their gods. . . . [After four days of preparation, they at last] took him to a small and poorly decorated temple which stood near the highway outside the city. . . . Upon reaching the foot [of the temple] the young man mounted the steps by himself. As he mounted the first step he broke one of the flutes he had played during the past year of his prosperity; on the second step, another, and so on successively until he had broken them all, and had reached the summit. There he was awaited by the priests who were to kill him, and these now grabbed him and threw him on the stone-block. After seeing him pinned down on his back with feet, hands, and head securely held, the priest who had the stone knife buried it deep in the victim's breast. Then drawing the knife out, the priest thrust one hand into the opening and tore out the heart, which he at once offered to the sun. . . . Thus ended the life of this unfortunate youth who had for an entire year been petted and honored by everyone. They said this sacrifice signified that those who possessed riches and pleasures in their lifetime would thus end in poverty and sorrow. (Book II, Chapter XXIV) [26]

[At the festival of Veytecuilhuitl] the dancing and singing of the woman [who was about to be sacrificed] was accompanied by the playing of an [unusual type of] teponaztli. [Unlike the ordinary teponaztli this one] had only one key on top [rather than the customary two keys. This single key on top was] matched by a similar key below it on the bottom side. To the bottom [key] was attached a cup such as might be used for drinking; for with this resonator cup the teponaztli produces a much stronger sound than if two keys [each sounding different pitches] are cut out on top, with none underneath. [This particular type of] teponaztli was called *tecomopiloa*, and it was so constructed that it could be fitted under the armpit of the musician carrying it. (Book II, Chapter XXVII) [27]

From the next short excerpt we learn that the young nobles in training for the priesthood at the Calmecac were required to learn vast numbers of hymns honoring the gods in the Aztec pantheon. The Calmecac was "a house of penance and tears, where nobles were reared to become priests of the idols." [28]

The fourteenth rule [of instruction] was to teach the boys all the verses of the songs to sing, which they called divine songs; these verses were written in their books by signs. (Book III, Chapter VIII)

In the next passage Sahagún offers a corroborating description of the fiestas in honor of the gods; since Sahagún's description differs in only a few details from Motolinía's the passage given below has been abridged. One interesting detail noted by Sahagún, but not by Motolinía, has to do with the capital punishment of musicians who made mistakes in performance. The meticulous preparation of the music cannot be wondered at if it was always true that a musician who erred was immediately withdrawn from the ensemble and executed.

> One thing that the chiefs took great pains with were the *areitos*, the dances which were festivals for the entire people. The leader of the singing first gave his instructions to the singers in his charge, and told them how to pitch their voices and how to tune them; the leader also told them what kind of ule [rubber] sticks they were to use in playing the teponaztli. He also gave orders for the steps and postures that were to be used in dancing. . . .
>
> Then they proceeded to the dance. If one of the singers made a mistake in singing, or if one of the teponaztli players erred in the execution of his part, or if one of the leaders who indicated the dance routine made a mistake, immediately the chieftain ordered him siezed, and the next day had him summarily executed. (Book VIII, Chapter XXVI) [29]

The last excerpt we offer from Sahagún's *Historia General de las Cosas* has often been quoted elsewhere; in it Sahagún tells some of the qualifications the Aztecs desired in an ideal singer.

> The worthy singer has a clear mind and a strong memory. He composes songs himself and learns those of others, and is always ready to impart [what he knows] to the fellows of his craft. He sings with a well-trained voice, and is careful to practice in private before he appears in public. The unworthy singer, on the other hand, is ignorant and indolent. . . . What he learns he will not communicate to others. His voice is hoarse and untrained, and he is at once envious and boastful. (Book X, Chapter VIII) [30]

FRANCISCO LÓPEZ DE GÓMARA (1511–1566?)

Gómara has suffered from the reputation of having lied. Bernal Díaz in writing his "True History" constantly berated him. Only in recent years has it been shown that Díaz himself was writing more of a *Relación de Servicios* than a precisely accurate account. As Díaz's own inflated reputation for strict veracity has declined, Gómara's has ascended.

Since Gómara was Cortés's own personal chaplain after about 1540, it has been thought his information concerning the conquest came largely from the conqueror himself. In describing the festival dances, Motolinía's description of which has already been given, Gómara said:

These two drums [teponaztli and huehuetl] playing in unison with the voices stood out quite strikingly, and sounded not at all badly. The performers sang merry, joyful, and amusing tunes, or else some ballad in praise of past kings, recounting wars and such things. This was all in rhymed couplets and sounded well and was pleasing.

When it was at last time to begin, eight or ten men would blow their whistles lustily. The drums were then beaten very lightly. The dancers were not long in appearing in rich white, red, green, and yellow garments interwoven with very many different colors. In their hands they carried bouquets of roses, or fans of feathers or of feathers and gold, while many of them appeared with garlands of exquisitely scented flowers. Many wore fitted feather-work hoods covering the head and shoulders, or else masks made to represent eagle, tiger, alligator, and wild animal heads. Many times a thousand dancers would assemble for this dance and at the least four hundred. They were all leading men, nobles and even lords. The higher the man's quality the closer was his position with respect to the drums. . . .

At first they sang ballads and move[d] slowly. They played, sang, and danced quietly and everything seemed serious, but when they became more excited, they sang carols and jolly tunes. The dance became more and more animated and the dancers would dance harder and quicken their pace. . . .

All those who have seen this dance say it is a most interesting thing to see and superior to the *zambra* of the Moors, which is the best dance of which we have any knowledge in Spain.[31]

FRAY ALONSO DE MOLINA (1515?–1585)

Molina was brought to New Spain as a small boy just shortly after the Aztec capital fell. His mother, who was soon left a widow, let him play with Indian children, and Molina therefore grew up speaking Nahuatl as a second tongue. His was the first dictionary of the Nahuatl tongue (first edition, 1555); this dictionary, a Spanish-Nahuatl and Nahuatl-Spanish dictionary, gives us several useful ideas (1) The Aztecs had no word simply meaning *music*, as we use that term; for music in the limited sense of singing they had a word, but none for music as a generic term. (2) Neither did they have a verb meaning *play*, in our sense of *play*ing on an instrument. (3) On the other hand, their language was immensely rich in specific nouns such as, for instance:

song sung by a soprano *tlapitzaualiztli*
song sung to compliment someone *tecuiqueualiztli*
song sung to insult someone *tecuicuiqueualiztli*
song sung to someone else *tecuicatiliztli*

and although they had no generic nouns meaning "musician," or "player," their language was extremely rich in specific nouns meaning "player on the huehuetl," "player on the teponaztli," "flute-player," "fife-player," "trumpet-player," and so on. (4) Their language was similarly rich in verbs with such varied specific meanings as "to sing in praise of someone," "to sing derisive songs," "to sing tenderly," or "to sing in a high voice." [32]

From Molina's dictionary, and from later dictionaries of the Nahuatl tongue, we can gather ample evidence to show that the ancient Mexicans wholly lacked our abstract idea of music as an art—an abstract idea, moreover, which in Western civilization originated as long ago as Pythagoras and Aristoxenus. If the aboriginal Mexicans lacked any abstract idea of music, it is of course a well known fact that their power of abstraction in other fields was limited also. Ethnologists, however, while pointing out the small number of abstractions the Mexican aborigines were able to make, have at the same time always called attention to the profuse number of concrete ideas they were able to verbalize. Music, then, according to the ethnologists, was only one of many life-experiences which they valued, but could not verbalize in any generic sense.

DIEGO DE LANDA (1524–1579)

Landa's *Relación de las Cosas de Yucatán* is the most complete account we possess of ancient Maya life. He has been described by the great Maya scholar, A. M. Tozzer, as a pioneer social anthropologist. No other Spanish writer of the sixteenth century, with the exception of Sahagún, so minutely described the social customs of the pre-Conquest aborigines. [33]

The Spanish penetration of Yucatán began in 1526, five years after

Cortés's conquest of Mexico; but because the lure of gold was not so potent in Yucatán the complete domination of the peninsula was delayed until twenty years later. Landa's *Relación* was written about 1566. Because of the burning of Maya writings, Landa has been known as the Attila of Maya culture, but he was in reality interested enough in it to provide the only key we possess to the Maya hieroglyphs.

Landa's enumeration of Maya musical instruments included:

> Drums which they play with the hand, and another drum made of hollow wood with a heavy and sad sound. They beat it with rather a long stick with a certain gum from a tree at the end of it, and they have long thin trumpets of hollow wood with long twisted gourds at the ends. And they have another instrument made of a whole tortoise with its shells, and having taken out the flesh, they strike it with the palm of the hand.[34] The sound is doleful and sad. They have whistles made of leg bones of deer; great conch shells and flutes made of reeds, and with these instruments they make music for the dancers.[35]

Landa's description of the Maya dances follows his description of their instruments. What he says about their dances tallies rather closely with Motolinía's and Gómara's descriptions of the dancing in Tenochtitlán. He says that men and women danced together only rarely. Erotic themes in pre-Conquest music are extremely difficult to find.

FRAY DIEGO DURÁN (1537–1588)

Durán, a Dominican missionary who immersed himself in Indian lore, was formerly thought to have been born in Mexico, but is now known from an Inquisition document (dated June 14, 1587) to have been born in Seville. His magnificent *Historia de las Indias de Nueva España*, like Landa's invaluable *Relación*, awaited the nineteenth century for its publication. Durán exactly dated his manuscript; the part of his history which we quote was finished in 1579. The *Atlas* appearing at the end of the history is actually a collection of pictures showing pre-Conquest customs; although the pictures post-date the Conquest they are considered authentic records.

In the extracts below Durán compares Indian and Spanish musical praxis; the second excerpt contains the earliest mention of the sarabande.

The old nobility all maintained professional singers who composed songs celebrating the important deeds of their ancestors . . . There were also singers who composed sacred songs in honor of their idols; these temple singers likewise received regular stipends. . . . Those who criticize Indian customs might well reflect that this custom of maintaining professional singers in no wise differs from the present-day practice of maintaining paid singers in the royal chapel, or a band of musicians in the chapel of the Archbishop of Toledo or of any other noble person. In New Spain there are yet today in certain towns members of the native nobility who still follow their ancient custom of maintaining singers. I myself do not think this old custom undesirable, but think rather that it conduces to good ends; for the traditions of these descendants of kings and chieftains are not unworthy. . . . Some of their songs that I have heard and some of their dances I have seen induced in me feelings of infinite sadness and melancholy [as I reflected on their vanished greatness].[36]

Since the young men were intensely eager to learn how to dance and sing well, and always wished to be leaders in the dancing and singing, they spent much time and effort mastering the particular types of body movement required. It was the custom of the dancers to dance and sing at the same time. Their dance movements were regulated not only by the beat of the music, but also by the pitch of their singing. . . . Their poets gave each song and dance a different tune, just as we employ a different tune when we are singing different types of poetry such as the sonnet or the *octava rima* or the *terceto*. Typical of the pronounced differences encountered in their dance music was the contrast between the solemn and majestic songs and dances performed by the nobility, and the lighter love songs danced by the youths. And still more different in type was another dance they performed which might have been derived from that lascivious sarabande which our own people dance with such indecent contortions of the body and such lewd grimaces.[37]

FRAY GERÓNIMO DE MENDIETA (1525–1604)

Mendieta came to Mexico as a youth of nineteen, and immediately began the study of Nahuatl, which he learned to speak with signal "elegance." He was commissioned by his order to prepare a history of the Indians and started the *Historia Eclesiástica Indiana* in 1571; the pressure of missionary duties, the involvement in unforeseen administrative responsibilities, and the interruption caused by a prolonged journey back to Spain, delayed its completion, however, until 1596.

Mendieta tells us (in the extract offered below) that the Aztecs ascribed a divine origin to their two most important instruments, the teponaztli and the huehuetl. The legendary account concerning the origin of these instruments runs like this: Teponaztli and Huehuetl were originally divine beings dwelling at the court of the Sun. A priestly messenger from earth invaded the heavenly precincts and poured forth in song the story of man's grief. The Sun, however, forbade his servitors to listen to the earthly messenger. Teponaztli and Huehuetl disobeyed the Sun, and for their disobedience were expelled from the heavens. They fell to earth and assumed the form of musical instruments. Ever since their expulsion from the skies they have assuaged man's grief with the sound of their music.

This legendary account is interesting if for no other reason than because it helps explain why the ancient Mexicans thought a magic power (having nothing to do with music) inhered in their instruments. Since they thought the teponaztli and huehuetl were actually divine beings temporarily condemned to earthly exile, they treated these instruments as idols. Even today the Indians in certain out-of-the-way places still hoard their teponaztlis, and venerate them as if they were sacred objects. The Church has, of course, tried to extirpate such vestiges of idolatry, but many contemporary Indians, like their pre-Conquest forbears, still ascribe mana to their teponaztlis and huehuetls; and the Church's campaign against idolatry has therefore not achieved full success.

Rodney Gallop (whose article on "The Music of Indian Mexico" appeared in the April, 1939, *Musical Quarterly*) reported several cases, all of which he had seen at first hand, involving the superstitious veneration of teponaztlis. According to Gallop, "There is a suspicion of idolatry in the reverence paid to the drums of San Juan Acingo, Tepoztlan, and Xico, which comes out even more strongly in other parts of the Sierras of Puebla and Hidalgo." Gallop continued by citing the case of an Aztec village, named Xolotla, where the chief sorcerer guarded a teponaztli which he kept wrapped in a garment, as if it were something human needing protection. The sorcerer, furthermore, called his teponaztli by a human name. "When the priest's back is turned this drum is sometimes smuggled into the village church and hidden behind the altar." [38]

The legendary account Mendieta gives also helps us understand how the Aztec priests acquired so terrible a stranglehold on the Aztec mind. In this story of the bringing of musical instruments as in other stories of other boons, the priests always pictured themselves as the bringers of every good gift man possesses. With music as with maize, the gift of the gods was only secured through the intercession of a priest in sorrowing man's behalf.

For the details of the legend which follows, Mendieta cited the authority of a pioneer Nahuatl grammarian, Fray Andrés de Olmos.

Seeing that they were utterly unable to prevail in their struggle with the newly-created Sun, the old gods of Teotihuacán in desperation decided to sacrifice themselves. Xolotl, the appointed sacrificer, opened each of their breasts with a large knife and drew out the heart; he then killed himself. By their deaths, the Sun's anger was appeased.

Each god bequeathed his sacred clothing to a priest who had worshipped him. Realizing the great weight of their responsibility for such sacred relics, the priests guarded the vestments most zealously. Their grief, however, on account of the deaths of their gods was not assuaged even though they now had in their possession the sacred vestments. Their grief instead of abating, in time grew insupportable, and they therefore decided to undertake a pilgrimage, hoping that somewhere they might find solace for their anguish.

After wandering about together for a time, they separated and one priest traveled toward the seacoast. When he arrived at the ocean he met there Tezcatlipoca, lord of being, who instructed him to proceed onward to the Court of the Sun, and there to beg the Sun for musical instruments. With songs and musical instruments man would be able fittingly to praise his new gods.

In order to assist him in this long journey to the Court of the Sun, various animals in the sea, among them the tortoise, the whale, and the sea-cow, formed themselves into a bridge so that the griefstricken priest might pass over them. When the priest arrived at the Court of the Sun he explained the motive of his visit. The Sun, however, not wishing to diminish his own retinue of followers, forbade any of his servitors to listen to the priest's entreaties.

But so eloquently and earnestly did the earthly messenger make his plea that two servants of the Sun, the one named Huehuetl and the other Teponaztli, disobeyed and listened. For their presumption in disobeying him, the Sun cast them forth from his presence in disgrace. They then accompanied the priest in his return to earth.

But the sound of the huehuetl and teponaztli must forever remain sorrowful; because forever they remember the sorrow they felt when first they heard the story of man's extremity, as the priest told it in heaven. If man's anguish because the gods of Teotihuacán are dead has now abated and if instead he has learned how to dance and make merry in song and dance, the sounds of the huehuetl and teponaztli still continue to remind him of the sighs Huehuetl and Teponaztli long ago breathed in heaven when first they heard the sad entreaties of the earthly messenger.[39]

SUMMARIES OF SIXTEENTH CENTURY OPINION

The best known writer on Mexican antiquities during the seventeenth century, Juan de Torquemada, said in his *Monarquía Indiana* (1615) little that had not already been said by his sixteenth century predecessors. It will therefore not be necessary to quote long passages from him or from such other later historians as Boturini Benaduci and Clavijero, both of whom like Torquemada summarized, rather than adding fresh information. Torquemada did, however, add a few glosses which must here be repeated: (1) He affirmed positively that part-singing of the kind practised in Spain was unknown in Mexico before the Conquest.[40] (2) He said that during their dances the Indians always sang in unison with the teponaztli tune.[41] (3) He stated that the teponaztli and huehuetl players during all the cult dances but one were placed where the dancers could see them, and thus better follow their beat—the one exception being the dance honoring the war-god, Huitzilopochtli. (4) He listed the instruments Montezuma particularly delighted in hearing at meal-time, clay-flutes, reed-flutes, conch shells, bones, and huehuetls, but said none of Cortés's men much cared for the emperor's favorite music, heard invariably at all the emperor's meals.

Among the scattered observations on Aztec music in Boturini Benaduci's 1746 *Idea de una nueva Historia General* the following is typical:

Not all of the songs sung in honor of the gods were accumulated from past tradition; the festival of Xochitl, for instance was solemnized with new songs in which it was forbidden to mix anything from older songs. . . .[42]

In this short passage, as in others, he merely confirmed from his own reading of Nahuatl codices a fact that Durán had previously noted. Francisco Clavigero, who wrote as lengthily on pre-Conquest music as Torquemada, seemed to say something new when discussing the different sizes of teponaztlis,[43] but as in the case of Torquemada's glosses, Clavijero's observation was founded on inference rather than fresh observation.

ABSENCE OF MUSICAL QUOTATIONS IN THE SIXTEENTH CENTURY CHRONICLES OF PRE-CONQUEST LIFE

It is highly probable that the missionaries and their Indian pupils wrote down various samples of indigenous melody. Shortly after the advent of the missionaries Christian texts began to be sung in such native languages as Nahuatl with indigenous tunes. Sahagún's *Psalmodia Christiana*,[44] already alluded to, comprises just such a collection of hymn-texts in Nahuatl, intended to be sung with indigenous tunes. This hymn-book, published in 1583, was (as he said in its preface) a collection of hymn-texts which he had composed several decades before actual publication; furthermore, according to Sahagún, many other missionaries had tried the same expedient of composing Christian texts in native languages, in order to give the Indians acceptable words to sing to their old tunes.

Acosta writing on this same subject said one of the popes had encouraged the missionaries to retain everything Indian that did not conflict with Christianity:

Our men that have conversed among them have labored to reduce matters of our holy faith *to their tunes,* the which hath profited well: for that they employ whole days to rehearse and sing them. . . . We must therefore conclude, following the counsel of Pope Gregory, that it was very convenient to leave to the Indians that which they had usually of custom, so as they be not mingled nor corrupt with their ancient errors.[45]

Regrettably, however, these indigenous tunes, like some of the original music composed by the Indians after the Spanish arrival,[46] seem to have been lost irretrievably. The only music with Nahuatl texts which still seems to survive from the sixteenth century is polyphonic music composed by Hernando Franco, chapelmaster at the Mexico City Cathedral between 1575 and 1585. Quite evidently Franco was not an Indian, and therefore we cannot adduce his polyphonic Nahuatl hymns as examples either of original music by a Mexican, or even necessarily as examples of adaptation from indigenous sources.

If no transcriptions of Aztec melodies noted down during the sixteenth

century have come to light, it need not however be concluded that none
so transcribed will ever be found. When it is remembered that such prose
accounts as Sahagún's, Motolinía's, Durán's, and Mendieta's were not
published until three centuries after they were written, that the texts of
the Nahuatl songs, *Cantares en Idioma Mexicano,* were not published
until 1899, that even yet no adequate attempt has been made to bring
these pre-Conquest songs into any modern language, that publication of
other important Nahuatl texts has been delayed, and that numerous manuscript sources in Indian tongues now resting in Spanish and Mexican
archives have scarcely been looked at by competent scholars, then it need
hardly be wondered at that no exemplars of Indian music—a much more
fragile kind of cultural remains than writing—have thus far been brought
forward.

In this connection it is pertinent to note that Francisco de Salinas (1513–
1590) published in 1577 a theoretical treatise, *De musica libri septem,*
in which was transcribed "the first Arab tune to be noted in western
musical notation." Salinas also included Portuguese, Spanish, and Italian
folk-songs in his *De musica.* In Mexico there were certainly musicians as
adequate as was Salinas for the task of noting down folk-songs. What may
easily have happened is simply neglect; there may now be in Spain or
in Mexico certain unexploited transcriptions of indigenous melody awaiting study and publication.

Only recently has it been discovered that a pioneer missionary in California, Fray Felipe Arroyo de la Cuesta, busied himself not only with
compiling a dictionary of the Mutsun tongue but also with the noting
down of texts and music of certain songs sung by the Indians whom he
was trying to convert. It is extremely probable such adept musicians as
Fray Pedro de Gante and Fray Bernardino de Sahagún similarly occupied themselves in sixteenth century Mexico. At the moment of this
writing, Arroyo de la Cuesta's jottings of California Indian melody remain unexploited in The Bancroft Library at the University of California
in MS. 35054. The neglect of this source of Indian melody in a state
where every scrap of historical information has been carefully collected
and studied, has possibly occurred because scholars dealing with local
history do not have time for peripheral matters; competent musicians, on
the other hand, do not usually have time or inclination to go foraging in
archives devoted to regional history simply on the bare chance that after

looking through a hundred manuscripts in obsolete handwriting an exceptional one with music will be found.

We say then again that the chances of discovering even at this late date a manuscript in an ecclesiastical archive in Spain, or in some such Mexican collection as the interminable Inquisition file, containing some scraps of Indian melody noted down during the sixteenth century have by no means been exhausted. Still other possibilities of arriving at an authentic indigenous melody exist. The writing of so-called parody masses using secular tunes was a common practice during the sixteenth century. Cristóbal de Morales, whose works were well known in sixteenth century Mexico, wrote several.[47]

Colonial composers in Mexico, such as Juan de Padilla, also wrote parody masses; these are just beginning to be transcribed into modern notation. Perhaps a complete corpus of Mexican masses and motets from the sixteenth and seventeenth centuries will enable us to identify melodic elements of non-Spanish origin upon which further deductions concerning the indigenous musical system can be based. Already it is being shown that Padilla, for instance, used certain melodic progressions which are hardly compatible with the European a cappella style; and when publication of his music has been achieved these non-typical traits will receive the attention due them. If Miss Alice Ray, to whom is due the discovery of Padilla's parodyings, does not isolate any Indian motifs in his music, it is entirely possible some other colonial composer's music will reveal an Indian *L'homme armé* theme. All the written evidence shows the missionaries favored preserving the Indian tunes wherever possible. Surviving written evidence proves, moreover, that the Indians who studied under such teachers as Fray Pedro de Gante soon learned the craft of music well enough to compose themselves, in certain cases composing polyphonic music that excited the admiration of their own Spanish mentors. If there were among the Indians individuals who could compose, certainly there must have been others with sufficient technical skill to write down the tunes used for the singing of such hymns as those included in *Psalmodia Christiana*.

Another as yet untried method in the study of the Aztec melodic system which may conceivably yield fruitful results should here be briefly explained. Certain early Nahuatl scholars, such as the Jesuit, Antonio del Rincón, stressed the fact that Nahuatl was recited with a pronounced up and down inflection in the pitch of successive syllables. Appropriate accent marks, according to Rincón in Book V of his *Arte Mexicana* (published in 1595),[48] showed the rise and fall of pitch in successive syllables. If such rules of pitch as Rincón gives were applied to a collection of Nahuatl songs, *Cantares en Idioma Mexicano*, for instance, a graph of the rise and fall in melodic line could be traced. The headings of the hundred-odd Cantares from this collection with teponaztli accompaniment tell us what the pitch pattern for the teponaztli accompaniment was; the mating of a graph showing the rise and fall of the voice with a graph of the rise and fall of the teponaztli accompaniment would afford us invaluable evidence upon which to base our conclusions concerning the Aztec musical system. The prevailing shape of Aztec melody might be deduced from such a study.[49]

THE MELODIC SYSTEM OF THE EARLY ABORIGINES

If it should seem that such methods as the last two we have named are unduly roundabout, we can only say in justification that at present the Achilles heel in all discussions of the Aztec melodic system is the actual lack of melodies transcribed in the Conquest period. Because no melodies of clearly provable antiquity have yet come to light, scholars have been forced to rely for their specific deductions concerning the Aztec musical system upon melodies noted down as recently as the end of the nineteenth century and the beginning of the twentieth by ethnologists working with phonograph in remote sections of Mexico where it has been hoped European influences had never effectively penetrated. A good example of such an ethnologist working with the aid of phonograph recordings is furnished us by Carl Lumholtz, whose *Unknown Mexico* appeared in two volumes at the beginning of this century (1902). Lumholtz's transcriptions of Huichol and Tarahumara Indian melodies were all made from phonograph recordings made in the field, and are therefore transcriptions that will withstand the most rigorous assay.

Lumholtz journeyed southward from Bisbee, Arizona. He first visited Sonora Indians, and then passed into Chihuahua where he investigated the habits of the isolated Tarahumaras. He proceeded thence down the western cordilleras through Durango and Zacatecas into Jalisco where he spent considerable time with the Huicholes. Obviously none of the tribes he visited were descendants of the Aztecs. Even had they been, it is too much to suppose that from 1519 until 1902 the musical culture of any people, however primitive, would have remained completely static. But since such transcriptions as Lumholtz provides have been frequently quoted in illustration of the aboriginal musical habits of the Mexicans, we shall here quote several musical examples from him, always bearing in mind, however, the date of his transcriptions, the source of his melodies, and the unlikelihood that these melodies recapture in any significant way the essential flavor of pre-Conquest music in Tenochtitlán, the proud heart of ancient Mexico.

The first three short melodies given below were taken by Lumholtz in Chihuahua during his stay with the Tarahumaras; prefacing the first song, he says:

> Although the Tarahumare, as a rule, has a harsh and not very power-ful singing voice, still there are some noteworthy exceptions, and the airs of the rutuburi songs are quite pleasing to the ear. These, as all their dancing-songs, are of great antiquity.[50]

Then he gives the following two rutuburi dances:

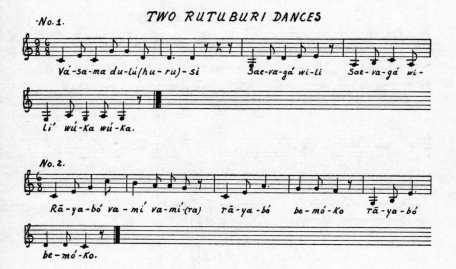

TWO RUTUBURI DANCES

Another type of dance popular with the Tarahumaras at the time Lumholtz visited them was the yumari. According to Lumholtz,

> The yumari songs tell that the Cricket wants to dance; the Frog wants to dance and jump; and the Blue Heron wants to fish; the Goat-sucker is dancing, so is the Turtle, and the Grey Fox is whistling. But it is characteristic of the yumari songs that they generally consist only of an unintelligible jargon, or, rather, of a mere succession of vocables, which the dancers murmur.
>
> Unlike the rutuburi, the yumari soon becomes tiresome, in spite of its greater animation. . . . According to tradition it [the yumari] is the oldest dance.[51]

Before setting down a yumari dance with two variants, Lumholtz explained that the accent sign $>$ in each of the following snatches meant a grunt rather than musical tone. It is a commonplace, of course, that no primitive music can adequately be transcribed in conventional Western notation. The manner of execution, which is all-important, cannot be reduced to paper with our conventional signs.

YUMARI DANCE

The next two musical quotations from Lumholtz were taken by him during a short stay with the Tepehuane Indians (who lived in the extreme southwest corner of the state of Chihuahua).

TEPEHUANE TRIBAL SONG

FEAST SONG SUNG AT APPEARANCE OF MORNING STAR

So-(só-) da-gi u - Ki-(ji-) ru in - vá-ni - mi.

The next several examples which we take from Lumholtz were collected during his excursion into the extreme northwesterly portion of Jalisco inhabited by the Huichol Indians. If we judge on the basis of Lumholtz's printed examples, this tribe seems strongly to have favored rhythmically free melodies founded on simple triad arpeggios.[52] Nearly all Huichol melodies have religious texts. As might be expected, both rain-songs given below invoke the aid of gods—the deer-god in the first song, and the mother-eagle goddess in the second.[53]

No. 1.   *HUICHOL RAIN SONGS*

O'- to Tá-wi me-ma-nó-ti Wa-wat-sá-li me-ma-no-tï Sa-Kai-mó-Ka me-ma-nó-ti

Ko-yo-(yo) ni me-ma-no-ti To-la-hú-li-pa me-ma-no-ti Sa-Kai-mo-Ka me-ma-no-ti

a - a.

No. 2.

Vae - li-Ka u-i-má-li Vae - li-Ka u-i-má-li (Va - vae-) me-mana Kaui Va

- vae me-má-na Kaui (Va-vae) me-má-na Kaui (Va-) ta-hae - má - me

(me-) má-na Kaui Va-ta-hae-má-me (me) ma-na Kaui (Va-

- vae-) me-má-na Kaui (Va- vae-) me-má-na Kaui (Va - vae-) me-má-na Kaui.

Lumholtz tells of having mightily pleased his Huichol hosts by learning several such rain-songs as the two just given.

Certain further excerpts of Huichol melody illustrate what seems to be a rather elaborate scheme of shifting rhythms. One of these was sung at the hikuli dance in honor of the mescal button [54] from which a highly intoxicating liquor was fermented (and the eating of which induces visions and ecstasies). The other was sung at the religious rites preparatory to a deer-hunt; during the deer-hunting season the hunters ate only sparingly, but had constant recourse to hikuli. Since the hikuli songs and dances obviously bordered on frenzy, Lumholtz again insists that he had made no attempt to transcribe them from actual ceremonial performances where he would have had only a flickering fire for light; these songs and dances he assures us were all recorded at the moment of actual performance and then later transcribed. Even so, our conventional notation can give no idea of the methods used in performance.

In the case of these last two songs, as with the other songs transcribed by Lumholtz, he reminds us that a principal feature of actual performance was the repetition over and over again of the same fragments of melody. From a Europeanized point of view this repetition became infinitely tedious at times, but since the songs were primarily sung for ritual purposes, their efficacy was thereby enhanced.

The Huichol instruments mentioned include the three-legged hollow cylindrical drum with a covering of deer-skin upon which the player rapped with his fingers; the four-hole flute; and the notched bone rasp. Wherever a Huichol song was sung with accompaniment the supporting instruments were usually percussive with a predominantly rhythmic function to perform. Since the typical Huichol *instruments* obviously resemble the typical Aztec instruments, many observers have chosen to draw parallels between existing Huichol and non-existent Aztec *melodies;* this inference is drawn easily enough: since the instruments are demonstrably similar, why should not the melodies sung in conjunction with the instruments have been similar? [55]

Since a sampling of melody from every tribe visited by Lumholtz would overcrowd us here, we now pause briefly in order to offer the general principles of indigenous melody which can be deduced from the Tarahumara and Huichol melodies: (1) melodies are pre-eminently pentatonic; (2) they are non-expressive in the Western sense; (3) they usually end on a note which we recognize as a satisfactory tonic; (4) their range is an octave or a tenth; (5) there is no sense of melodic climax; (6) a strong rhythmic propulsive force informs all their songs; (7) nearly all are cult or ritual songs; (8) dance and song are twins in the native culture areas.

Lumholtz, a Norwegian, was soon followed by K. T. Preuss, whose Mexican travels culminated in a book entitled *Die Nayarit-expedition*, published at Leipzig in 1912. Preuss worked among the Cora Indians. Frances Densmore, the well-known American student of Indian music, contributed two valuable articles, one on Pápago music and another on Yaqui music in 1929 and 1932, respectively.[56] The literature on indigenous music has been significantly enriched in recent years by such Mexican authorities as G. Baqueiro Fóster, Jesús Romero, and Vicente T. Mendoza. The Mexicans all agree that whatever may be ascertained regarding the melodic system of the pre-Conquest peoples must be inferred from examples recently collected.

One more sample of indigenous melody may aptly be quoted here before we take final leave of these "modern" melodies on which theories regarding ancient indigenous melody have trellised themselves. The final example given below is presented in three versions, the first Baqueiro Fóster's version, the second Saldívar's version, and the last Mendoza's version. The melody in question was first noted down by Baqueiro Fóster, who remembered hearing it as a child in Mérida; he assumed it was a native Maya melody, as it may well have been. The title has been translated, "Ribbon Dance," although the Maya words themselves mean, "Come on, come on, children, the sun is setting." The rhythmic disparities in the following transcriptions probably indicate individual interpretations rather than mere inadvertences in copying.

Xtoles

If it were to the point we could continue our quotation of indigenous melodies, as they have been picked up by zealous investigators in recent years, ending this chapter with a thesaurus of aboriginal melodies. An appendix for good measure could then be added to the chapter in which would be contained all the variants encountered in such cases as that of the melody just quoted, *Xtoles*. Such a thesaurus would include samples of Otomí melody picked up by Rodney Gallop,[60] of Mixtec melody recorded by Matéo Hernández,[61] of Maya melody transcribed by Luis Sandi and Francisco Dominguez after their 1934 visit to the Chiapas; [62] and of Yaqui, Seri, Tarahumara, and other tribal melodies picked up and recorded by folklorists in more recent years for such institutions as the Library of Congress at Washington. Such a thesaurus would, however, unduly extend the chapter; the ten examples already given will perhaps suffice. They give us enough evidence so that we can form at least a tentative opinion concerning the reiterate melodies still precariously surviving in isolated and remote areas of Mexico.

CONCLUDING SUMMARY

What can be made of these melodies? We have already said that scholars have used them in order to reconstruct the melodic system and even the rhythmic system of the ancient indigenes. Lest this use seem unduly inferential, we hasten to point out the use made of such fragments of ancient Greek melody as the Delphic Hymns to Apollo (written about 130 B.C.) and of the so-called Seikilos Song (written still later); such Greek fragments are nowadays used by writers who are attempting to reconstruct the musical system in vogue among the Greeks of the Periclean age. As long as modern scholars permit themselves the liberty of using music of the late Alexandrinian epoch in their discussions of music during the age of Aeschylus or Sophocles, they should undoubtedly admit the equal propriety of using such indignous fragments as Lumholtz collected, in discussions of the melodic system in vogue among the Mexican aborigines of an earlier epoch.

If we ask the same question, what can be made of these melodies? this time, however, asking it not as musical antiquarians, but as practical musicians, we can speak much more enthusiastically in their behalf. In a country such as Mexico, which even today contains a larger group of Indians than of persons with pure European blood, the indigenous expressions in art and music assume almost the value of national palladiums. As symbols of Indian cultural achievement in a nation so largely made up even yet of pure-blooded Indians, any fragment or shard of Indian music gathers to itself a spiritual significance that far transcends its objective value in the eyes of foreign musicians. Only those who have troubled to acquaint themselves with the divided character of the Mexican national soul can realize how important it is to the formerly oppressed Indian now to assert himself spiritually and artistically, even if in so doing he seems to stress the musical value of aboriginal specimens that, objectively considered, lack transcendent worth.

In the United States where a competent musician such as Edward MacDowell in his 1890 *Second Orchestral Suite* or Charles T. Griffes in his *Two Sketches for String Quartet* has used Indian themes, the musical result has had to stand on its own merits and not on its appeal to lineal descendants of Powhatan and Squanto. In Mexico, however, even an Indian name, such as Candelario Huízar affixed to his symphony entitled *Oxpaniztli*—whether Indian themes are actually used or not—guarantees a certain type of success that we who are unfamiliar with the spirit of Cárdenas's Mexico have no way of properly anticipating. If a return to the speaking of Nahuatl as a national language has not yet been suggested in Mexico, it is certain that in the minds of many leading artists and musicians the effacement of all other cultural intrusions that have occurred since 1519 would be heartily desired, even if it meant the utter annihilation of every monument of Mexican colonial art. It is not to be wondered at in such a climate of opinion that aboriginal music stimulates enthusiasm.

The most widely known and the most universally admired composition founded on aboriginal melody is undoubtedly Chávez's eleven-minute *Sinfonia India*. Yet in this unique achievement it seems hardly possible to claim any greater distinction for the melodies which Chávez used than can be claimed for the fragments of melody Lumholtz collected. It may be interesting to compare the Huichol melody heard at the opening of this one-movement symphony [63] with other Huichol melodies:

Objectively considered, this particular Huichol melody seems as limited in expressive content as either of Lumholtz's rain-songs; its musical substance is even thinner than that of the hikuli songs already presented. Not the melody itself, but rather Chávez's treatment of it, impresses the international music public.

If no particularly intriguing charms of the kind found everywhere in European folk-music are presently discernible in the Indian themes used by Chávez or other modern Mexican composers, still Indian themes are to be revered and valued simply because they constitute symbols of the heroic Indian past. Authentic Mexican aboriginal music of the kind recorded under Henrietta Yurchenco's supervision for the Library of Congress album [64] entitled "Folk Music of Mexico" may not seem very promising raw material for a symphony, but since Chávez and others less well known have shown it can be done, this music deserves to be highly regarded if not for its intrinsic qualities, at least as a convenient totem. A sympathetic hearer will not count the hundred-odd times a simple triad arpeggio may be sung at a Huichol Fiesta del Peyote, but will rather make a serious effort at transporting himself into the culture area in which the music originated. Only by so doing will he begin to realize why the indigenous music of Mexico is so much more highly regarded by Mexico's serious composers than are the innumerable jarabes, huapangos, sandungas, and bambas, that pass in this country as the only authentic Mexican folk-music.

The connecting of Mexico's present-day Indian music with the Indian music of the pre-Conquest past, as has already been admitted, may involve us in an egregious historical fallacy. But other historical errors have proved fruitful of good result in music history. The birth of opera, for instance, can be directly attributed to a mistaken notion of Greek drama and music in which certain Florentine gentlemen who gathered at the palace of Count Giovanni Bardi during the late sixteenth century fondly indulged themselves. They were certainly as mistaken in their notions of the Greek past as Columbus was in 1492 when he thought he had landed on the coasts of Asia. However wrong the modern Mexican musician may be in thinking he has arrived at a true understanding of the Aztec past by contemplating the features of contemporary indigenous music, still a desirable result may have been achieved by making such a connection.

Contemporary Mexican composers have been stimulated by an ideal, as it were, of a Homeric age in Mexican music; and in their mouths has been placed a rallying cry. As far as practical results are concerned it hardly matters whether such ideas on Aztec music as Chávez has propagated are really accurate or not; as long as they are accepted and believed they deserve considerate attention, whether they are strictly provable or not. Because they have been believed, Mexican musicians for the first time in the long history of music in Mexico have ceased pining for European glamor, and instead have taken a certain indispensable pride simply in being *Mexican* musicians. The Aztec past has ceased to be any longer a disgraceful and regrettable incident in national history. Instead it is now regarded as a moment of national grandeur; scenes from the Aztec past are the culminating glory of Mexico's history, as Diego Rivera has painted them in his highly idealized versions of pre-Conquest life now on view at the National Palace.

With this spirit now abroad, Mexican musicians are ready to go back to the earliest aboriginal music, and play a fortissimo *da capo*.

NOTES

1. Laurence E. Schmeckebier, *Modern Mexican Art* (Minneapolis: The University of Minnesota Press, 1939), p. 4.
2. Bernal Díaz del Castillo. *The True History of the Conquest of New Spain* (London: The Hakluyt Society, 1912), IV, 142, 149–50, 154.
3. Alba Herrera y Ogazón, *El Arte Musical en México* (México: Dirección General de las Bellas Artes, 1917), p. 9. Continuing in the same strain, she commented: "During the rites when hapless victims by the hundreds were cruelly offered to their gods, the eerie light of the sacrificial fires, the vivid color of freshly spilt human blood, the ghastly shrieks of the captives, and the insane frenzy of the diabolical priests must together have combined to produce a truly terrifying spectacle. The lugubrious accompanying music for these ceremonies must undoubtedly have been wild, incoherent, and macabre; since in it was expressed the ferocious passions of the untamed savage."
4. Otto Mayer-Serra, "Silvestre Revueltas and Musical Nationalism in Mexico," *The Musical Quarterly*, April, 1941, p. 127.
5. Jesús C. Romero, *Música Precortesiana* (México: Talleres Gráficos de la Editorial Stylo, 1947), pp. 252–3.
6. Hubert Herring and Herbert Weinstock (editors), *Renascent Mexico* (New York: Covici-Friede, 1935), p. 234. Rivera wrote for this book a chapter entitled "Plastic Art in Pre-Conquest Mexico," in which he gave it as his opinion that most of the Spaniards who invaded Mexico were "very close to living on the Neolithic level." The Spaniards were too "barbarous" to appreciate the advanced "mental development" of the race they destroyed, according to Rivera.

7. Romero, *op. cit.*, pp. 256–7.

8. For a discussion of the Bonampak paintings as revelators of Mayan musical practices, see Vicente T. Mendoza, "Música Indigena de México," *México en el Arte*, 1950, IX, 58. On pp. 59 and 62 appear color reproductions of the Maya instruments in the Bonampak paintings. Because of the inaccessibility of the Lacanya Valley (State of Chiapas) where the Bonampak temples are located, the Mexican government commissioned Agustín Villagra to execute full-scale color duplicates for the Instituto Nacional de Antropología at Mexico City. For the story of the spectacular Bonampak discovery see Charles M. Wilson, "Open Sesame to the Maya," *Bulletin of the Pan American Union*, July, 1948, pp. 376–84.

9. D. G. Brinton in *The Güegüence* . . . (Philadelphia, 1883), pp. xxx–xxxii, advanced the theory that multi-keyed teponaztlis were used in Mexico; he reproduced in evidence a picture from Durán's *Atlas* (Mexico, 1880), Trat.º 2.º, Lam.ª 6.ª, Cap.º 8.º, showing a teponaztli player crouched before a five-keyed instrument. It is of course well known that both the *Codex Florentinus* (issued in 1905 under the editorial supervision of Francisco del Paso y Troncoso at Madrid) and Durán's *Atlas* contain post-Conquest paintings that cannot be accepted as definitive in minor details; the paintings in both clearly show Spanish influence.

10. See Daniel Castañeda and Vicente T. Mendoza, "Los Teponaztlis . . ." and "Los Percutores Precortesianos," *Anales del Museo Nacional de Arqueología, Historia, y Etnografía*, 4a epoca, Tomo 8 (Mexico, 1933), especially pp. 281–2.

11. Antonio Peñafiel (editor), *Cantares en Idioma Mexicano* (México: Secretaría de Fomento, 1899). An English version containing 27 of these *cantares* (but in an unreliable translation) was published in Daniel G. Brinton's *Ancient Nahuatl Poetry* (Philadelphia, 1890).

12. H. T. Cresson, "Aztec Music," *Proceedings of the Academy of Natural Sciences of Philadelphia*, Part I, 1883, pp. 86–94.

13. Miguel Galindo, *Nociones de Historia de la Música Mejicana* (Colima, "El Dragon," 1933), pp. 100–1.

14. Herbert Weinstock, *Mexican Music* (New York: Museum of Modern Art, 1940), p. 8.

15. The Bonampak "trumpets" were actually made of wood rather than of clay, and included what appears to be a separate mouthpiece. Since fingerholes were not shown, only natural harmonics could have been produced. The paintings show the lips of the players tightly pursed, with the bell of the "trumpet" held at an angle above the heads of the players. Undoubtedly the Bonampak instrumentalists played in concert with each other, rather than as soloists, if the paintings are to be trusted. Since the "trumpets" were made of wood, a more nearly equivalent European instrument would no doubt be the now obsolete cornett (zink). For further discussion see Mendoza, *op. cit.*, p. 58.

16. Eduard Seler, *Collected Works* (Englished under the editorial supervision of J. E. S. Thompson for the Peabody Museum, Cambridge, Mass., 1939), Vol. III, Part 2, Section 2, pp. 28–33.

17. Marshall H. Saville, *The Wood-Carver's Art in Ancient Mexico* (New York: Museum of the American Indian, 1925), pp. 64–74.

18. *Ibid.*, p. 67.

19. *Renascent Mexico*, pp. 203–8.
20. *Ibid.*, p. 203.
21. *Ibid.*, p. 208.
22. Sylvanus G. Morley, *The Ancient Maya* (Stanford University Press, 1946), pp. 261–2.
23. On the "burning of books," see Alfred M. Tozzer (ed.), *Landa's Relación de las Cosas de Yucatán* (Cambridge: The Peabody Museum, 1941), pp. 77–8. Acosta's statement appears on p. 78.
24. This phrase was inserted, along with several other explanatory phrases, into Mendieta's transcription of Motolinía's account. See Gerónimo de Mendieta, *Historia Eclesiástica Indiana* (México: Antigua Librería, 1870), pp. 140–3.
25. Toribio de Motolinía, *Memoriales* (México: García Pimentel, 1903), pp. 339–43.
26. Bernardino de Sahagún, *Historia General de las Cosas de Nueva España* (México: Imp. del Alejandre Valdés, Bustamente ed., 1829), Tomo I, pp. 101–4.
27. *Ibid.*, I, 137.
28. *Ibid.*, I, 276.
29. *Ibid.*, II, 314–5.
30. *Ibid.*, III (1830), 21.
31. Francisco López de Gómara, *Historia de Mexico, con el descubrimiento dela Nueva España* (Antwerp, 1554), pp. 106–7.
32. Alonso de Molina, *Vocabulario en lengua Castellana y Mexicana* (Mexico, 1571), p. 24.
33. Tozzer, *op. cit.*, p. vii.
34. From this statement we should infer that the tortoise shell was more of a gong than a rasp.
35. Tozzer, *op. cit.*, p. 93.
36. Diego Durán, *Historia de las Indias*, II, 233.
37. *Ibid.*, II, 230.
38. Among the instruments Gallop encountered which he classified as idols was a teponaztli "that is kept mysteriously hidden all year long at Tepoztlan and played on only three occasions during the year." The figure carved on this teponaztli was Xochipilli. He encountered a sorcerer at Xico in the Sierra de Puebla who guarded a drum to which a hymn in Aztec was sung as to the god, Xochipilli. See *Musical Quarterly*, April, 1939, p. 218.
39. Mendieta, *op. cit.*, pp. 79–80. See also Gabriel Saldívar, *Historia de la Música en México* (Mexico, 1934), pp. 4–5.
40. Juan de Torquemada, *Veinte i un libros rituales i Monarquía Indiana*, 2nd edition (Madrid: Nicolas Rodriguez Franco, 1723), I, 229.
41. *Ibid.*, II, 265.
42. Lorenzo Boturini Benaduci, *Idea de una Nueva Historia General de la America Septentrional* (Madrid, 1746), p. 90.
43. Francisco Clavijero, *Storia antica del Messico* (Cesena, 1780), II, 178.
44. The only work of Sahagún published during his lifetime, it is now excessively rare. A copy is in The Huntington Library. When Icazbalceta compiled his 16th

century bibliography, he was under the impression that he possessed the only surviving copy. See J. García Icazbalceta, *Obras* (México: V. Agüeros, 1896), III,
175. The hymns in *Psalmodia Christiana* were all written at a considerably earlier
stage in Sahagún's life than the publication date of 1583 would suggest; it is
known that he began writing them twenty-five years before they were published.
Only adequate study of the metrics of these hymns will give us any inkling of the
kind of music to which they were set; the tunes have all been lost. The loss of the
tunes, which were not printed, can hardly be surprising when copies of the printed
book have so precariously survived.

It must not be thought that the words are paraphrases of the Davidic psalms;
in actuality the words (as one can easily infer from the numerous wood-blocks
that illustrate the text) are hymns of devotion to Christ and to the saints.

45. José de Acosta, *Historia Natural y Moral de las Indias* (Seville, 1590), p. 447.
See also *The Naturall and Morall Historie . . .* (London, 1604), p. 492.

46. Concerning the original music written by the Indian converts during the earliest
Conquest period see García Icazbalceta, *Colección de Documentos para la Historia
de México* (México, Librería de J. M. Andrade, 1858), I, 210.

47. Morales wrote two *L'homme armé* parody masses, and others on the secular
tunes, *Mille regretz, Caça,* and *Tristezas me matan.* His pupil, Guerrero, also
wrote parody masses.

48. Antonio del Rincón, *Arte Mexicana* (Mexico, 1595; new ed. by Antonio Peñafiel, 1885), Libro V, capítulo primero. (In Peñafiel's edition, pp. 61–6.)

49. Vicente T. Mendoza, "Música Precolombina de America," *Boletín Latino-
Americano de Música* (Bogotá, 1938), IV, 244 ff. Mendoza thinks he found a
clue to the prevailing direction of pre-Conquest melody; but his results have been
imperfectly corroborated.

50. Carl Lumholtz, *Unknown Mexico* (New York: Charles Scribner's Sons, 1902),
I, 338.

51. *Ibid.,* I, 339–40. Both rutuburi and yumari dances have been linked to the
same peyote cult Lumholtz later found a prominent feature of ceremonial life
among the Huichol Indians (see his references to the hikuli dance).

52. The Huichol melodies recorded in the "Folk Music of Mexico" album (issued
by the Library of Congress) show the same marked preference for reiterate melodies
founded on simple triad arpeggios.

53. Lumholtz, *op. cit.,* II, 10 and 18.

54. A species of narcotic cactus plant.

55. Auguste Génin, in his "Notes on the Dances, Music, and Songs of the Ancient
and Modern Mexicans," *Annual Report of The Smithsonian Institution,* 1920,
pp. 657–8, strongly opposed the tendency to identify present usages and customs
with those of the remote past, and also the tendency to identify the usages of
one contemporary tribe with the usages of another contemporary tribe—especially
where the two tribes live far removed from each other. On the other hand, E. Seler
in "The Huichol Indians of the State of Jalisco" (*Coll. Wks.,* Eng. tr., Vol. III,
Pt. 3, Sec. 2, pp. 2 and especially 7) strongly endorsed the use of parallels between the Huicholes and the ancient Mexicans in our endeavor to understand the

culture of ancient Mexico. Particularly interesting is Seler's endorsement of the parallels between Huichol and Aztec instruments—parallels, he points out, which extend beyond mere externalities, and have to do with much more intimate matters, such as the proper use of instruments in religious ceremonies. See also in this connection Seler's article in *Globus, Illustrierte Zeitschrift für Länder und Völkerkunde*, August 19, 1899, pp. 109–12, treating of the likenesses between Mexican and Maya instruments.

56. Frances Densmore, *Papago Music* (Washington, U.S. Govt. Printing Office, 1929); *Yuman and Yaqui Music* (Washington, 1932).

57. Baqueiro Fóster, *Revista Musical Mexicana*, January, 1942, p. 16.

58. Saldívar, *op. cit.*, p. 72.

59. Mendoza, "Música Indigena de México," p. 63.

60. Rodney Gallop, "Otomi Indian Music from Mexico," *The Musical Quarterly*, January, 1940, pp. 87–100. Gallop strongly felt that what indigenous melody still existed possessed little artistic worth. Compare his attitude with that of Chávez, who in his chapter, "The Music of Mexico," written for Henry Cowell's symposium, *American Composers on American Music* (Stanford University Press, 1933), spoke glowingly of "the knowledge of music possessed by the contemporary Indians who still, in many regions of the country, preserve the manner of execution and the forms of the most ancient traditions." (p. 170)

61. Mendoza, "Música Indigena de México," p. 60.

62. *Ibid.*, p. 62.

63. A short introduction actually precedes this quotation of Huichol melody. No source is given in the program notes supplied by Chávez for either the Huichol, Yaqui, or Seri melodies which he quotes in the course of *Sinfonia India*.

64. See Henrietta Yurchenco, "Grabación de Música Indigena," *Nuestra Música*, May, 1946, pp. 65–78. In contrast with Rodney Gallop, who complained of the paucity of indigenous examples, she stated (p. 78): "My collection of indigenous music represents only a small sampling of the vast treasury of aboriginal melody which can still be heard in out-of-the-way places in Mexico and Guatemala. Centuries after the Conquest and after the initial contact between Spaniard and Indian, numerous Indian groups still preserve intact their ancient musical culture. . . . I hope the album which the Library of Congress will soon issue will (though it contains only a small fraction of the recordings I have taken) be of use not only to comparative musicologists, but also to practical composers, and also to anthropologists and linguists."

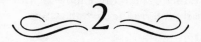

THE TRANSPLANTING OF EUROPEAN
MUSICAL CULTURE

The amazing speed with which European music was taken up and mastered by the Indians immediately after the arrival of the Conquerors affords us convincing proof of the innate musicality of the aborigines. Such chroniclers as we quoted in the previous chapter unite in extolling the readiness and talent of their Indian charges in mastering the European musical system. The Indians could hardly have so soon mastered Gregorian chant and so readily embraced polyphonic singing had they not already among themselves built up a strong musical tradition. Because the Indians showed such inordinate fondness for the music the missionaries brought with them, the first bishop of Mexico instructed the missionaries within his diocese to teach music wherever they went as "an indispensable aid in the process of conversion."

A number of Cortés's own men, as will later be shown, were competent singers and instrumentalists. Wherever Cortés traveled he carried professional Spanish minstrels along with his army in order to entertain himself and his soldiers. The Indians were everywhere fascinated with the music of these sixteenth-century USO entertainers and began to imitate them as soon as possible. Certain ones among Cortés's followers who were gifted musically began to teach after their warring days had ended, and a number of amusing stories have descended to us from the chroniclers of the Conquest period telling how speedily the Indians wheedled out of their masters all their best professional secrets. But none of the Indians could have progressed so rapidly in music as the chroniclers testify had they not already been rather generously endowed with what, for lack of a better word, is usually referred to as "talent."

Even at the moment of their initial contact with the Indians the Spaniards emphasized the primacy of music in worship. One can hardly imagine today a group of three hundred would-be conquistadores stopping their negotiations with emissaries of Montezuma in order to build an altar where their chaplain could not say, but sing Mass. Bernal Díaz, however, tells us that the very first Sunday after they set foot on the spot later re-christened Veracruz two Indian governors arrived on an embassage from Montezuma; before any business could be transacted Cortés ordered an altar built, after the hasty erection of which Fray Bartolomé de Olmedo, "who was a fine singer, chanted Mass." [1] Symbolically this chanting of Mass was an excellent prelude to the later efforts of the missionaries who everywhere they went sang their services. What the Indians failed to grasp in words was at least partially conveyed in music.

Cortés's own chaplains because of their duties with his troops were unable to give more than incidental attention to the Indians; missionaries specifically assigned to Indian work soon arrived, however. In the summer of 1523, two years after the fall of Tenochtitlán, the first three missionaries specially picked for the task of converting the Indians arrived. One had spent fourteen years as professor of theology at the University of Paris; another was a Fleming who had been employed in state business by his relative, Charles V, before his conversion and joining of the Franciscan order; the third claimed Scottish antecedents. All three had spent several years in a Franciscan house at Ghent before applying to Charles V for permission to go as pioneers to Mexico. The second of the trio, Pedro de Gante (1480?–1572),[2] was himself originally a native of Ghent, where he had grown to maturity. He therefore had lived in the atmosphere which produced masters such as Des Près, de la Rue, Mouton, and Gombert. Fray Juan de Tecto, the Frenchman in the trio, was at the time the three asked permission to go himself serving as Charles's personal chaplain. The journey from Ghent to Seville before embarking was taken in Charles V's company. Charles wherever he traveled always carried about with him his own private chapel choir,[3] which included several of the most illustrious musicians of the age. When Pedro later wrote his near-relative, Charles V, claiming the Indians under his charge had already gained sufficient skill to rival the chapel singers in Charles's own private chapel, he was therefore pitting them against a choir which he already knew to be superlative.

The first two or three years after their arrival in Mexico they busied themselves with the learning of Nahuatl, the language of the Aztecs. Fray Pedro soon founded a school at Texcuco which has been called the first school for the teaching of European subjects in America. He also instigated the founding of the first church for the Indians, the Church of San José de Belem, which stood not far from the present location of the famous American restaurant in Mexico City, Sanborn's (busy Gante street nearby still reminds one of Pedro de Gante). The Indian chapel itself was later chosen the scene of the most impressive pageantry in sixteenth century Mexico. Because it was the finest and largest church in the city (larger than the primitive cathedral) it was chosen for such great ceremonial occasions as the commemorative services after Charles V's death in which participated the entire civil and ecclesiastical hierarchy. Adjacent to the chapel was a school for Indians founded by Fray Pedro soon after his removal from Texcuco to Mexico City.

Although music was only one of several arts which were taught in the San Francisco school founded by Fray Pedro, his surviving portraits all carry a notice to the effect that his music teaching was the subject in which he gained his most phenomenal results.[4] His own early background in Flanders prepared him for his role as music mentor. He came to Mexico a man of forty-odd years, with a long background of exceptional musical advantages. His own epoch was, moreover, one during which church musicians everywhere throughout Europe looked for inspiration to the celebrated Flemish masters. Fray Pedro was assisted in his music instruction by others who were not Flemings, Fray Arnaldo de Bassacio, listed as a Frenchman, and the venerable Spanish priest, Fray Juan Caro, for instance.[5] But they were all united in their belief that music provided an indispensable adjunct to worship. The music they approved for instructional purposes included the finest European art-music of their period.

The remarkable success which Fray Pedro de Gante achieved with the Indians may be ascribed to certain other factors than mere goodwill: he first learned the Nahuatl language; the school he then proceeded to found alongside the San Francisco monastery was modeled on those maintained by the celebrated Brethren of the Common Life in Flanders; he taught

the Indians and not the children of the Spanish invaders thus eliminating
the possibility of racial friction. His importance as an educator has been
stressed by recent historians of education in Mexico.[6] The best tribute he
has been paid, however, has been the widespread adoption given his educational plan by other missionaries.

A memorable letter written in October of 1532, just nine years after
the advent of the band of three in Mexico, tells in Pedro's own words
what he felt had been accomplished in music since his arrival:

> I can tell Your Majesty [Charles V] without exaggeration that there
> are already Indians here who are fully capable of preaching, teaching, and
> writing [in behalf of the faith]. And with the utmost sincerity I can affirm
> that there are now trained singers among them who if they were to sing
> in Your Majesty's Chapel at this moment would do so well that perhaps
> you would have to see them actually singing in order to believe it possible.[7]

If Pedro had been alone in his enthusiasm for music his labors would
soon have ended abortively. But others perceiving his results wholeheartedly seized upon his educational plan. Numerous other missionaries
wrote letters describing their successes in music education. Fray Martín
de Valencia, leader of the band of twelve that came out the year after
Fray Pedro's arrival in Mexico, wrote a letter to the Emperor in November of 1532, endorsing music as a prime aid in the task of conversion.
A short excerpt from this particular letter will show why he valued music
instruction. The training given the natives in music helped to wean them
from their former beliefs; music was the sweetening added to make their
new instruction more palatable.

> Likewise we take all the children of the caciques (insofar as we are able
> to get these nobles to send us their children), and also children from other
> of the more influential Indian families. We take these children in order
> that we may separate them from heathen influences by rearing and edu-
> cating them in our monasteries. We devote much time to them, teaching
> them not only how to read and write, but also how to sing both plainchant
> and polyphonic music. We teach them how to sing the canonical hours
> and how to assist at Mass; and we strive to inculcate the highest standards
> of living and conduct.[8]

Motolinía, one of the original band of twelve that came over in 1524
with Fray Martín de Valencia as leader, gave in his *Historia de los Indios*

several remarkable instances showing how avidly the Indians took to the music of the friars.

At the time when the Indians began to learn the Ave Maria and the Pater Noster the friars in order to make the learning easier and more pleasurable gave them these and other prayers, along with the Commandments, in their own tongue and set to a pleasing plainchant melody. They were so eager to learn, and there were so many of them, that they fairly piled up in the courtyards of the churches and shrines and in their own sections of the town, singing and learning prayers for three or four hours on end; and their haste was so great that wherever they went, by day or by night, one could hear them on all sides singing and reciting the whole catechism. The Spaniards were amazed.[9]

In another excerpt from his *Historia de los Indios* he commented at length on the astounding facility with which the Indians mastered even the most complicated elements in the European music system.

Their understanding is keen, modest, and quiet, not proud or showy as in other nations. They learned to read quickly, both in Spanish and in Latin, in print and in manuscript. . . . They learned to write in a short time. . . . The third year we started to teach them singing and some people laughed and made fun of it, both because the Indians seemed to be singing off pitch, and because they seemed to have weak voices. It is undoubtedly true that they do not have voices as strong or as sweet as the Spaniards. Probably this comes about because they go barefooted, with unprotected chests, and eat food that is poor fare. But since there are so many of them to choose from, the Indian choirs are all reasonably good.

It was quite a sight to see the first man who began to teach them [part-] [10] singing. He happened to be an old friar who knew scarcely anything of the Indian language, only Castilian, and he talked with the boys as correctly and sensibly as if he were talking with intelligent Spaniards. Those of us who heard him were beside ourselves with laughter as we watched the boys standing openmouthed to see what he meant. It was marvellous that, although at first they did not understand a thing and the old man had no interpreter, in a short time they understood him and learned to sing so that now there are many of them so skilful that they direct choirs. As they are quick-witted and have an excellent memory, most of what they sing they know by heart, so that if the pages get mixed up or the book falls while they are singing this does not prevent them from singing on without the slightest error. Also, if they lay the book on a table, the ones who see it upside down or from the side sing just as well as those who are in front of it. One of these Indian singers, an inhabitant of this city of Tlaxcala, has composed unaided a whole Mass which has been approved by good Castilian singers who have seen it.

Instead of organs they use flutes playing in harmony, and the sound resembles that of a pipe organ because of the large number of flutes playing together. Instrumentalists who came from Spain taught them how to play; so many instrumentalists arrived together that we asked them to divide themselves up among the Indian towns where they might receive pay for their lessons, instead of becoming a burden on one community. The Indians have learned to make chirimías [double-reed instruments] though it cannot be said that as yet they know how to produce from them a satisfactorily tuned scale. . . .

Notably to be valued in these Indian students is their exceptionally good deportment. The teacher has to expend very little effort, for they are so eager to learn that they are soon ready to teach themselves. Indian instructors are used along with the friars in such schools as San Francisco de México and Santiago de Tlatelolco.[11]

Motolinía finished his history in February, 1541. For a considerable period of time anterior to its completion he had centralized his missionary activities in Tlaxcala,[12] the capital of the province where Cortés had found his staunchest Indian allies. It was but natural that the people of this province, who had always remained loyal to the Spanish, should more speedily than their neighboring tribes have acquired a Neo-Hispanic cultural outlook. Motolinía selected the 1538 festival of Corpus Christi at Tlaxcala in order to illustrate the rather considerable success the people of this province had shown in weaving into the fabric of their own indigenous culture certain Spanish strands.

On the holy day of Corpus Christi in the year 1538, the Tlaxcaltecas held a very solemn festival which deserves to be recorded, because I believe that if the Pope and Emperor had been there with their courts they would have been delighted. . . . This was the first day that the Tlaxcaltecas used the coat of arms which the Emperor granted them when the town was made a city. This favor has not yet been granted to any other Indian town but this one, which well deserves it, for its people greatly assisted Don Hernando Cortés, acting for His Majesty. . . . In the procession there marched a large choir trained to sing polyphonic music of considerable complexity; their singing was accompanied by music of flutes which duplicated the [treble] parts, and also by trumpets and drums, sounding together with bells, large and small. Since all these instruments sounded together at the moment of their entering and at the moment of their leaving the church, it seemed just then that the very heavens were falling. . . .

On the following Monday they presented four one-act plays . . . written in prose. . . . One scene ended with the singing of *Benedictus Dominus Deus Israel.*

Motolinía then proceeded in this section of his history to set down a narrative of the Easter celebration in Tlaxcala the next year (1539).

These Tlaxcaltecas have greatly enlivened the divine service with polyphonic music written for voices and for groups of instruments. They have two choirs which alternate with each other in singing the divine office. Each choir has more than twenty singers; they have also two groups of flutists who accompany these choirs, and they also use in their performances the rebec and a certain type of flute (copied from the Moors) which aptly imitates the sound of the organ. Besides these they also have skilful drummers who when they sound their drums conjointly with the bright, jingling bells they carry, create a delightful effect. . . .

The Wednesday of the Easter octave . . . they had a play ready to be performed. It represented the fall of our first parents. . . . When the angels brought two garments, very clever imitations of the skins of animals, and dressed Adam and Eve, the most striking thing was to see them go out into exile weeping, Adam escorted by three angels and Eve by another three. As they went out they sang together a polyphonic setting of the psalm *Circumdederunt me.*[13] This was so well performed that no one who saw it could keep from weeping bitterly. . . . Consoling the disconsolate pair, the angels went off singing, in parts, by way of farewell, a *villancico* [14] whose words were:

> Oh, why did she eat
> —that first married woman—
> Oh, why did she eat
> The forbidden fruit?
>
> That first married woman
> —she and her husband—
> Have brought Our Lord down
> To a humble abode
> Because they both ate
> The forbidden fruit.

This play was performed by the Indians in their own tongue.[15]

Among the other plays mentioned by Motolinía some two or three seem to have shown considerable imagination and skill in construction; music, as he described them, was considered a necessary incidental in all these plays. Most of them were of the *auto sacramental* type, whose enormous popularity spread from Spain to New Spain during the sixteenth century. The blending of the various arts—scenic, literary, dramatic, and musical—into a unified whole seems to have been well contrived, despite the inexperience of the Indians who presented them. Motolinía was understandably proud of the friars' contribution to the Indian cultural advance. Although the period between 1519 and 1538 saw the decline of many artistic customs which must have been ideal expressions of the aboriginal spirit, the assimilation of Spanish customs compensated at least partly for the loss of certain older modes of cultural expression.

The first bishop of Mexico, Fray Juan de Zumárraga (appointed in 1528), though by no means as exclusively concerned with the problems of Indian welfare as was Motolinía, nevertheless applied himself earnestly to the problems involved in converting them. Because he learned soon after his arrival in the New World that no inducement had proved so alluring to the Indians as the music of the friars, he wholeheartedly endorsed the program of music instruction that Fray Pedro had already set up in the school attached to the San Francisco monastery, and also encouraged the founding of several other schools where reading, writing, and especially music, could be taught the Indians. He was not so successful as he would have desired in instituting a full musical program in the primitive cathedral; but he appointed Canon Juan Xuárez (who arrived in 1530) chapel master,[16] and for a quarter of a century Xuárez labored with the Indian youths preparing and rehearsing them for musical service in the cathedral.

Zumárraga, despite his own Franciscan vow of poverty, perfectly understood the necessity of paying a trained resident choir and hiring instrumentalists, if the cathedral were properly to be served. In order to adorn his cathedral, which was at first a dependency of Seville in Spain, he spent the whole revenue of his bishopric during four years.[17] His ideal for a physical plant was a cathedral which in every detail of appearance and appointment would equal that of the parent church at Seville.[18] In musical matters he was equally ambitious. A letter which he wrote April 17, 1540, to Charles V, illustrates at one and the same time his understanding of the unusual value of music as a tool for plowing and furrowing the Indian mind, and also his understanding of the necessity for paid choirs.

He began his plea for paid choirs with no little astuteness. He pointed out to the Emperor (Charles V was more than usually devout and ended his days in a monastery at Yuste) that the Masses appointed for the members of the royal house and more particularly for Charles himself were celebrated with insufficient solemnity. Zumárraga's line of reasoning ran thus: "I believe the deed of erection for these Masses obliges us to sing them, not merely recite them. The Cabildo, however, disagrees with me. But it seems to me that it is preferable to err on the side of more rather than less in such important matters. However, since there are insufficient funds to pay the singers, and since the Indians who are now singing under Canon Xuárez's direction can only devote a small part of their time (for they must do outside work), I appeal to you for stipends for the singers." Zumárraga also pointed out to Charles in this letter other values which would accrue from a costlier music program.

At present we are simply singing together simple music [in familiar style] and everyone is of the opinion that this is the most satisfactory thing to do since we have such gaps in our choir. Numbers of the clergy are absent on business elsewhere during the week, and some that remain do not know how to sing plainchant properly.

. . . . . .

Experience has taught us how greatly edified the Indians are by sacred music; indeed the fathers who work directly with them and who hear their confessions tell us that more than by preaching the Indians are converted by the music. They come from great distances in order to hear it, and they ardently desire not only to learn the fundamentals but also to become really proficient in it. We are not able to pay them. It would be well, however, for those who sing in the choir to be freed from other business so that the Masses may be celebrated with befitting solemnity.[19]

Zumárraga did not simply content himself with pleas to the Emperor, however; he himself while detained in Spain on a lengthy visit engaged professional church musicians and purchased manuscript choirbooks for use at Mexico City.

Music having proved its value as a tool in missionary work among the indigenes in the Valley of Mexico, it was but natural that elsewhere in

New Spain the same emphasis upon music should have manifested itself. In 1569 Fray Alonso de Paraleja wrote from Guadalajara:

> We support an Indian master in every religious house the duties of whom consist in teaching reading, writing, arithmetic, and music. Music is taught all those who wish to learn it, and because most Indians have a natural flair for it, many become skilful singers and players. We are unfortunately, however, unable to pay them for their services in church. If Your Majesty would order these singers who compose the choirs of our churches and monasteries to be paid, it would be accounted a deed glorious in the sight of God, and would enhance our work with those who still remain heathen. A suggested stipend would be, let us say, ten pesos annually.
>
> .   .   .   .   .
>
> We are extremely careful to see that in our churches and monasteries the Office . . . is sung daily, and also on saints' days to see that the Office is sung with suitable solemnity. On festival days polyphonic music is sung, accompanied by chirimías and flutes, and the Indians find all this extremely attractive.
>
> .   .   .   .   .
>
> We are also careful to see that the Indians know how to sing in their own houses at night [after work is over] suitable Christian hymns.[20]

One final account may suitably be reproduced here. The Council of the Indies, the supreme governing body in Spain, sent over to Mexico in 1568 an inspector whose duties included the gathering of reports from the various religious orders on the progress of their missionary labors. The longest account we have of the Indian musicians who played and sang in the mission churches probably occurs in the report prepared by the Franciscans for this visiting inspector, Licenciado Juan de Ovando. The section reproduced below carries the heading, "Singers and Instrumentalists."

> The Indian singers and instrumentalists who play in church gather together every day in order to rehearse their singing and playing, using our schools for a place to practice. We recommend the continuation of this custom: for one thing, because without daily practice they do not progress in their singing, and for another, because they soon forget what they have learned already if they stop practicing. They can hardly practice elsewhere than at our schools.

It is customary in the towns large enough to warrant the stationing of clergy for the singers to divide themselves into two choirs, and the players to form two bands; choirs and bands alike alternate weekly so those in the groups who are married and have families may see them regularly. Also they need every other week free so they earn enough to pay their taxes. It would be cruel for us to allow them to serve continuously in church, doing nothing but singing. They are all so long-suffering that we feel conscience-stricken not to give them any financial aid. In each of the two choirs there are ordinarily fifteen or sixteen Indians. While a lesser number might suffice, still the thinness of their voices prevents them from sounding well unless there are at least that many. . . . Finally, it is their custom to sing Mass and the Divine Office in all the churches attached to monasteries. They sing plainchant and polyphony with agreeable skill. In some of the more favored towns where time and circumstance propitiously unite, they perform the Offices of the church with as great solemnity and with as impressive music as can be encountered in many of the Cathedral churches of Spain itself.

Polyphonic music is the vogue everywhere, and accompaniment of flutes and chirimías is common. In a number of places lutes [dulzainas] and reeds [orlos] along with viols [vihuelas de arco] and other types of instruments are used. Organs are also found in a number of places.

The Indians themselves play all these instruments, and their harmonious sounding together is truly a wonderful allurement towards Christianity as far as the generality of the natives is concerned. The music is most necessary. The adornment of the church itself and all the beauty of the music lifts their spirits to God and centers their minds on spiritual things. They are naturally inclined to be careless and forgetful unless they are reminded of the unseen by the seen and the unheard by the heard. Because of their very tendency to forget and to neglect, their own governors during the times of their infidelity made a point of occupying them incessantly in the building of huge and sumptuous temples, and also in the adornment of them with numberless beautiful flowers; requiring them, moreover, to offer gifts of gold and silver, and to participate in endless sacrifices and ceremonies, more severe and arduous than those imposed by the law of Moses.[21]

Most of the passages thus far quoted have had to do with the missionary labors of the Franciscans. Theirs was, of course, the first order commissioned to undertake the conversion of the Indians. The Dominicans, however, arrived in force during 1526, and the Augustinians followed in 1532. Juan de Grijalva's *Crónica de la Orden de N. P. S. Agustín en las provincias de la Nueva España . . . desde el año de 1533 hasta el de*

1592 contains a passage in which music is endorsed with the same emphasis as the best allurement to Christianity. After the three orders already named, a fourth, the Society of Jesus, entered Mexico in 1572. Father Pérez de Rivas (1576–1655), a prominent Jesuit, testified a century after the Conquest that in his experience music instruction and performance were still one of the best means of attracting and holding the Indians. The Jesuit Indian work was done in northwestern Mexico; they together with the Franciscans worked also in California and New Mexico.

It is quite probable the level of musical ability declined among the missionaries sent out during the later colonial period. Only a few of the later missionaries in what is now the southwestern part of the United States can have come into the field with such an extensive background of training as Pedro de Gante.[22] But where one did appear in California, Father Arroyo de la Cuesta for example, musical emphasis was still found an invaluable aid in the conversion process. Elsewhere in the New World during the later colonial period music training when given by competent instructors still proved invaluable. Anthony Sepp (who had received his own thorough musical training at Augsburg) found that "one secret of [his] popularity among the Indians was his decided talent and love for music."[23] Sepp's "brilliant success in the musical training of the Indians" won him a large "harvest" of converts, and "being the first to have introduced harps, cornet[t]s, clari[o]nets, and organs into these parts, [he] has earned for him [self] undying praise."[24]

Many other notable examples of missionary success traceable, on the human level at least, to emotional conditioning through music can be culled from Jesuit missionary documents in the *Archivo General de la Nación* at Buenos Aires. The honors that priority in applying a successful missionary technique brings rightfully belong to Pedro de Gante in Mexico, however, for it was he who first showed the way.

THE RESULTING SUPERFLUITY OF INDIAN SINGERS
AND INSTRUMENTALISTS

The gathering of further statements attesting the Mexican Indian's extraordinary fondness for music would be an easy task, simply because so many of the friars who wrote concerning the conversion of the tribes in central Mexico mentioned the role music played in winning them to Christianity. But if we understand why the early friars so gladly inaugurated music instruction, we still perhaps cannot quite understand why such large numbers of Indians gladly undertook careers as professional church musicians, especially when the friars were not usually able to pay them living wages. The problem of oversupply in the number who presented themselves for service as church musicians was studied by the president of the famous second audiencia, Bishop Sebastián Ramírez de Fuenleal. Fuenleal ascribed the plethora of church musicians *1* to the prestige they enjoyed among their fellow-Indians by virtue of their profession, and *2* to the privilege of exemption from taxation which they often enjoyed. Both these advantages descended to them from their pre-Conquest antecessors. As Fuenleal remarked: "Among the Indians [before the Conquest] instrumentalists and singers were highly esteemed, because by means of songs their musicians preserved the memory of the past; and not only was respect given those who devoted themselves to music but also the privilege of exemption from taxation." [25]

The first official notice of the excessive number of singers and instrumentalists was taken at the initial church council called by Archbishop Alonso de Montúfar. The printed provisions of this council, which were published in 1556, the year after the meeting of the council, explain what had taken place.

The great excess in our archdiocese of musical instruments, of chirimías, flutes, viols, trumpets, and the great number of Indians who spend their time in playing and singing obliges us to apply a remedy and to place a limit on all this superabundance. We therefore require and order that from henceforth trumpets shall not be played in churches during divine service, and require that no more be bought; those which are already in possession of the churches shall be used only in outdoor processions, and not as accompaniment for the liturgy. As for the chirimías and flutes, we require that they be stored in the principal towns and only distributed for use in the villages on festival days of their patron saints; and as for viols and other instruments, we request that these too be no longer used; we urge all the clergy to install organs everywhere so that indecorous and improper instruments may be banished from the church. The organ is the correct instrument for use in the church, and we wish its use to become universal in Mexico.

We charge all clergy in our archdiocese and all other clergy in Mexico residing outside our archdiocese but under our spiritual jurisdiction, carefully to limit the number of singers throughout our jurisdiction so that no more than are necessary shall continue to spend their time simply in singing. Those who are permitted to continue must be able to sing plain-chant intelligently. They shall sing polyphonic music only when their singing conforms to standards which we consider acceptable.[26]

. . . . .

Because of the vast number of churches which have sprung up every-where in our archdiocese, proper regulation has proved difficult. . . . We therefore decree that only those which in the judgment of the ordinary seem really necessary shall be permitted to continue; the others shall be taken down. Those that remain shall be decently equipped with all the proper furnishings and ornaments. No more Indians than are absolutely necessary shall be permitted to become choristers and custodians. They should be few in number, and should live lives that are without blemish or spot. They moreover should know the doctrines of our holy faith and the traditional customs of the church. They should be married and not bachelors, and they should be persons who know how to give sound in-struction in doctrine to those who are still ignorant.[27] . . . Indian catechists who work in villages where there are no priests must be able to sing the various prayers, so they can teach the people.[28] . . . The Indian singers shall be examined by the clergy who know the native lan-guages, and shall not be permitted to sing songs that remind the people of their old idolatrous customs; they shall sing nothing that savours of heathenism or that offends against sound doctrine.[29]

. . . . .

The Indians of this nation continue to delight on the kind of dancing, of festivity, and of mirth-making which they delighted in during the days of their heathenism; but in order to avoid contamination from customs that may contain seeds of evil, we ask (as said the Apostle Paul) that the appearance of evil be avoided.[30] . . . Furthermore they shall not begin dancing before the hour of High Mass; they may dance, however, during the afternoon and in the evening.

No more convincing proof need be given than these extracts from the printed proceedings of the council to show with what extravagance the Indians had taken to the music of the friars. One chronicler caustically remarked the Indians liked Mass best when it was an instrumental con-cert as well. But churches in Mexico during this period were by no means unique in allowing a wide assortment of wind and string instruments. They were a commonplace even in the chapel music at Charles V's court.

His chapel payroll included salaries for eight trumpeters and four drummers [31] in addition to salaries for woodwinds and strings. The decision of the First Mexican Council to exclude all these was, however, in line with the eventual dictates of Philip II, who in 1572 finally abolished all instruments from his chapel.[32]

What deserves particular notice in the decisions of the First Mexican Council is not, then, simply the fact that instrumental music was a commonplace in the newly founded churches, but rather that Indian instrumentalists and singers had multiplied beyond reason. Philip II was not slow in adding the force of his secular authority to the decisions of the bishops. In February of 1561 he issued to the president and oidores of the royal audiencia a cedula which read in part:

> Because of the cost of maintaining the present excessive number of instrumentalists who consume their time playing trumpets, clarions, chirimías, sackbuts, flutes, cornetts, dulzainas, fifes, viols, rebecs, and other kinds of instruments, an inordinate variety of which are now in use in the monasteries, . . . and because the number of musicians and singers is reported to be increasing constantly in both large and small towns, . . . and because very many of those reared simply to sing and play on instruments soon become lazy scoundrels whose morals are reported to be extremely bad, . . . and because in many places they do not pay tribute and resist lawful authority, we require a reduction in the number of Indians who shall be permitted to occupy themselves as musicians.[33]

Even Philip's strongly worded cedula, enforcing as it did the decisions of the First Mexican Council, failed however to procure the desired results; the Second Mexican Provincial Council meetings in 1565, a decade after the First Council, was again forced to occupy itself with the same problem. In addressing itself to Philip, the Second Council petitioned:

> Item, that Your Highness order a further abatement in the excessive number of Indian singers; . . . the small payment they now receive almost always is insufficient for them even to eat, much less pay tribute.[34]

In general it would be correct to say that the opinion of the prelates and of the secular clergy favored throughout the sixteenth century a drastic curtailment in the numbers of Indians whom the regulars, that is to say the friars, were willing to place in such semi-official church positions as janitors, building custodians, church decorators, music instrument makers, and players and singers in church services. With the division of opinion that existed it was but natural that the friars wherever they were in complete control should not have paid overmuch heed to the musical injunctions issued by Montúfar. Since Montúfar was himself a Dominican, the members of his own order perhaps took his injunctions seriously, but the Franciscans and even the Augustinians seem at times blandly to have disregarded him. Admirable men often disagreed on vital points of missionary procedure during the sixteenth century as the violent disagreement of such leaders as Las Casas and Motolinía on the correct method of baptizing Indians illustrates. Because of this possibility of disagreement, then, one finds that Indian musical life did continue to flourish, at least in Franciscan environments, long after church councils had ordered an abatement and after Philip II had himself intervened in order to halt the excess.

The reasons high secular and ecclesiastical authorities tried to limit the spawning of Indian choirs were exactly the same reasons that induced so many Indians to offer themselves as church musicians. The Indian singers had to be reminded continuously, even as late as the end of the century, that they could no longer expect the tax exemptions which their pre-Conquest forbears had enjoyed. And they had similarly to be reminded that, whatever kindnesses had been done them by the friars, in the minds of bishops their place in God's economy was as hewers of wood and drawers of water rather than as children of the covenant.[35]

Saldívar, the foremost living authority on Mexican colonial music, found an interesting petition presented by a group of Indian singers who prayed Viceroy Martín Enríquez in 1576 for relief from the tribute. Enríquez roughly reminded them that they must pay it like every other Indian, no matter how poor they were or how little they received for their services as church musicians. Saldívar also unearthed evidence to show that the cash salaries paid a sampling of 1,376 Indian singers averaged during Enríquez's administration only a little more than two pesos annually. Even this munificent cash salary was, however, begrudged by Spanish self-styled grandees. It is of course well-known that many prelates came to regard the Mexican church simply as a choice haven for impecunious immigrants. In the 123 towns whose records Saldívar studied the average number of Indian church musicians was 11.2, a figure which represented in some cases instrumentalists as well as singers. Since the towns which he included in this count were in many instances mere hamlets or villages numbering their total population in the hundreds rather than thousands, a figure of eleven musicians for each is quite sufficient proof that Mendieta and Torquemada knew their arithmetic when they boasted of the tremendous interest the Indians took in music. But the average cash salary paid the 1,376 Indian singers whose records Saldívar studied reached only about one percent of the average cash salary paid Spanish and creole singers who functioned at the same time in the important metropolitan churches of New Spain.[36]

THE MUSICAL ACHIEVEMENT OF EARLY COLONIAL INDIAN CHOIRS

As Torquemada summed up the achievement of sixteenth-century Indian choirs when he came to write his *Monarquía Indiana* (published in 1615) their record seems notable.

I. Without receiving any direct gifts of choirbooks, the Indians nevertheless were able to create splendid libraries of church music by painstakingly copying books brought over by Zumárraga and his deputies.

> After they had learned to write, they then learned how to draw lines on paper and write music notes; they then made excellent copies both of plainsong and of polyphonic music in large letters suitable for use in choirs. Their copies were used by the friars as well as by themselves, and were beautifully done with illuminated letters throughout.

II. By sharing among themselves teaching which certain privileged ones were able to get from Spanish masters, musical culture of the European type became sufficiently diffused for them to develop respectable choirs even in their smaller villages.

> Nowadays every town of one hundred population or more contains singers who have learned how to sing the Offices, the Mass, Vespers, and are proficient in polyphonic music; competent instrumentalists are also found everywhere. The small towns all have their supply of instruments, and even the smallest hamlets, no matter how insignificant, have three or four Indians at least who sing every day in church. Especially is this true in the provinces of Michoacán and Jalisco.[37]

III. Because the Indians in addition to making their own instruments soon developed among themselves the art of fabricating clever imitations of European instruments brought over by the invaders, they were able to develop instrumental accompanying ensembles with unique and unforeseen tone color possibilities.

The first instruments of music manufactured here were flutes, then oboes, and afterwards viols and bassoons and cornetts. After a while there was no single instrument used in churches which Indians in the larger towns had not learned to make and play. It became unnecessary to import any of these from Spain. One thing can be asserted without fear of contradiction; in all Christendom there is nowhere a greater abundance of flutes, sackbuts, trumpets, and drums, than here in New Spain. Organs have also been installed here in nearly all the churches which are administered by the orders. However, with these, not the Indians but rather Spanish builders have taken charge of construction, since the Indians do not have capital for such larger enterprises. The Indians make the organs under supervision, and they play the organs in our monasteries and convents. The other instruments which serve for solace or delight on secular occasions are all made here by the Indians, who also play them: rebecs, guitars, trebles, viols, harps, monochords.[38]

IV. The Indian musical accomplishment was by no means limited simply to clever imitation of European performance, but included also a certain amount of original creative activity in the European idiom.

With this I conclude (and this is an important observation): only a few years after the Indians began to learn the chant, they also began to compose. Their villancicos, their polyphonic music in four parts, certain masses and other liturgical works, all composed with adroitness, have been adjudged superior works of art when shown Spanish masters of composition. Indeed the Spanish masters often thought they could not have been written by Indians.[39]

MUSIC PRINTING DURING THE SIXTEENTH CENTURY

An aggregate of approximately 220 books are known to have been published in Mexico during the sixteenth century. A very large proportion of these sixteenth century Mexican books were printed in Indian tongues. Grammars, dictionaries, and religious tracts were published in at least nine different Indian languages—including Nahuatl, Otomí, Tarasco, Maya, Zapotec, Huastec, Mixtec, Utlatec, and Chuchon. Those who controlled the press obviously had no intention of neglecting the Indian. The books published in Spanish included treatises on navigation, on medicinal herbs, on surgery, instruction leaflets on how to teach reading, on elementary arithmetic, records of notable current events such as earthquakes, stories of voyages and explorations, and a large number of devotional texts.

Of these 220-odd Mexican imprints, twelve are known to have been liturgical books containing music. The first book containing music appeared in 1556, thirty-five years after Cortés crushed the Aztec nation. The remaining eleven of these dozen Mexican liturgical books containing music were published between 1560 and 1589. Several circumstances conspire to make the printing of a dozen music books in Mexico during the sixteenth century a notable achievement. During the half-century between 1550 and 1600 only fourteen liturgical books with music were published in Spain, the home country. During the entire century, twenty-nine liturgical books with music were published in Spain.[40]

If we look more closely at the publication record in Spain we discover that from only one publishing center—Toledo—were as many liturgical books with music issued during the entire century as were published in Mexico City during the brief span of thirty-three years between 1556 and 1589. Six such books were published in Salamanca (where Francisco de Salinas occupied the chair of music during the latter years of the century). One each was published in Seville (the seat of the archdiocese on which the diocese of Mexico depended until 1546), and in Madrid (the newly established capital). Even Toledo would not have matched the publication record of Mexico City during the century had not the great Cardinal Ximénez de Cisneros, a prelate of vast learning and Biblical zeal, dedicated himself to the restoration and propagation of a rite—the Mozarabic—which differed from the more usual Roman rite.

The number of books with music published in Mexico is significant not only in comparison with the number of such books published in Spain during the same epoch, but also because Mexico was the only Hispanic colony throughout the entire colonial period in which any books of liturgical music were printed. Even at Lima in Peru where another viceroyalty whose importance equaled that of Mexico had its seat, no music books were printed. Printing of books started in Lima just forty-five years after printing began in Mexico. In most other respects, except the printing of music books, both Lima and Mexico presses followed a similar course of development. In both capitals the first book was a manual of Christian doctrine in an Indian tongue. The 1539 *Breve y mas compendiosa doctrina* published at Mexico City in the language of the Aztecs was the counterpart of the 1584 *Doctrina christiana* published at Lima in the language of the Incas. The first printers in both capitals were Italians; printing from the beginning in both capitals was rigidly circumscribed by government regulations. From presses in both capitals flowed a stream of titles having to do with similar cultural interests. The literary life in both capitals followed a parallel course; a long heroic poem such as Pedro de Oña's *Arauco domado* (1596), published in Lima, was soon followed by another similarly ambitious poem on a New World theme, Bernardo de Balbuena's *Grandeza Mexicana* (1604), published in Mexico. These comparisons between the cultural life of Mexico and of the other Hispanic colony nearest it in political importance, Peru, are offered simply in order to reinforce the capital importance of the music books which we are now about to discuss more specifically. If it is not realized that in no other Hispanic colony of the colonial period were such publication ventures involving music attempted; and if it is not realized that during the particular period when these books were printed Spain herself scarcely matched her colony, New Spain, one cannot properly appreciate the true significance of these twelve music books which are now submitted for individual examination.

DESCRIPTION OF SIXTEENTH CENTURY MEXICAN IMPRINTS
CONTAINING MUSIC

Four of the dozen music books printed in Mexico before 1600 contain the plainchant portions of the Mass sung by the choir; these portions include not only the Ordinary of the Mass, that is to say, the invariable portions such as the Kyrie eleison, Gloria, and so forth; but also the Proper, that is to say, the portions which change from day to day. These four books bear the collective title, *Graduale Dominicale*.

The word "Dominicale" in the title does not mean "Dominican" as some imperfectly informed Latinists have supposed. The Dominican order did most certainly import choirbooks during this particular epoch to fulfill its own individual needs in Mexico. A shipment of forty boxes of books to Mexico in 1584 contained, for instance, twelve Dominican liturgical books,[41] seven of which were specifically listed as books published in Venice. The Dominicans used an order of the Mass which was their own, and differed then as now from the standard Roman arrangement of the elements in the Mass. But their own individual liturgical needs could be met by importing books into Mexico, rather than by undergoing the expense of printing them in the colony. "Dominicale" in the title, *Graduale Dominicale*, simply means that the choirbook in question contains the plainchant sung in all Sunday and feast-day Masses.

The second largest group among the dozen with music printed in Mexico comprised three antiphonaries. These antiphonaries contained the plainchant sung during the canonical hours.

The singing of the canonical hours, a practise as old as St. Benedict, occupies the singer's entire day. The canonical hours include matins (sung before dawn); lauds (sung at dawn); prime (sung shortly after daybreak); terce (sung in mid-morning); sext (sung at noon); none (sung in mid-afternoon); vespers (sung at nightfall); and compline (sung just before retiring). During the canonical hours psalms and antiphons are sung. These psalms and antiphons change from day to day and often from hour to hour. Moreover, the music (for the antiphons especially) is often extremely florid. Nowadays the hours are sung only in monasteries and conventual churches, but in sixteenth century Mexico they were sung everywhere. In village churches where there were only six or seven singers, an abbreviated and easy Office of *Nuestra Señora*, Our Lady, was sung; [42] elsewhere the Office in unabbreviated form was attempted.

The other seven liturgical books with music include two manuals, or directories, for the proper administration of the sacraments; a missal (which contains the music sung by the celebrant at Mass, rather than the music sung by the choir); a passion-book (containing in this particular case the music sung during the last three days of Holy Week); and a directory for novices who were being prepared for the priesthood (containing brief excerpts of music for the priest to sing at Mass: giving only a tabloid version, however, of all he was supposed to sing).

I. The first of these twelve books published in Mexico was the simplest as far as music was concerned. Its printer was not named, but the date of publication, 1556, appeared on the titlepage. From the Latin title of this first book containing music one learns that it was designed to serve as a directory of worship for members of the Augustinian order; moreover, that this directory of worship had been purified of errors which had crept into other directories of a similar character; that though the ceremonies were purified the chants in their old form were retained. On its titlepage was printed the following: *ORDINARIUM* / *sacri ordinis heremitarū* / *sancti Augustini episco/pi &* *regularis obser/uātiẹ, nunc denuò* / *correctū, sique* / *nō secūdum* / *morē* *an/tiquū* / *ce/remoniẹ fiant, sed se/cūdū choros altos.// Mexici. anno* / *dni.* *1556* / *idibus* / *Iulij.*

The total number of pages in this book, or booklet, amounts to only eighty. But a large number of essential matters in the conduct of public worship are included; the titles of the first several chapters will afford some idea of the contents: (1) How and when to ring bells, (2) When to face the altar, (3) When to stand and when to sit, (4) The times for singing, (5) Proper tones for benedictions and absolutions, (6) When to kneel while in choir, (7) When to genuflect, (8) When to bow, (9) Versicles, invitatories. The music scattered through the *Ordinarium* does not supply a complete version of all that a priest should sing at Mass throughout the entire year. It simply gives the intonations which the priest should sing at various classes of church feasts throughout the year. These feasts are classified under such conventional headings as "minora simplicia," "maiora simplicia," "minora semiduplicia," "maiora semiduplicia."

As inspection clearly reveals, this *Ordinarium* was intended to serve as an instruction manual for young Augustinian seminarians whose destined field of service was Indian work in Mexico. From it the seminarian could learn the basic rules of church etiquette. After studying it he would know not only the intonations for the Kyries, Glorias, Sanctuses, and Agnuses, which he should sing at various classes of feasts, but he would know also how to form processions, what colors of ecclesiastical vestments he should wear throughout the church year, how to swing incense, proper melodic formulas for the intoning of gospels, how to be a subdeacon or a deacon at Mass, how to give the *pax,* what to do when the bishop visited his church. As an instruction manual its virtues are manifest; rules are clearly set down in simple language, the easiest rules are given first with an orderly progression towards more difficult rules, only the bare essentials are stressed with all superfluous verbiage stripped away.

All the melodies in the book were, as the titlepage of the book itself suggested, several centuries old at the time the book was compiled. From datings supplied by the Solesmes scholars it is apparent that none of the chants printed in this 1556 book can have originated later than the twelfth century. This *Ordinarium,* moreover, contains no Creed-melodies. But though Creed-melodies are omitted, the 1556 book does supply melodies for the *Ite missa est* sung by the priest at the end of Mass. In consonance with the instructional purpose of the book, most of the melodies included are of an easy syllabic rather than a melismatic type.

In order to show how nearly the 1556 melodies approximate those printed in such an easily accessible book as the 1934 edition of the *Liber Usualis*, we present below for comparison the opening phrases of four different Kyries, the first Kyrie in each pair being the 1556 version and the second being the Solesmes version. The Solesmes monks, of course, made no claims to infallibility, but they did attempt to determine the exact shape of a given melody at the time it was originally divulged. If a melody as printed in 1556 closely adhered to the version arrived at by the Solesmes scholars after painstaking collation, one may safely say that the 1556 version was "uncorrupted." Nearly all recent liturgiologists have made a great point of the supposed corruption of plainchant during the Renaissance. It would be interesting then to see from a study of the melodies as they appear in sixteenth century Mexican imprints whether this corruption was as universal as has been supposed.

The building on Isabel la Católica Street in Mexico City now used to house the Biblioteca Nacional was originally a part of the building used as headquarters for the Augustinian order in New Spain. As one thinks of the sixty-nine Mexican incunabula already shelved as rare books at the Biblioteca Nacional, it would seem particularly appropriate that a copy of the 1556 *Ordinarium* should be among them, and more especially as one thinks of the order under whose auspices this first music book appeared. As yet, however, the Biblioteca Nacional does not possess a copy. Perhaps in the future a copy will come to light somewhere which can become the property of the Biblioteca Nacional; the only copy in the United States is one which was formerly owned by a resident of Titusville, Pennsylvania, and which is now in the possession of the New York Public Library.

II. The second book with music published in the New World was the *Manuale Sacramentorum secundum usum ecclesię Mexicanę* . . . printed in 1560 by Juan Pablos. This manual was by no means the manual for beginners that the 1556 *Ordinarium* was; it contained 354 pages, and its use was made mandatory throughout the archbishopric of Mexico by Montúfar. This particular *Manuale* did not present a liturgical usage drawn from any one continental usage. Montúfar and the other bishops who sat at the First Mexican Council (1555) had no way of knowing what kind of liturgical usage would finally be prescribed by the Council of Trent, then in adjourned session. The bishops under Montúfar's presidency committed themselves in 1560, then, to a liturgical use drawn not from any one source, but rather to an eclectic use derived from the usages of Rome, Toledo, Salamanca, Seville, Granada, "y otros." The music of this 1560 manual has not yet been studied in detail; presumably it too was drawn from a diversity of sources, and in order to locate the exact provenience of the plainchant melodies contained in it, liturgical books in use at the various named Spanish centers would need to be consulted. A certain unexpected liturgical independence, a Neo-Hispanic "Gallicanism," if one will call it that, seems manifest not only in this sacramentary "according to the use of the Mexican Church," but in several later liturgical books which were issued before Pius V's bull *Quod a nobis* "swept away all the numerous variations and exuberances then common in the Roman Rite, and established one uniform Mass, and one uniform method of saying Mass." [43]

III. In 1561 was published a *Missale Romanum Ordinarium* which has been called the handsomest book issued from the Mexican press during the sixteenth century.

The most splendid product of the Mexican press, a volume whose pre-eminence has been challenged only two or three times during the centuries which have elapsed since its publication, is the *Missale Romanum Ordinarium*, printed in the city of Mexico in 1561. It is a magnificent folio volume of 330 leaves, printed in red and black, with historiated initials and occasional woodcut borders.[44]

Music printing appears on 52 pages in this 1561 *Missale*. The notes themselves are printed in black; the five-line staff in red. The music, like that of the 1556 *Ordinarium*, has been chosen from the repertory of simpler chants; both books were printed for the use of priests rather than choirs, and therefore florid chants were quite naturally excluded. The majority of the melodies in the 1561 *Missale* are syllabic. Neumes of two notes appear frequently enough (podatus and clivis), but three-note neumes are rare (torculus and climacus). No such niceties as liquescent neumes or the quilisma appear anywhere throughout the book. Even so, the music could never have been sung by a mere tyro in plainsong. The kind of background in plainsong that clergy in New Spain were expected to have may be gauged not only from the character of the melodies in this book, but also from certain rules already promulgated by Archbishop Montúfar five years before the printing of this *Missale*. In the 1556 *Constituciones del arçobispado* Montúfar required that candidates for minor orders must "know the fundamentals of plainchant, and at the very least must be able to sight-sing creditably." Candidates for the diaconate were expected to show that they had mastered all the rules for singing set down in the breviary. Those ordained to the priesthood were required to demonstrate a still higher degree of accomplishment as plainchanters. If these rules were at all implemented, then Montúfar had a right to expect that the music notes printed in the 1561 *Missale* would serve more than a mere decorative purpose.

García Icazbalceta, the great Mexican bibliographer, compared the 1561 Missal with standard missals in use in his own day. Since he was not interested in musical problems he confined his study to textual variants.[45] He found that the editors of the 1561 *Missale* had selected their text from no single European source, but had pieced together material from a large number of different sources. Having chosen a preface or a postcommunion or other matter, the editors however adhered faithfully to the source from which they were at the moment copying. Insofar as the music in the 1561 *Missale* can be compared with the music in contemporary European missals the same thing holds true. An exhaustive search has not been made, but at present it seems certain the music editor no more committed himself to copying the music *in toto* from any single European source than did the editors of the *Missale* text. What is perhaps significant, however, is the fact that though eclectic in choosing his source-books, once having committed himself to a particular melody he copied it with utter fidelity. Although then he assembled his music from a wide variety of sources, as do modern hymn-book editors, at least it seems that once having selected his source for a particular antiphon, introit, or other melody, he then copied it without tinkering.

Some such antiphon as the one given below will show how faithfully a model was copied, once it had been selected.

The underlined notes in the 1497 Missal differ from those in the 1561 Missal; otherwise these two examples are identical.

IV. The fourth Mexican book with music was published seven years after Espinosa's much-praised *Missale*. In 1568 a French printer named Pedro de Ocharte published a *Manuale secundum usum Almae Ecclesiae Mexicanae*. This was the first music book published under a ceiling price regulation. Diego de Sansores, the gentleman at whose cost the book was printed, was enjoined not to sell it in a paper-back covering for more than four pesos de oro común. The publication of another book traversing almost the identical territory covered by the 1560 *Manuale* proved necessary in 1568 because during the intervening eight years a pontifical commission had recommended certain revisions of the sacramentary.

V. The exact dating of the next imprint, a *Graduale Dominicale*, has proved difficult because in the one extant copy both title page and colophon are missing.[46] Formerly this particular mutilated copy, now shelved at the Biblioteca Nacional in Mexico City, was thought (for reasons that will appear later) to have been printed in 1576; now, however, it is recognized that this mutilated copy was printed before 1572.

VI. The next two books were printed by Pedro de Ocharte. A Frenchman from Rouen, he had fallen heir to the business started by Juan Pablos, the first printer in Mexico (by marrying Pablos's daughter). Probably because he was envied and disliked by certain Spaniards he was denounced to the Inquisition at the very moment he was in process of completing an order for one hundred passion-books, Passionarios, ordered by Juan Diego de Rincón, bishop of Michoacán, and Tarasco linguist. Because Rincón's order was pressing, Ocharte while still in prison implored the printer who was his rival, Antonio de Espinosa, to finish printing these books. In a letter to his wife, Ocharte described the contents, which included music for Maundy Thursday, Good Friday, and Holy Saturday.

The documents collected by the Inquisition authorities during their investigation include several which bear on Ocharte's passion-books. In all he printed 310 of them, and for each one he asked a handsome sum—twenty pesos.[47] This was five times the price placed on his 1568 *Manuale*. The Inquisition file reveals, moreover, who read proof, who took charge of delivering the books while Ocharte was in prison, and even the name of the person who pulled sheets while he was awaiting trial. We know when Ocharte was apprehended, and we know therefore that the printing of the *Passionario* was completed shortly before March 1, 1572. Yet despite all this specific information not one copy is extant today. Where did 310 books selling for such an extraordinary price disappear? The story of the Inquisition trial and the documents appertaining to it became known shortly before the first World War when the Archivo General de la Nación published the pertinent materials. But no one had ever seen a copy of the *Passionario* itself.

Finally in the late 1930's several battered sheets of a Passion According to St. John in plainsong setting were found in a tiny Indian village near Tlaxcala. Here at last was a possible fragment from Ocharte's *Passionario*. Along with the eight pages of passion music was found a fragment of a *Graduale Dominicale* which was later identified as one of the issues of 1576. Interest rose in the passion fragment. A collecter named Conway and another named Federico Gómez de Orozco shared possession of the battered sheets which had been found.[48] The assistance of expert Mexican bibliographers was secured and the eight questioned sheets were finally pronounced authentic fragments of a sixteenth century passion-book which could be none other than Ocharte's, since none other is known to have been printed in Mexico during that century. Specimens of type from the known Ocharte books proved it had been printed at his press. His own letter saying he had printed only the portions of the passion used on Maundy Thursday, Good Friday, and Holy Saturday clinched the matter; the only Passion narrative that would be sung during any one of those three days would be the Passion According to St. John—and that was the gospel portion found in the Indian village.

The finding of these several sheets demonstrated once more the hazards that have beset Mexican sixteenth-century imprints. It is no wonder that only one copy of the 1556 book, one copy of the 1560 book, two copies of the 1561 book, and one or two copies of certain other books here mentioned have come into the possession of libraries in the United States, despite the high prices paid for them. The British Museum and the Biblioteca Nacional in Madrid have acquired occasional copies offered for sale by private Mexican collecters, but even the National Library in Mexico still lacks some of the most important music imprints. In view of the scattered places in which the books now exist—some at the Biblioteca Nacional in Mexico City, others at the University of Texas in the García Icazbalceta collection, others at the New York Public Library, and other individual items at the Newberry Library in Chicago, at the Huntington Library in San Marino, and at the Library of Congress in Washington— it is not surprising that so little is actually known concerning these Mexican music imprints. Henry R. Wagner, whose studies in Mexican bibliography are definitive, has more than once called attention to the inadequate canvassing of Mexican music imprints, simply because of the wide dispersal of the books and the difficulty of making comparisons.

VII. The next book with music has disappeared altogether. We know, however, of its existence through the same set of Inquisition documents which revealed the existence of an Ocharte *Passionario*. Along with a passion-book, he spoke of an *Antiphonario Dominical* which he said Espinosa was in process of printing for him while he was imprisoned. Although we cannot now fix an exact terminal date for its completion, it must have been finished not much later than the summer of 1572. In March Ocharte ordered his friend and factotum, Diego de Sansores, to give Espinosa all the paper "de marca mayor" —of superior quality—which he had still at his shop in order that Espinosa might finish the *Antiphonario* without delay.[49] The next mention of this particular antiphonary occurs in the record of the Cabildo Eclesiástico which met on February 12, 1577. On that date the Cabildo ordered that Pedro de Ocharte (whose imprisonment had ended in 1574) be paid 40 pesos de tepuzque for an antiphonary that had already been delivered to the cathedral authorities at an earlier unspecified date.[50]

VIII, IX, X.   In 1576 at least three (and possibly four) [51] editions of a new *Graduale Dominicale* were issued. One of these 1576 editions was printed by Espinosa "at the charges of Ocharte"; Ocharte himself published the other two editions of the same book. The issue of three different editions of an immense book—comprising more than four hundred large folio pages—all in one year needs explanation. Such a book printed throughout in two impressions, black over red, with music of the more elaborate plainsong variety printed on nearly every page, must have been hugely expensive to produce. The pressure of a real emergency is needed if we are satisfactorily to account for the simultaneous issue of three editions. No decision independently made by the Mexican hierarchy was responsible for the sudden and urgent need for new choir books. Rather it was Pope Pius V's decree issued in 1571 concerning the reform of the missal and with it of the gradual that made necessary the immediate acquisition of new missals and graduals everywhere. Pius V's decree implemented liturgical decisions already made by the Council of Trent, and in issuing it he stipulated that henceforth all liturgical books should be printed under the direct supervision of the Roman See. Although the purpose of this ruling was to halt all liturgical printing undertaken elsewhere, Philip II soon overrode the stipulation that all books should be printed at Rome. But the requirement for new missals and graduals exactly conforming to papal requirements stood, and in Mexico as elsewhere new books had immediately to be procured.

The capacity of any one press to produce new books within a given length of time was severely limited during the sixteenth century. When a sudden need arose for quantity production of any one book, the work had to be divided between two printers. In England, for instance, when a new prayerbook was adopted by Parliament in 1548, and its use throughout the whole realm became mandatory on or before Whitsunday in 1549, a sufficient number of books could only be produced by dividing the work between two printers, Whitchurch and Grafton. In Mexico the commission for new graduals was divided between Ocharte and Espinosa. Ocharte alone may have produced three editions, but in any event he undertook two. The evidence for the production of two rests on the differing typography of two *Graduales*, each bearing Ocharte's name as printer, and each bearing the 1576 imprint date.

How does this extraneous information concerning printers and publication dates add significantly to our knowledge concerning music in sixteenth century Mexico? In this fashion: from the different bits of information now assembled one can arrive at a fairly accurate estimate of the number of choirs in Mexico which in 1576 were capable of doing in elaborate plainsong version the entire liturgy of the church. Mendieta and Torquemada boasted of an incredible development of Indian choirs. The evidence pieced together here proves that they were entirely correct in their boast.

In 1572, as we have seen, Ocharte stated that he had just finished printing 310 *Passionarios*, of which one hundred had been ordered by the bishop of Michoacán. If in 1572 with no pressure upon him to produce more than one hundred books he was able to print an extra 210, then certainly he was able to turn out no less than twice 310 when he produced two editions of the *Graduale*. Espinosa's contribution of a third batch of graduals in 1576 means we should multiply 310, our test figure, by three. The result, 930, can be accepted as a minimal figure; probably the actual number was in excess of 1,000. Because all these 1576 Graduals were "libros de facistol" only one copy for each choir was required. That a thousand choirs with singers all trained to sing the full service in the elaborate plainsong version of the 1576 *Graduale Dominicale* should have existed in New Spain at that time seems indeed astounding. In all New Spain in 1580 there were only 14,711 Spaniards.[52] If every Spaniard in the realm had been singing plainchant there would have been scarcely enough of them to fill the choirs for whose specific use the 1576 *Graduales* were printed. But the records of the Metropolitan church at Mexico City, as they have been collected by Dr. Lota M. Spell, clearly show that Spanish singers were notoriously difficult to come by; only a few of the cathedrals, such as those at Mexico City, at Puebla, and at Guadalajara, can have used any Spanish singers at all. Nearly all of the 10,000 or more choir singers who began singing the service out of the 1576 *Graduales* were Indians. Perhaps never at any time in any colony has so quickly and thoroughly been applied a bright polish of European musical culture as in sixteenth century Mexico.

The music of the 1576 *Graduale* is substantially the same music as that which is printed in current editions of the *Graduale*. Copies of the 1576 Gradual may now be seen in Mexico at the Biblioteca Nacional (collocation number o/I/7/2), and in the United States at the Newberry Library in Chicago and at the Library of Congress. The congressional copy, which lacks title-page and colophon, differs in small details from the Newberry copy (especially in the use of wood-cuts); the congressional copy also differs in certain small details from the Biblioteca Nacional copy; each of the three copies is individually different from the other two. But all three 1576 Graduals conform exactly to the Tridentine decrees; the 1571 Biblioteca Nacional Gradual does not.

XI, XII. Two more Mexican imprints with music were published before 1600: the *Psalterium Amphonarium* [sic] *Sanctorale, cum Psalmis et Hymnis* . . . , printed by Ocharte in 1584, and finally an *Antiphonarium*, printed also by Ocharte (1589). Both these last two books contain music for the revised breviary; although the revised breviary had been announced by Pius two years before the announcement of the revised missal, the less immediate demand for music for the Office delayed the final issue of antiphonaries. In a copy of the 1589 *Antiphonarium* now preserved at the University of Texas marginal notations are given for an organ accompaniment. The cutting of the margins in order to prepare this particular copy for binding has pared away some essential writing, but enough remains to provide clues as to performance practice.

PRESENT-DAY SIGNIFICANCE OF SIXTEENTH CENTURY MUSIC IMPRINTS

The present-day significance of these music imprints can be summarized under six headings: (1) These were the first books containing music printed in the New World. (2) They were the only liturgical books with music published in any of the Spanish colonies. (3) They provide superb examples of the printer's art in sixteenth century America. (4) The plainchant printed in them is less "corrupted" than had previously been thought universal in sixteenth century liturgical books. (5) From them can be ascertained the general level of musical culture in churches of New Spain during the epoch. (6) From circumstances connected with their publication can be adduced corroborating evidence concerning the number, the geographic spread, and the performance ability of Indian choirs.

SIXTEENTH CENTURY BACKGROUND IN SPAIN

If the evidence of these printed books shows that Mexico fully participated in the musical culture of the home country as far as monody was concerned, the evidence of the choirbooks preserved in such cathedrals as those at Mexico City and Puebla proves the colony fully participated in the polyphonic activity of the home country. A brief preliminary outline of Spanish polyphony will clarify the later discussion of Mexican polyphony. Formerly it was thought no school of polyphonic composers flourished in Spain before the sixteenth century. The publication of several codices such as the Calixtinus and the Huelgas has proved, however, that Spanish polyphony developed without aid from exterior influences at a much earlier date than the older music historians thought possible.

The immediate antecessors of the sixteenth century Spanish polyphonists were not only the Flemings in Philip the Fair's chapel establishment, and the Flemings such as Gombert who spent time in Spain during Charles V's residences in the peninsula, but also such Spanish composers as those included in Barbieri's *Cancionero de palacio.* The advent of such an exceptionally meritorious composer as Cristóbal de Morales (1500?–53) was prepared by the many earlier Spanish polyphonists such as Anchieta, Peñalosa, de la Torre, and Escobar, who were not content simply to copy the Flemings but insisted rather upon establishing a peculiarly Spanish polyphonic tradition. The most distinguished follower of Morales in the so-called Seville group of polyphonists was Francisco Guerrero (1527–99). In terms of influence, Morales and Guerrero must be accounted the two most important Spanish polyphonists as far as Mexico is concerned. The works of these two were brought to Mexico in manuscript copies during the mid-century, and were widely dispersed. The cathedral archives at both Mexico City and Puebla show an overwhelming preponderancy of these two over all other Spanish polyphonists of their epoch.

The reason Tomás Luis de Victoria, even better known today than Morales, is poorly represented in Mexican church archives stems from the fact he was not connected at any time during his career with either the parent cathedral of Mexico City—Seville, or the parent cathedral of Puebla—Toledo. Morales and Guerrero, on the other hand, were both natives of Seville, upon the musical archives of whose cathedral Mexico City depended for manuscript copies. Morales, moreover, was chapelmaster at Toledo after his return from Rome in 1545.

Some other background facts concerning Spanish music during the sixteenth century may be usefully summarized: music theory had been expounded in a remarkably progressive way by Ramos de Pareja, a Spaniard who taught at Bologna during the latter years of the fifteenth century. Several Spanish theorists of the sixteenth century produced distinguished works on musical theory; numbered among them were Juan Bermudo, Diego Ortiz, Tomás de Santa María, and Francisco de Salinas (whose pioneer labors as a collector of folk-songs have been noted in the previous chapter). The virtuoso vihuelists of the century included Luis Milán whose *El Maestro* (1535) was an epoch-making publication, Narváez, Fuenllana, Pisador, and Daza. Together with such keyboard artists as Cabezón and Venegas de Henestrosa these virtuosi succeeded in producing a Spanish instrumental literature that has not been surpassed in any subsequent century.

Historically Spanish music is seen as reaching its most vital epoch during the seventy-five year period between 1525 and 1600. This period of musical vitality therefore exactly coincided with the age of Spanish empire-building. The colony of New Spain was the happy recipient of numerous composers whose early life had been spent in the orbit of such masters as Morales, Guerrero, Salinas, and others of like notability. No other Spanish colony—not even Peru—enjoyed the same overflow of musical vitality that streamed from Spain during her best epoch.

Among the controlling forces that Hilarión Eslava listed when he sought reasons for the flowering of Spanish musical culture were several which had their effect in New Spain as well.

> [When we think of the reasons for the flourishing estate of Spanish religious music during the sixteenth century] we will do well to bear in mind that clergy who were appointed as singers in chapel and cathedral establishments were invariably expected to compose as well as sing. . . . Moreover we should remember . . . that many of the chapel establishments in Spain were [at that time] heavily endowed with funds for the maintenance of musicians; these [lucrative] posts were awarded in open competition, and appointment was therefore made on the basis of true merit. All these various factors should be borne in mind if we wish clearly to understand why Spain was not a laggard but rather in the vanguard, musically speaking, during the sixteenth century.[53]

SYNOPSIS OF NEO-HISPANIC POLYPHONIC DEVELOPMENT

The landmarks in the development of Neo-Hispanic polyphony during the sixteenth century may profitably be listed here in chronological order:

1527 Fray Juan Caro begins to teach the Indians in the mission school at Texcuco how to sing in parts.

1530 A small Indian choir trained in Pedro de Gante's Indian school sings every Sunday and feast-day at the newly established Mexico City Cathedral. Their more ambitious part-singing is supported by an organ just brought over from Seville.

1531 Bishop Zumárraga praises the skill of Indian singers who have been trained in part-song.

1532 Zumárraga commends the rapid progress his Indian choir has made in the singing of part-music, and praises the Indian copyists who deftly transcribe music from European sources.

1533 Canon Xuárez of the cathedral staff is assigned to teach young Indian choristers polyphonic singing.

1534 Zumárraga returns from a trip to Spain bringing back with him several part-books of Masses and motets for the use of the growing cathedral choir.

1536 Two cathedral canons are dispatched to Spain, one of whom secures several important choirbooks from the Seville Cathedral, and the other of whom locates a printer with music type who is willing to come to America.[54]

1538 Youths of Spanish blood are for the first time mentioned as members of the Mexico City Cathedral choir.

1538 A brilliant festival held at Tlaxcala provides Indian singers an opportunity to demonstrate their superior ability in performing polyphonic psalms, motets, and villancicos.

1539 "Canon Juan Xuárez is appointed chapel master at a salary of 20 pesos de minas, beginning the 1st of February of this year." Antonio Ramos is appointed cathedral organist, November 15.[55]

1540 Polyphonic music in preference to the prescribed plainchant is frequently sung in the Mexico City Cathedral.[56]

1543 Diego Perez Gordillo Negron, sixteen years resident in Michoacán, is singled out for praise in an official letter to Charles V because of skill in both plainchant and polyphonic music, which he teaches the Indians.

1544 Morales's 1544 Masses (Liber I), now preserved in a handwritten copy at Puebla Cathedral, is the oldest surviving polyphonic music anywhere to be encountered in an existing Mexican archive today.

1554 Instrumentalists (*los tañedores*) form an important part of Mexico City's cathedral ensemble; the salaries of the instrumentalists other than the organist are not, however, specified.

1554 An alumnus of Salamanca University, Lázaro del Álamo, is appointed cantor in the Mexico City Cathedral at an annual salary of 60 pesos de oro.[57]

1556 Álamo is promoted to the chapelmastership.

1559 The cathedral choir sings several important works of Morales at a commemoration service for Charles V. They also sing several original polyphonic compositions by Álamo.

1559 The number of paid choristers at the Mexico City Cathedral is set at twelve.[58] These participate in all daily services.

1560? Archbishop Montúfar promulgates an *Orden que debe observarse en el coro* containing 42 rules for the organization and conduct of the cathedral choir at Mexico City.[59] This rule-book is modeled after the 59 *Constitutions of the Pontifical Choir* given in 1545 by Pope Paul III.

1564 Álamo is mentioned as rendering important and valuable service to the archbishop by composing original motets, villancicos, and chanzonetas for use at Christmas, Easter, and Corpus Christi.

1564 A *Psalterium secundum sacro sancte Romane ecclesie consuetudinem* is published at Seville (in folio, 520 pages) for specific use of the Augustinians in Mexico.

1570? Juan de Victoria from Burgos, Spain, is named Álamo's successor in the chapelmastership.

1570 Guerrero's *Motteta* published by Gardano at Venice is the oldest polyphony in original printed form still extant in any Mexican archive.

1574 A play interspersed with choral and solo singing is performed by the Mexico City choirboys in honor of the new archbishop, Moya y Contreras. This musical play is but typical of many of its type; the choirboys sing at most important public functions in the capital during this epoch.

1575 Hernando Franco, the first Neo-Hispanic composer for whose music claims to lasting importance have been made, is appointed chapelmaster at an annual salary of 600 pesos de oro común.

1575 Moya y Contreras writes Ovando, president of the Council of the Indies, explaining the difficulties he encounters in securing cathedral singers because of the poor pay offered. The archbishop complains he cannot hold open competition for the posts as is held in Spain, nor can he submit a list of candidates to the viceroy, because none offer themselves.[60]

1575 The cathedral orchestra is significantly enlarged.[61]

1582 Salaries of singers are reduced because of the mounting costs of the

new cathedral building which has been started. The singers strike, however, and the archbishop is forced to restore them their former
wages.

1585 Mexican bishops in conclave enact important church music rules.[62]

1587 Fray Alonso Ponce, Franciscan Father Commissary visiting from
Spain, is deeply impressed by the music he hears in New Spain; he
hears the indigenes singing both plainchant and polyphony.

1589 A catalogue of the cathedral choral library at Mexico City made
this year reveals that works of Morales, Guerrero, Orlando di Lasso,
and Palestrina, are in the repertory.[63] Three Masses by Morales are
sung.

1592 Puebla, already an important center for sacred music instruction,
limits the personnel of the cathedral choir to "youths born of Spanish
parents." [64]

1599 A commemoration service for Philip II duplicating the pomp and
circumstance of the 1559 service for Charles V is held at Mexico City.

A tabulation of this sort emphasizes the musical life of the capital. This
emphasis is, however, almost inevitable during the first century. In the
first place, Mexico City even before the Conquest was the cultural center
of the territory dominated by the Aztecs. All the principal lords of Mexico
maintained town houses in Tenochtitlán where they resided during at
least a portion of the year.[65] Even though partially destroyed by Cortés,
Tenochtitlán—now Mexico City—still remained the capital. In New
Spain, as in every other political entity, the administrative center attracted
to itself the leading artists, musicians, and literary men of the day.

A comparison of the musical time-table in sixteenth century Mexico
with the European time-table reveals that the full apparatus of European
music culture was transferred to New Spain within only one generation
after the Conquest. The intimate liaison between colony and mother
country never at any later time during the colonial epoch redounded so
favorably to the musical advantage of the colony as during the first hundred years; the obvious reason is that Spain herself was at her all-time
cultural peak during those hundred years.

NEO-HISPANIC POLYPHONY AS "GEBRAUCHSMUSIK"

In the fullest sense of the term as Hindemith's school has used it, all
early Neo-Hispanic polyphony was *Gebrauchsmusik*—music for use. Since

the forum in which this "music for use" was heard seems always to have been some church occasion, we may predispose ourselves to a more favorable view of the remnants which survive if we first make an effort to understand the kinds of use to which polyphonic music was put in Neo-Hispanic church life. The formal public worship of the church provided most of the opportunities available for the performance of part-music. However there were also numerous non-liturgical occasions sponsored by the church such as processions, public acts of mourning, welcome ceremonies for new viceroys, or congratulatory acts staged for important public officials, when polyphonic music was required. The non-liturgical occasions which appealed most to the humbler classes were without doubt the processions where popularized part-music, such as hymns to the Virgin, or villancicos in honor of the saints, or chanzonetas of thanksgiving were sung. On the other hand, the non-liturgical occasions during which more pretentious types of part-music were attempted were the welcome ceremonies for new viceroys or the acts of mourning for deceased emperors such as Charles V (died 1558) and Philip II (died 1598).

MUSIC IN COMMEMORATIVE ACTS

A detailed account of the commemorative pageant honoring the memory of Charles V occurs in the 52-page pamphlet published at Mexico City in 1560 entitled *Túmulo Imperial*. Its author, Francisco Cervantes de Salazar, though not a musician but rather a professor of rhetoric in the newly founded (1553) University of Mexico, was nevertheless well qualified to discuss the musical aspects of the pageant. Born in Toledo and a professor in the University of Osuna before emigrating to Mexico, he had while in Osuna enjoyed the friendship of so eminent an authority as Juan Bermudo, the famous music theoretician, who not only held him in high personal esteem but also asked him to write the introduction to his 1550 music manual, *El Arte Tripharia*. Correspondence between the two evidently continued after Cervantes came to the New World, for it was at the latter's suggestion that Bermudo added a section of his original organ pieces in the second (1555) edition of his well-known treatise, the *Declaración de instrumentos*. In this second edition Bermudo (folio 113ᵛ) gratefully acknowledged the request for the addition of his own original compositions which he had received from the New World.

Cervantes de Salazar's description of the commemorative ceremony in Mexico City shows it to have been an occasion when the colonials set out to surpass if possible the pomp and circumstance of the commemorative acts already staged at Brussels and in the peninsula. Because Charles V had died at Yuste in the odor of sanctity, church authorities in Mexico as elsewhere were eager to do his memory every possible homage. *Túmulo Imperial*, because of its contemporaneity, because of the vividness with which it describes individual details, because of its specific mention of performance methods, and more especially because of its references to the music of Cristóbal de Morales and Lázaro de Álamo, deserves close scrutiny by every student who would understand sixteenth century music in New Spain. The extracts below by no means exhaust the passages which might interest a music student.

Having discussed the matter with the audiencia and with the archbishop, the viceroy [Luis de Velasco] decided to stage the ceremonies in the Church of San José [the first church erected for the use of Indians] and in the adjoining patio between it and the monastery to which it belongs [San Francisco monastery].

The Church of San José was chosen rather than the cathedral because the cathedral is entirely too small to accommodate any great throng; and moreover because its ceiling is too low to permit the erection of a suitably imposing funeral monument. Also the viceregal palace is so close to the cathedral that a procession could hardly have started moving before it would have reached the cathedral door.

The Order of the Procession on the Afternoon of St. Andrew's Day (November 30)

The procession from the viceregal palace was divided into four sections; in the first were the Indians, many of whom when they neared the monastery broke into audible sobs (as if they had been personally indebted to their sovereign). Before the Indian procession was carried aloft a cross covered with black cloth. Flanked on both sides with candles, this processional cross was borne aloft before the governor of Tlaxcala; he was selected for this honor because of the faithfulness of the Tlaxcalans. . . . The Indian governors of Tacuba, Texcuco, and Tlaxcala, along with the Indian governor of Mexico, all wore formal mourning attire. Each governor carried the standard of his province showing on it a coat of arms; the personal tokens of appreciation sent by His Majesty to each of the Indian governors were woven into these standards with intricate designs of gilt and silver thread running over a black background. . . . More than two hundred caciques marched in solemn procession with their governors, all observing ceremonious silence. Approximately two thousand were in the Indian line of march, including all the principal personages from the Indian tributary villages. The onlooking Indians who awaited the procession in the patio and in the streets adjacent to the monastery numbered at least forty thousand. This tremendous Indian procession [and the motley crowd gathered to see it] was kept under control by interpreters who knew their languages and by peace officers from the local constabulary. Upon arriving at the monastery patio the four Indian governors—those of Mexico, Tacuba, Texcuco, and Tlaxcala—laid their banners at the four corners of the memorial monument. . . .

The procession of the clergy included the archbishop, the bishop of Michoacán, the bishop of Nueva Galicia, and provincials of the Orders of St. Francis, St. Dominic, and St. Augustine; along with these marched a host of inferior clergy.

. . . . . .

The dignitaries having finally entered the Church of San José and having seated themselves (the procession itself lasted two full hours) the vigil proper began. Outside and inside the church stood a huge crowd of onlookers. The cathedral choirmaster [Lázaro del Álamo] began by directing one of his choirs (his singers were divided into two antiphonal choirs) in the singing of the invitatory, *Circumdederunt me*, by Cristóbal de Morales; and then the other in the singing of the psalm, *Exultemus*, also by Morales. Both settings by Morales are polyphonic throughout, and the choirs sang them with the utmost sweetness. The vigil began then with a devotional fervor that elevated the minds of everyone present.

After the invitatory eight cope-bearers intoned the first antiphon in plainchant; the succentor [precentor's assistant] then started the first psalm, *Verba mea auribus percipe, Domine*, and the same eight cope bearers then sang the verses antiphonally with a chorus made up of friars and clergy, carrying it through with utmost solemnity. After the psalm, *Verba mea*, there followed an antiphon sung by the choirs in a polyphonic setting, and then another antiphon sung by the cope-bearers in a polyphonic setting.

Next the succentor started the psalm [*Domine ne in furore*]; when he reached the mediation, a small group of boys responded to him in a four-part setting of the remainder of the first psalm-verse. The rest of this psalm was antiphonally sung according to this plan: verses in plainchant sung by succentor and cope-bearers in unison alternated with verses in polyphonic setting sung by the boy choir. This boy choir was directed by the cathedral choirmaster [Álamo] who himself had composed the music they

sang. After the psalm, *Domine ne in furore*, another antiphon and psalm
followed, sung again in the same way with polyphony and plainchant alternating. Then another antiphon, and still another psalm, in the middle
of which last psalm the cope-bearers advanced to the main altar.

There the archbishop [Montúfar] started the *Pater noster;* after the
Pater noster Morales's polyphonic setting of *Parce mihi Domine* was sung,
the beauty of which enthralled everyone. The response was sung in plainsong; the cope-bearers remained at the main altar during the singing of
the verses of the response. There they remained also during the second
lesson which was read by the bishop of Michoacán [Vasco de Quiroga].
After the second lesson *Qui Lazarum resuscitasti* (in polyphonic setting)
was sung; then the archbishop began the last lesson. . . . At its conclusion the cope-bearers began the psalm, *De profundis*, during which the
clergy and the friars prepared to form their recessional. At the conclusion
of *De profundis* the singing of the response, *Libera me*, aroused the deepest
devotion. The response completed, the archbishop . . . and all the choristers . . . joined in the final prayer; the vigil service thus came to an
end with the profoundest solemnity.

Early Mass the next day [December 1] was sung by thirty friars with
such great fervor and pathos that tears involuntarily started in the eyes of
those present. . . . High Mass later during the day was sung in a five-
voice setting.[66]

A generation later the exequies of Philip II provided the colony with
another opportunity for an ostentatious display of public grief. Dr.
Dionysio de Ribera Flórez, canon of the metropolitan cathedral, wrote
the official account in his *Relación historiada de las Exequias Funerales
. . . del Rey D. Philippo* which was printed in 1600. Though not as
informed a person, musically speaking, as Cervantes de Salazar, Ribera
Flórez nevertheless emphasized the role of music in the pageantry. After
the death of every subsequent Spanish sovereign a similar public act was
staged in Mexico, and then the account printed for distribution in Spain
as well as the colony. Among its rare books the Biblioteca Nacional in
Madrid now houses a series of these accounts; the musical extracts from
them enable the reader to gain an accurate idea of the shifting currents
of musical taste in the colony.

SIXTEENTH CENTURY DEVELOPMENTS IN INSTRUMENTAL MUSIC

As has been already noted in the chronological synopsis, an orchestra
formed part of the musical ensemble at the Mexico City Cathedral as

early as 1554. Despite Montúfar's eagerness to suppress all instrumental music except that of the organ, orchestras continued to exist everywhere, even in his own cathedral. The very year Montúfar's successor, Moya y Contreras, was consecrated (1574), the orchestra at the metropolitan cathedral was further enlarged, and a director of instrumental music, Bartolomé de Luna, engaged at an annual salary of 200 pesos. The next year three more expert instrumentalists were added to the cathedral staff, Luna's salary enlarged, and 1,000 pesos budgeted annually for instrumental music. Brass as well as woodwind instruments are mentioned as components of the cathedral orchestra at the end of the century. If even the metropolitan cathedral, long after the warning voice against noisy and frivolous instruments had been sounded, still continued to use trumpet, trombone, flute, cornett, and harp, small wonder the less restrained parochial churches throughout New Spain took fullest advantage of the implied license.

That the use of instruments was not merely confined to relief or variety is proved by the numerous notations scribbled over manuscript copies of polyphonous and monodic music still preserved in such archives as those at the Puebla and Mexico City cathedrals. It is coming more and more to be recognized, of course, that performance practice even in the more influential European centers was not exclusively confined to *a cappella* singing. What Michael Praetorius suggested as an acceptable way of performing a double-choir ten-voice motet, *Quo properas*, by Orlando di Lasso, although his evidence dates from the earliest years of the seventeenth century rather than from the years immediately preceding di Lasso's death in 1594, is nevertheless of interest here.[67]

He suggested the following "orchestration" for the successive sections of this motet:

Choir I	Choir II
1. cornett or voice, with four trombones	1. cornett or voice, with four trombones
2. voices alone	2. cornett and four trombones
3. voices alone	3. five viols da braccio
4. voices alone	4. two flutes, two trombones, bassoon
5. five viols da braccio	5. flute and four trombones
6. five viols da braccio	6. two flutes, two trombones, bassoon
7. two flutes, two trombones, bassoon	7. cornett and four trombones

Just these very instruments, as a matter of fact (with the exception of the *viola da braccio*), are to be encountered in the Mexico City orchestra as early as 1575, evidently performing the same function in Franco's antiphonally conceived music. In Mexican as well as European chapel establishments during the late sixteenth century

> the chapel master was left free to adapt, arrange, and orchestrate the music. The written notes were used only as a guide to an end result determined by the conductor: a result often diverging widely from the original textual significance of compositions.

The variety of instruments available in sixteenth century New Spain and the generally high quality maintained in their manufacture may be learned from a municipal ordinance passed by the Mexico City cabildo on August 30, 1568, and confirmed by the audiencia a month later.

> No carpenter, no engraver, no joiner, no maker of musical instruments, shall set up shop in this city or in its environs without passing the officially prescribed examination. . . . An instrument-maker must show by examination that he knows how to construct the organ [without pedals], the spinet, the monochord, the lute, the various different kinds of viol, and the harp; and he must know not only how to make these instruments but also must be able to demonstrate the correct method used in playing them.
>
> The examination shall be given under authority of the alcalde, and of the municipal supervisor of construction. A fine of ten pesos shall be levied against anyone who opens a shop without first passing his examination. . . . Special care shall be exercised to see that no one presumes to make the various classes of viols unless he knows how to attend to the most minute details and can fashion a truly presentable instrument. . . . Every four months an official examiner shall overlook the stock of instruments carried by an instrument-maker, and shall confiscate all those which are faulty in workmanship.[68]

The enactment of such an ordinance in 1568 (and its renewal in 1585) [69] shows instrument-making had developed into a thriving industry during the latter half of the sixteenth century. Where did a market exist in New Spain for a stready stream of new instruments? The springing up of an instrument-making industry subject to legal regulation certainly implies that a market did exist. In 1568 Bernal Díaz wrote that it was not private individuals but rather churches which acquired a plethora of trumpets (of the loudest and shrillest kind), a plentiful supply of "flutes, oboes, sackbuts, and lutes," and also organs when financial resources permitted.[70] With all the other evidence that can be gathered showing the universal use of instruments in Neo-Hispanic churches—from foremost cathedrals on down to humblest village chapels—it seems obvious that the sonorous ideal even during the so-called golden age of Neo-Hispanic polyphony was not one of unaccompanied (*a cappella*) vocalism, but rather was that of "broken music." [71]

SECULAR MUSIC

In Aztec society (historians now universally agree) religion swathed every cultural manifestation. With the advent of the missionaries the Indian was baptized but not secularized. He exchanged one mode of expression for another, his creative energies were re-channeled, and instead of praises to Huitzilopochtli and Texcatlipoca he sang praises to God and the saints.

> After the Conquest the Christian Indians were extremely eager to exult in their new-found religion with songs. . . . Don Francisco Placido, lord of Atzcapotzalco, with his Tecpan subjects, celebrated the enthronement of the blessed image of Our Lady of Guadalupe with such newly composed songs; he initiated a custom which continued for a century.[72]

Indian secular art was not yet born. If we wish information concerning secular music, as we designate it, we must turn to the records of the Spaniards who came to Mexico, rather than hoping to find it among the Indians.

Of the original band of three hundred who came with Cortés from Cuba in 1519, six were excellent musicians, according to Bernal Díaz, who uses such phrases as "a fine singer," "an excellent performer on the viol," "a great musician," in describing them as individuals. A soldier in the original expedition, Ortiz by name, taught dancing and viol-playing in Mexico after 1521.

Díaz tells of certain other nameless Spanish musicians who joined Cortés on his 1524 expedition to Honduras.

> Cortés brought along five players on the oboe, sackbut and dulcimer, and an acrobat and another who did sleight of hand tricks and worked puppets. . . . I must refrain from telling in detail all the hardships we

endured. . . . The players on the oboes, sackbuts, and dulcimer, whom Cortés had brought with him, as I have already recorded, and who were accustomed to dainties in Castile and knew nothing of hardships, had fallen ill through hunger and made no music, excepting one of them, and all the soldiers cursed the sound of it and we said it was like foxes and jackals howling and it would be better to have maize to eat than music.[73]

In several places Díaz dwells on Cortés's fondness for music. At a banquet given in Cortés's honor by the first viceroy, for instance, "singers at each seat of honor, and trumpetry and all sorts of instruments, harps, guitars, violas, flutes, dulcimers, and oboes" provided music which rivaled the best any of the guests had ever heard at home in Spain.

Formerly it was thought that Cortés introduced a new dance into Spain during his first visit after the Conquest. He arrived in Castile during December of 1527, weighted with trophies from Mexico, and bringing along in his entourage certain Indian entertainers and jugglers. These entertainers delighted the members of Charles V's court, and Cortés forthwith sent them along with a lieutenant of his in order to display themselves before Pope Clement VII. The dance which some writers have thought was introduced by these Indian entertainers (dance-steps, not the dance-music) was the pavane; eventually the pavane became the most important dance-form of the century. Compan (*Dictionnaire de danse*, 1787) identified the pavane as of New World origin, and said the steps imitated the courtship of a turkey-cock approaching his hen. Other writers have taken up Compan's idea concerning the origin of the pavane, among them Chávez and Saldívar.[74]

The first pavanes printed in Spain appeared in Milán's *El Maestro* (1535–6). Milán, however, spoke of imitating Italian pavanes. Italian publications of the period alternately entitle the same dances *padovanas* (*paduanas*) and *pavanas*. The confusion in dance titles makes it difficult to decide just when either dance was actually introduced. Petrucci published padovanas (paduanas) as early as 1508. If it is now indiscreet to accredit Cortés's Indians with any decisive part in introducing the pavane (despite the opinions of Chávez and Saldívar), it is on the other hand certain that two other dances of capital importance were derived from the New World—the sarabande and the chaconne.

Curt Sachs in his *World History of the Dance* stated sometime ago that both the sarabande and chaconne were of New World origin and offered ample proof for his statement. To the evidence he presented showing the

New World origin of these two dance-forms should now be added another most important bit of fact. Sachs stated legislation prohibiting the dancing of the sarabande enacted in 1583 was the first dated reference to the sarabande.[75] Actually, however, Diego Durán, the Dominican historian writing a history of the Indians whose remarks we have already had occasion to quote, mentioned the sarabande four years earlier—in 1579. Thus, the first dated reference to the sarabande now becomes one contained in a history written by a friar in Mexico. In a passage describing the dances of the Indians Durán said they had one called the *cuecuecheuycatl* which was almost as lewd and offensive as a dance "que nuestros naturales usan" called the *zarabanda*.[76] Durán's 1579 reference clearly shows that the sarabande, though danced by the native-born in Mexico, was nevertheless not an Indian dance. The "native-born" would refer to Spaniards born in Mexico.

The references which Sachs collected will be summarized here. He mentioned Mariana's imprecations on the sarabande, Cervantes's horror of it, and Marino's disgust with it. Giambattista Marino in 1623 published a long poem entitled *L'Adone*[77] in which he identified and described dances which he called twins, the sarabande and the chaconne. He said in both dances obscene motions and lewd gestures were used. He called down the wrath of heaven on the lascivious inventor of these vulgar dances. Both dances he said were imported from New Spain. The dancers he found pantomimed the ultimate intimacies of the conjugal act. Their dancing, according to him, was accompanied by the sound of castanets played by wanton maidens who alternated the loud clack of the castanets with the snapping of their fingers, beating out the rhythm meantime with their feet. The men dancers beat on tambourines. Far from the staid dances they later became Marino knew them as frenetic orgies accompanied only by noise-making instruments.

Sachs listed several references from other authors such as Cervantes, Lope de Vega, and Quevedo Villegas, all of which show the chaconne as well as sarabande to have come from New Spain. In 1599 a certain writer named Simon Agudo included in a farce of his "an invitation to go to Tampico in Mexico and there dance the *chacona*." Lope de Vega in *La prueba de los amigos* introduced a band of musicians. They are being importuned to play. "Play what?" they ask. "Play that chaconne with the words beginning: 'Go to Tampico',"[78] comes the reply. In another Lope de Vega comedy, *El amante agradecido* (1618), a troop of musicians start singing: "A jolly life, a jolly life we lead, dancing the chaconne. It came over from the Indies by mail, and now it dwells here in this house as its home; here it will live and die." [79]

From a study of his references, Sachs came to believe that the sarabande and chaconne, clearly Neo-Hispanic in origin, showed negroid influence. Negroes came along with the conquistadores; one of Cortés's gunners was a Negro. After Las Casas suggested substituting Negro labor for Indian labor (in order to save the Indian population from extermination) they were brought over in ever-increasing numbers. In 1580 there were slightly less than 15,000 Spaniards in New Spain, but over 18,500 Negroes, and almost 1,500 mulattoes. Throughout the colonial epoch we shall have occasion to note the importance of negroid influences; the dance forms of the *tierra caliente*, the rumba, the bomba, and even the huapango, all show easily recognizable Negro traits.[80]

NOTES

1. Bernal Díaz del Castillo, *op. cit.*, I, 138.
2. For full biographical details see J. García Icazbalceta, *Obras* (México: Imp. de V. Agüeros, 1896), III, 5–39.
3. Higinio Anglés, *La música en la Corte de Carlos V* (Barcelona: Instituto Español de Musicología, 1944), p. 20.
4. Jesús Romero Flores, *Iconografía Colonial* (México: Museo Nacional, 1940), p. 90.
5. Mendieta, *op. cit.*, pp. 412, 414.
6. Ezequiel A. Chávez, *El primero de los grandes educadores de la América* (México: Editorial Jus, 1943), pp. 49–60.
7. *Cartas de Indias* (Madrid: Ministerio de Fomento, 1877), p. 52.
8. *Ibid.*, p. 56.
9. J. García Icazbalceta, *Colección de Documentos* (Mexico, 1858), I, 50. See also E. A. Foster, *Motolinía's History of the Indians of New Spain* (Berkeley: The Cortés Society, 1950), p. 52.
10. *Col. de Documentos* (1858), I, 109. "Fray Juan Caro, un honrado viejo, el cual introdujo y enseño primero en esta tierra el castellano y el *canto de organo* . . ."
11. *Ibid.*, I, 209–11.
12. E. A. Foster, *op. cit.*, p. 8.
13. Psalm 114.3 (Vulgate) = 116.3 (A.V.): "The sorrows of death compassed me, and the pains of hell gat hold on me . . ." This same psalm in a polyphonic setting by Morales was sung by the Mexico City Cathedral choir at the funeral commemoration for Charles V in 1559. Although Motolinía does not say who composed the version the Tlaxcalans sang, it might well also have been Morales's setting. (The oldest polyphony of Morales still extant today in a Mexican church archive is his *Liber missarum*, I, 1544.)

14. During this epoch in Spanish history the villancico was a poetic form beginning with a refrain (estribillo), continuing with a stanza (copla) which is immediately repeated, then the refrain, then a second stanza which is immediately repeated, then the refrain, and so on. A diagram of the form: $E - C^1C^1 - E - C^2C^2 - E - C^3C^3 - E$ et cetera. The pattern can go on as long as desired. The music fits the words, of course.

15. *Col. de Documentos* (1858), I, 79, 81–2, 84–7.

16. J. Jesús Estrada, "Clásicos de Nueva España," *Schola Cantorum* (Morelia), July, 1945, p. 91. The date of appointment to the chapelmastership was February 1, 1539, but Xuárez had filled various musical posts since his arrival almost a decade earlier.

17. *Col. de Docum.* (1858), I, 24–5.

18. See Lota M. Spell, "Music in the Cathedral of Mexico in the Sixteenth Century," *The Hispanic American Historical Review*, August, 1946, p. 296.

19. P. Mariano Cuevas, *Documentos Inéditos del Siglo XVI* (México: Talleres Gráficos del Museo Nacional de Arqueología . . . , 1914), pp. 98–9.

20. J. García Icazbalceta, *Nueva Colección de Documentos para la Historia de México* (México, Imp. de Francisco Díaz de Leon, 1889), II (*Codice Franciscano*), p. 169.

21. *Ibid.*, pp. 65–6.

22. Rafael Montejano y Aguíñaga, "La Conversión de los indios por medio de la Música," *Schola Cantorum*, September, 1947, pp. 134–6.

23. Angela Blankenburg, "German Missionary Writers in Paraguay," *Mid-America* (Chicago), January, 1947, p. 43n.

24. *Ibid.*, p. 44. (Quoted from a letter written June 15, 1729, by Matthias Strobel.)

25. Quoted from Henri Ternaux-Compans, *Voyages, Relations et Mémoires* . . . , XVI, 218, in Montejano y Aguíñaga, *op. cit.*, p. 134.

26. *Constituciones del arçobispado . . . de Tenuxtitlan Mexico* (México: Juan Pablos, 1556), fol. xxxiii recto (cap. 66).

27. *Ibid.*, f. xix recto.

28. *Ibid.*, f. xxxiii verso.

29. *Ibid.*, f. xxxv recto.

30. *Ibid.*, f. xxxiv verso.

31. H. Anglés, *op. cit.*, p. 23.

32. *Ibid.*, p. 10.

33. Genaro García, *Documentos . . . para la Historia de México* (1907), XV, 141–2.

34. *Colección de Documentos Inéditos . . . del Archivo de Indios* (Madrid, 1870), XIII, 287.

35. For a striking illustration of the changed attitude towards the Indian, see Alonso de Montúfar, "Carta del Arzobispo de Mexico al consejo de Indias . . . ," *Anales del Museo Nacional de Arqueología, Historia y Etnografía*, 1934, p. 355.

36. Gabriel Saldívar, *op. cit.*, pp. 90–94.

37. Juan de Torquemada, *Veinte i un libros rituales i Monarquía Indiana* (Madrid, 1723), III, 214.

38. *Ibid.*, III, 214.

39. *Ibid.*, III, 214. Most of what Torquemada says in this passage comes from Mendieta, pp. 412–3.

40. Juan F. Riaño, *Critical and Bibliographical Notes on Early Spanish Music* (London: Bernard Quaritch, 1887), pp. 81–94.

41. *Libros y Libreros en el Siglo XVI* (México: Publicaciones del Archivo General de la Nación, 1914), pp. 263–281.

42. Mendieta, *op. cit.*, p. 412.

43. William R. Bonniwell, *A History of the Dominican Liturgy 1215–1945* (New York, Joseph F. Wagner, 1945), p. 295.

44. Samuel A. Green, *A Second Supplementary List of Early American Imprints* (Cambridge [Mass.]: University Press, 1899), p. 20. (Quotation from George P. Winship.)

45. J. García Icazbalceta, *Bibliographia Mexicana del Siglo XVI* (México: Librería de Andrade . . . , 1886), p. 124. Variants from modern usage were found in the prefaces of St. John Baptist, St. Francis, St. Augustine, and in the use of benediction at requiem; this latter was a custom continued by the Dominicans into the next century.

46. Emilio Valtón discovered this Gradual and dated it 1571; see Henry R. Wagner, *Nueva Bibliografía Mexicana del Siglo XVI* (México: Editorial Polis, 1940), p. 25.

47. *Libros y Libreros en el Siglo XVI*, p. 139.

48. H. R. Wagner, *op. cit.*, p. 273.

49. *Libros y Libreros* . . . , p. 139.

50. García Icazbalceta, *Bibliografía* . . . , p. 329.

51. Lota M. Spell, *op. cit.*, p. 315, especially note 116. When Archbishop Francisco Plancarte in 1916 presented the Newberry Library in Chicago with a copy he stated he himself had seen copies of each of the *four* editions of the 1576 Gradual.

52. Gonzales Aguirre Beltrán in his article, "The Slave Trade in Mexico," *Hispanic American Historical Review*, August, 1944, quotes this population figure, p. 414.

53. Hilarion Eslava, *Música Religiosa en España* (Madrid, 1860), p. 63.

54. L. M. Spell, *op. cit.*, pp. 298–9.

55. *Ibid.*, p. 299. Ramos, the organist, had come from Seville the previous year. His son came with him and immediately started singing in the choir (p. 300).

56. Cuevas, *op. cit.*, p. 98.

57. Estrada, *op. cit.*, p. 91.

58. Spell, *op. cit.*, p. 305 (note 62).

59. Francisco Antonio Lorenzana, *Concilium Mexicanum Provinciale III* (México: Typ. Josephi Antonii de Hogal, 1770), Part II, pp. 115–130.

60. *Cartas de Indias* (Madrid: Ministerio de Fomento, 1877), p. 192.

61. Spell, *op. cit.*, pp. 310, 316.

62. Lorenzana, *op. cit.* (Part II), "De Magistri Capellae officio, & Cantoribus," pp. 66–70.

63. Spell, *op. cit.*, p. 317.

64. Steven Barwick, "Sacred Vocal Polyphony in Early Colonial Mexico," Harvard Ph.D. Dissertation, 1949, p. 60.

65. Gonzalo Fernández de Oviedo y Valdés, *Historia General y Natural de las Indias* (Madrid: Imp. de Real Academia de Historia, 1853), III, 304.

66. Cervantes de Salazar, *Tumulo Imperial dela grand ciudad de México* (México: Antonio de Espinosa, 1560), folio 3 verso, 23 v., 24 r., 25 r., 25 v., 26 r. The only extant copy of this book is now in the Huntington Library at San Marino, California.

67. See Michael Praetorius, *Syntagma Musicum, Vol. II*: Translated by Harold Blumenfeld (New Haven, 1949), p. ii ff.

68. Juan Francisco del Barrio Lorenzot, *Ordenanzas de gremios de la Nueva España* (México, Dirección de Talleres Gráficos . . . , 1920), pp. 80–5.

69. According to Saldívar, *op. cit.*, pp. 185–6.

70. Díaz del Castillo, *op. cit.*, V, 266. Sackbuts must be identified as precursor trombones.

71. Barwick, *op. cit.*, p. 135, states: "Although I do not believe that the texts were omitted only in places where parts for instruments were intended, I do feel that instruments were used in the performance of this music. . . . I have noted specific indications in some manuscripts as to which instruments were to play the different parts."

72. Lorenzo Boturini Benaduci, *Idea de una nueva Historia General* . . . , p. 91.

73. Díaz del Castillo, *op. cit.*, V, 16.

74. Herbert Weinstock, *Mexican Music* (1940), p. 9 quotes Chavez's opinion. For Saldívar's see his *Historia de la Música* . . . , p. 159. See also *Grand Dictionnaire Universel du XIXᵉ Siècle* (P. Larousse, 1874), XII, 444, col. 3.

75. Curt Sachs, *World History of the Dance* (New York: W. W. Norton, 1937), p. 367.

76. Diego Durán, *Historia de las Indias de Nueva España* (México: Imprenta de I. Escalante, 1880), II, 230.

77. Giovanni Battista Marino, *L'Adone* (Turin: G. B. Paravia & Co., n.d.), p. 376. The stanzas in question are in Canto Ventecismo, 83–85.

78. Ricardo del Arco y Garay, *La Sociedad Española en las Obras Dramáticas de Lope de Vega* (Madrid: Escelicer, S. L., 1942), p. 916.

79. *Ibid.*, p. 915.

80. See Saldívar, *op. cit.*, "La Influencia Africana," pp. 219–229.

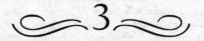

3

THE CULMINATION AND DECLINE
OF NEO-HISPANIC MUSIC

SOURCES

The student of Mexican colonial architecture or colonial painting will
find interesting remains almost everywhere he travels in central Mexico.
From Oaxaca and Mérida on the south and southeast to Zacatecas and
Durango on the north and northwest, and from Jalapa on the east to
Guadalajara on the west, he will find in almost every town of any size
or importance a colonial monument or two well worth study.

But with music the case is different. Colonial music manuscripts by an
unkind fate have disappeared nearly everywhere, and in only the barest
handful of Mexican centers do any still exist. In many a town where a
now disused colonial organ may sit, still testifying to the important role
music once played in the life of that town, all music manuscripts and
printed music books will have vanished forever. Why this loss of colonial
manuscripts and books? The reasons are principally these: neglect and
wilful destruction.

Priceless music manuscript books containing the greatest European and
colonial polyphony of the sixteenth and seventeenth centuries have on
occasion fallen into the hands of persons who knew nothing of their value.
As an instance the so-called Valdés Codex may be cited. Some years ago
a priest, Padre Octaviano Valdés from Tacubaya, came upon a group of
Indians in the small village of Cacalomacán who had in their possession
a 280-page music manuscript book bound in worn parchment. Thumbing
through its leaves Padre Valdés was suddenly startled when he came

upon the name of Palestrina. He looked further through the book and found that it contained no less than five Masses attributed to Palestrina: *Aeterna Christi munera, Ave Regina coelorum, Già fu chi m'ebbe cara, Quem dicunt homines,* and *Christus resurgens.* The Indians who had owned the book thought it was only worthless paper, and gladly gave it up; one of them told the padre that but a short time before they had owned another music book of the same kind, but that they had lost it.

When he took it back to Mexico City, Padre Valdés found that four of the Masses attributed to Palestrina in his newly acquired codex were indeed authentic Masses, published originally in 1590, 1599, and 1600 collections; but the fifth, *Christus resurgens?* Is it a Palestrina Mass hitherto unknown? one that should be added to the canon of 94? That question is still unsolved. But what of the other compositions in Padre Valdés's find? Two of them turned out to be the only polyphonic pieces with Aztecan (Nahuatl) text still preserved; these two pieces were simple four-part hymns in honor of the Virgin whose music later in this chapter is transcribed into modern notation. Other compositions by early Neo-Hispanic composers and by their European contemporaries made this book as exciting a discovery as the finding of a genuine but uncatalogued Stradivarius.

If by chance the Valdés book was recovered, many more of similar worth have perished simply through neglect. And still other music books have perished during the periodic storms that have swept bands of soldiers into such cathedrals as those at Morelia and Mérida where they have been for a time quartered, only to leave after the cathedral had been stripped of its artistic treasures as well as the gold on the altar. Just as during the period of Cromwellian stress military occupation of churches and cathedrals took a heavy toll of cultural monuments such as organs and stained glass, so during the periods of revolution in Mexico military occupation has resulted in many irreparable losses.

The two cathedrals which have perhaps suffered least have been those at Puebla and at Mexico City, and it is to these two principally that the traveler in search of musical materials from the colonial period will go. The *tesoros artísticos* at these two great cathedrals still contain enough Neo-Hispanic polyphony to afford a basis for judging the magnitude of the colonial achievement. Though perhaps that which still remains is in comparison with that which has been lost as the visible part of an iceberg is to the subsurface invisible part, still the extant Neo-Hispanic repertory is of sufficient magnitude to warrant judgments concerning style, musical substance, technique of composition, and even performance methods.

THE PRINTING OF PART-MUSIC

No Neo-Hispanic polyphony was printed during the colonial epoch. Some monodic music continued to be published in the seventeenth and eighteenth centuries: the 1604 *Quatuor Passiones* by Juan Navarro, the 1725 *Breve Noticia del Canto Llano* by Manuel Sánchez,[1] and the 1770 *Missa Gothica seù Mozarabica et Officium itidèm Gothicum* edited by Francisco Lorenzana,[2] for instance. But polyphony was not published, partly because printing of all types became inordinately expensive after 1600, and also of course because the market for some of the very difficult part-music written by such Neo-Hispanic masters as Franco and Padilla must have been quite limited.

It was not exclusively the monopolistic practices of the home country which prevented New Spain from developing a music printing industry. Even in the home country the printing of polyphonic music lagged. No Attaignant or Gardano settled early Spanish music printing of part-music on a firm basis, and consequently all of Morales's music was published abroad, as was also all of Guerrero's sacred music, except one book. Victoria published his first Spanish collection as late in his career as 1600. The first polyphony published in the Spanish capital was Philip Rogier's book of Masses (1598); Victoria's *Missae, Magnificat, Motecta, Psalmi* . . . (1600) was second, and Alfonso Lobo's *Liber Primus Missarum* (1602) was third. These books were immediately sent over to Mexico, and a copy of Rogier's book is still preserved at Puebla. Five copies of the Lobo 1602 book are scattered over Mexico, one each at Mexico City, Puebla, Oaxaca, Guadalajara, and Morelia.

If at the same time a printer of polyphony was found for Madrid one had been found for Mexico City an entirely different story of Neo-Hispanic culture might now be known. Instead of only literary personages such as Alarcón and Sor Juana Inés de la Cruz as the bright ornaments of Neo-Hispanic culture, we should perhaps have heard also of composers such as Franco, Bermúdez, and Zumaya. The superlative reputations of the two literary figures we have just named rest not upon any pronouncedly "Mexican" traits in their writing. Alarcón even returned to Spain and so thoroughly devoted himself to Spanish themes that without a knowledge of his biography no one would ever guess he had attended the University of Mexico. Spanish approval has assured these two authors their international reputations. But Spanish approval was perforce denied the composers we have named because their works have had no way of reaching European eyes.

Even yet the bulk of Neo-Hispanic polyphony seems destined to remain unpublished. The issuance of such renowned historical editions as the *Denkmäler der Tonkunst in Österreich* and *in Bayern* was in every instance promoted in the same spirit that a public monument to a dead national hero is promoted. Logically the publication of Neo-Hispanic musical monuments now would redound more to the advantage of Spain than to the advantage of Mexico. In this connection it is interesting to note that the only large-scale publication venture involving a Neo-Hispanic master currently in the offing is being editorially supervised by a prominent Spanish expatriate now resident in Mexico.[3] Although his work is subsidized by the Departamento de Bellas Artes, his interest in the project and background for it stems from his own Spanish antecedents, undoubtedly.

If the publication of the total extant repertory were now to be attempted, a subsidy of the magnitude provided for the *Tudor Church Music* ten-volume series by the Carnegie Trust would be needed. The presently known music from the sixteenth and seventeenth century polyphonists would, according to informed estimate, involve six or seven volumes if printing in the style of *Tudor Church Music* were attempted.

THE EXTENT OF THE REPERTORY

In conspectus the Neo-Hispanic polyphonic repertory of the sixteenth, seventeenth, and early eighteenth centuries consists of the following works:[4]

Hernando Franco (fl. 1580) . . . . 7 Magnificats, 2 Salves, miscellaneous psalms, hymns, and responsories

Juan de Lienas (16th cent.) . . . . 3 Masses (one a Requiem), a Magnificat, 4 motets, a set of Lamentations

Pedro Hernández and Fructos del Castillo (1600?) . . . . One motet each

Pedro Bermúdez (fl. 1605) . . . . 4 Salves and a psalm
Bernardo de Peralta (1640?) . . . . Magnificat
Francisco López y Capilla (fl. 1645) . . . . 3 Masses, 2 Magnificats, 12 motets, a set of Lamentations
Juan de Padilla (fl. 1650) . . . . 5 Masses, 5 Magnificats, a passion, miscellaneous motets and villancicos
Antonio de Salazar (fl. 1690) . . . . 7 hymns for the church year, 2 psalms, miscellaneous villancicos
Manuel Zumaya (fl. 1720) . . . . 3 Magnificats, 2 Misereres, 2 sets of Lamentations, miscellaneous villancicos

The bunching of Neo-Hispanic composers suggests that the period of greatest activity lay between 1575 and 1650. During that particular 75-year period colonial life had sufficiently stabilized itself so that a full musical apparatus could be provided in the chief centers of population. The silver and gold mines of the colony had established it as the richest in the Spanish empire, and composers emigrated as readily to New Spain as they have emigrated to the United States during the present century.

HERNANDO FRANCO

Although the lives of most Neo-Hispanic composers remain yet to be investigated, Hernando Franco has emerged from anonymity. During the early 'thirties Jesús Estrada, eminent organist of the Mexico City Cathedral, first began the laborious task of transcribing Franco's music into modern notation. In 1934 Saldívar after studying the *Actas del Cabildo Eclesiástico* at the metropolitan cathedral published a valuable summary of the information he found there. More recently two American scholars have expanded our knowledge of cathedral music in Mexico during the sixteenth and seventeenth centuries, and have both discovered new facts concerning Franco. The following summary therefore represents a composite of information derived from Estrada, Saldívar, Lota Spell, and Steven Barwick.

Like most early colonial chapelmasters at the Mexico City Cathedral, Franco was imported from Europe. Although his birthdate has not yet been fixed he is known to have been born in the village of La Serena near Alcántara [5] (Alcántara lies on the Tagus River a few miles from the Portuguese border). That information concerning his early life should be lacking does not surprise us when we consider that little or nothing is known of the early lives of such more important composers as Morales and Guerrero. Franco during 1542, or thereabouts, was in Espinar (approximately 23 miles from Ávila). Espinar was the home of the Álamo family, and Franco during his sojourn there knew Lázaro del Álamo [6] who later (1556) was to become chapelmaster at Mexico City.

Franco's arrival date in the New World, though like his birthdate still uncertain, may have occurred in 1554. The patron who sponsored his coming was a civil functionary, Sedeña by name, an oidor, who later became rector of the University of Mexico. At first after his arrival in the New World Franco settled in Guatemala, but soon after Álamo's chapelmastership ended (1570) he was invited to Mexico City. The invitation was promoted by Sedeña, but Álamo's personal acquaintance may have had something to do with it.

Franco's immediate predecessor in the Mexico City chapelmastership, Juan de Victoria, was so unwise as to allow his choirboys to appear in a farcical interlude [7] (December, 1574) satirizing the viceroy's taxation policy. A collector of the newly imposed (and thoroughly hated) alcabala tax appeared on the scene and tumbled some nude choirboys out of bed. The moral taken by the thoroughly amused audience was that the new tax would strip everyone naked. For this little venture in topical satire de Victoria was allowed to languish a few days in prison, and although the archbishop soon enough secured his release, he either died shortly thereafter or was relieved of his chapelmaster responsibilities and retired to obscurity. In any event Franco was engaged as his successor on May 20, 1575, with a stipulated salary of 600 pesos de oro común. [8] Along with him was hired his cousin, Alonso de Trujillo, who as precentor was engaged at an annual salary of 200 pesos de oro común. These salaries may be compared with the dean's (1,800) pesos, a canon's (1,200), a prebendary's (840), and an unbeneficed clergyman's (240).

Franco wisely abstained from choirboy plays, thereby avoiding all danger of affronting the viceroy. However, his career did not move with perfect smoothness. Within four years after his appointment to the chapelmastership he had incurred such huge debts that the ecclesiastical cabildo only saved him and his cousin, Trujillo, from dire consequences by ordering paid in their behalf the sum of 500 pesos in partial satisfaction of a 4,000-peso debt which these two had run up with the corregidor. The cabildo in ordering this 500-peso partial payment noted the value of

Franco's services to the cathedral "and agreed to take care of the bills as a special favor." [9] The bills in aggregate equaled Franco's and Trujillo's combined salaries for five years. Someone has asked, how could these two, both in orders (all Spanish church musicians, Morales, Guerrero, Victoria, and all the rest, were in orders) have run up such huge debts? The most often-mentioned vice of the clergy in New Spain during this epoch was gambling.[10] Since the cabildo accepted responsibility for the debts without demurring no serious derelection must have been involved. A gambling debt might furnish a plausible explanation for such a large sum.

On September 1, 1581, Franco was appointed a prebendary to fill a vacancy left by the death of a certain Manuel de Nova. A little later during the same month (September 19) the cabildo quashed a penalty against him for having violated a holy day. Franco, it seems, had actually taken his young choristers to a fiesta on a day set aside for remembering the seven dolors. The next year, 1582, Archbishop Moya y Contreras asked the cabildo to reduce the salaries of singers and instrumentalists because the expenses of the new building program were eating up the archdiocesan revenues.

When in July Franco learned that he was to be reduced to 300 pesos, a fifty per cent reduction in salary, and his cousin Trujillo also learned he was to be correspondingly reduced, the pair resigned.[11] Twice again during the month they affirmed to the cabildo their intention of quitting. On July 19 Franco even told the cabildo to go ahead and keep the amount of his salary that he had already earned during 1582 before the reduction was announced—in a spirit of bravado, no doubt. With his musicians all out on strike and no volunteer songbirds to fill their places, the archbishop a month later (in August) changed his mind on salary cuts and asked all of the singers to come back. They did, but in February, 1583, a cut in Franco's salary was again announced, this time not to 300 (as had been announced the previous year), but to 400. In September of 1583 his salary was mulcted another 100 pesos "because he had failed to give the choirboys proper instruction."

Most of the information concerning Franco is of this financial type, simply because the cabildo records dealt so extensively with money matters. In May, 1584, Franco was raised to 450, and his subordinates in the musical establishment were all boosted to what they had earned before any cuts were made in 1582. But Franco was enjoined to teach singing to the choirboys; he failed to fulfill his duties as a teacher, however, and later in the year 50 pesos were taken from the 450 and given to another priest who taught the choirboys not only reading and writing, but also singing in addition. In November of 1585 Franco was ailing; on the 22nd he attended the last session of the cabildo and on the 28th he died. As a mark of honor he was buried in the main chapel of the cathedral back of the viceroy's seat.[12]

The cathedral in which Franco's music was first heard stood where the present sagrario stands. The present imposing cathedral, one of the world's largest, was not started until 1573,[13] just two years before Franco was hired. During his incumbency, therefore, the archbishop well needed every peso he could lay hands on; approximately 200 workmen were constantly employed during the last quarter of the century in the initial building operations. The zócalo, where now rise the present cathedral edifice, the Palacio Nacional, and other important buildings, was then still an island, just as it had been since Tenochtitlán was founded in the mythical year, 1325. Building materials therefore had to be brought over in canoes, and the constant hum of Indian workmen laying the foundation of the new cathedral was a part of Franco's everyday existence during his decade as chapelmaster.[14]

In his cathedral the choir sat in the central nave surrounded by gilded railings.[15] The placement of the choir in the middle of the central nave is, of course, normal procedure in Spanish cathedrals, but for those who have never seen such an arrangement, seems novel. The long central nave with a continuous sweep of vision which we associate with Gothic cathedrals was therefore missing; instead the choir bisected the nave. To the west of Franco's choir was the altar of pardon and the door of pardon. To the east was another altar and door. In the choir itself sat not only the singers, but all the dignitaries also. With their stalls separated, half on one side and half on the other, the choir members constantly sat facing each other. The answering back and forth such an arrangement makes possible is an everlasting presupposition in all Neo-Hispanic (and Spanish) polyphony.

The music was of two types, of course: plainsong and polyphony, with the precentor in charge of plainsong and chapelmaster in charge of polyphony. Most sixteenth century music we now know—such as Palestrina's *Pope Marcellus Mass* or his *Stabat Mater*—does not require the intoning of interspersed sections in plainsong. Only the Mass sections beginning with "Et in terra pax" and "Patrem omnipotentem" require plainsong intonations—and those are usually left out in performances. As a consequence, present-day students, even those who have heard some Palestrina, know nothing of his or anyone else's vast numbers of compositions where plainsong and polyphony alternate. Nearly all the Neo-Hispanic polyphony that has descended to us is of the alternating type—a verse in plainsong, then one in polyphony, one in plainsong, and one in polyphony, and so on. This alternation back and forth establishes a kind of large duple rhythm that is extremely important to the success of the music. This oscillation between two antiphonal choirs—one singing a verse in polyphony, the other a verse in plainsong—reminds one of a swinging pendulum. Our first example shows how this principle of alternation worked in the singing of a penitential psalm (Psalm VI).

Domine, ne in furore (Psalm VI)

Puebla Choirbook No. 3, folio 76 v. 79 r.   Hernando Franco

The reliance on antiphony as a principal artistic device was especially suited to the texts chosen by most Neo-Hispanic composers whose music survives. Their Magnificats, their Salves, their Lamentations, and their psalms, all employ texts which seem naturally to call for antiphonal treatment. It is a well known fact that Hebrew poetry, even in translation, preserves a large duple rhythm. Cognizance of this fact is taken today when ministers of religion in both Hebrew and Christian denominations read the psalms responsively. The very structure of the poetry itself suggests such answering back and forth. Even with only a cursory glance at the words of some such psalm as that just transcribed from Franco one can see how each verse divides itself naturally into two balancing halves and how each odd-numbered verse alternates with each even-numbered verse in going back and forth over a single idea. The Magnificat and certain other poetic passages from Scripture show this same tendency towards parallelism; all students of Hebrew poetry recognize this structural device as a commonplace. Recognizing this basic structure in the texts, one can understand why the composers so often wrote music that "tends to sound like a striped peppermint bar"—to carry out the analogy, with the white stripe representing the plainsong, and the red the polyphony.

Particularly notable in Franco's psalm-setting just given (Mode VIII) is his subtle handling of such words as *morte* in verse 5 with the unexpected b flat in the bass, and his vigorous melisma—distributed among all the voices—on *furore oculos* in verse 7. The ending of the psalm (not given) leads immediately into the *Requiem aeternam*.

THE MAGNIFICATS

Franco's most artful compositions are his seven Magnificats. He undoubtedly composed eight—one for each tone—but the Magnificat for the Third Tone seems to have been lost. In order properly to evalue his achievement it is necessary to know something of the way Magnificats were written during his century. Most musicians today, if they know any Magnificat-setting at all, know J. S. Bach's. Much more helpful, however, for an understanding of the Magnificats now about to be discussed, would be a knowledge of Morales's or Guerrero's. The list of sixteenth century composers who wrote important Magnificats is very large; certain procedures were followed by everyone who wrote them—Palestrina, Lassus, de Monte, de la Rue, Duarte Lobo—to name composers of different nationalities. According to a recent scholar's analysis (Carl Heinz Illing in a 1936 doctoral dissertation, *Zur Technik der Magnificat-Composition des 16. Jahrhunderts*): (1) the composer was not at liberty to pick his themes at random out of the air but had to use the psalm-tone melodic formulae; (2) each short section of the Magnificat had to end on a chord whose root was the final of the "tone"; (3) the more learned devices such as extended canon or imitation by inversion were usually reserved to the Gloria Patri at the end.

Palestrina wrote 35 Magnificats, Lassus 100, yet each of these composers only once set *all* the verses of the Magnificat.[16] The common procedure was to set alternate verses. Occasionally the odd verses were set, but much more commonly the even verses were set. Morales, however, in his first collection of five Magnificats published at Venice in 1542 set all dozen verses consecutively. Franco chose to follow Morales's primitive practice, and each of his seven still preserved Magnificats therefore includes all the verses consecutively set. It is known that Palestrina's eight-part Magnificat (the one in which he provided continuous music for all twelve verses of the Magnificat) was designed for the Papal Choir as an extremely choice work;[17] the other 34 Magnificats were designed for the Julian Choir and the St. John Lateran Choir—less important choirs. Franco's settings speak well for the pretensions of his choir, and for the seriousness of his own purpose.

The fidelity with which Franco followed the plainsong intonations in constructing his themes deserves note. The openings (cantus part) of his Magnificats illustrate this fidelity.

That Franco was but following the universally prescribed custom in generating his own melodies from plainsong formulae can be proved by comparing his Magnificats with those of any other Neo-Hispanic composers one may choose to examine. Below, for instance, are the beginnings of two Magnificats by López y Capilla and of one of Bernardo de Peralta.

Having committed himself to the traditionally accepted idea that a Magnificat should simply ring changes on an already thrice-familiar melodic formula, the sixteenth century composer's task then became one of demonstrating his taste and skill as a variationist. The utter familiarity of the formulae redounded to his advantage because it allowed him to indulge in much more subtle types of variation than a modern composer working with a theme the audience does not know is allowed. The variation-devices were of several types. Palestrina often chose to intersperse extraneous notes or rests between successive essential notes in the formula. Henry Coates in his study of Palestrina (1938) showed how "each part of the psalm tone generates contrapuntal melodies," [18] and gave the following example. (The asterisks stand above notes which belong to the plainsong formula.)

Franco used the same means of extension by interpolation; the opening of the cantus part in his *Magnificat I* shows such an extension.

A favorite device with such Flemings as de la Rue and de Monte [19] consisted in stating the melodic formula as an inner voice cantus firmus in long notes. Meanwhile they contrived a play of imitation between or among surrounding voices, but the imitative fragments usually were

melodically unrelated to the psalm-tone formula. Another device sometimes used consisted in stating the psalm-tone formula first in long notes,
then in successively shorter notes. The Gloria Patri from Franco's *Magnificat* (*Tone VIII*) shows such a speed-up in note values at the end.
The Sicut erat from the same Magnificat shows a canon worked out on
the notes of the psalm tone.

Magnificat Tone VIII (Sicut erat)

Franco's technical competence is beyond dispute; if he has nothing quite as elaborate to show as Palestrina's double canon at the octave and fifth in the Sicut erat of *Magnificat IV* (Lateran Magnificats), or the canon cancrizans at the end of *Magnificat V*, or the canon by inversion at the end of *Magnificat VI*, neither for that matter do Morales or Guerrero in their Magnificats. The various refinements that acute students of sixteenth century counterpoint have been led to expect in all the better-fabricated works of the period are certainly there: his handling of the nota cambiata is at all times meticulous; accented syllables are always placed on notes, or groups of notes, with longer values than weak syllables in the same word; the ambitus of the voices in their respective modes are carefully preserved; the rhythmic problems involved in what we are now pleased to call "ties" are all handled in approved fashion; the rhythmic balance between voices is well contrived; the melodic and harmonic progressions will satisfy the most fastidious text-book theorist.

Students who are unfamiliar with the convention that required the ending of every section in the Magnificat with a complete or incomplete chord built on the final of the formula may perhaps cavil at twelve short sections all coming to rest with chords on the same root. The taking of exception, however, to this procedure is as anachronistic as the taking of exception to the dances in a Bach keyboard suite because they all "are in the same key." Franco, like most of his contemporaries, stayed away from the "chord" with which each section was required to end until the final cadence in the section. It may be worthwhile to remind those who are disposed to look at Magnificats that I and II Tone Magnificats end on a D chord (G if one flat is in the signature); III Tone end on an A chord; IV Tone on E; V on A; VI on C (or F if one flat is in the signature); VII on A; and VIII on G.

In his Magnificats as in his other preserved works he showed exquisite sensitiveness in his timing of cadences. In a long motet like the one in familiar style he wrote using Job:16b–21 for a text, he included twenty cadences, but only one—the penultimate—comes to rest on the crucial "F-chord" which gives the Phrygian mode its distinctive flavor. We are not anachronistically imputing to him a chordal sense, and use the word *chord* simply as a convenience, but are commending his manipulation of harmony as well as melody.

His word-painting is neither more nor less obtrusive than is the word-painting in such other polyphonists of his time as Morales and Guerrero. As is well known, Bach was stimulated by the Magnificat text to some of his most literal word-painting. Where the word "omnes" occurred all the voices burst in. Where the word "inanes" occurred two flutes ended on an unresolved chord. Nothing quite as literal as that should be expected from Franco, but for words like "misericordia" [20] he chooses a gliding rhythm; for "exaltavit" [21] he chooses an upward thrusting scale-line;

for a phrase like "deposuit potentes" he chooses a widely skipping bass line with an implication of strong accent. In order to see his word-painting in its clearest aspect it is useful to contrast his setting of "fecit potentiam" in the IV Tone with the immediately following three-voice "esurientes": [22] in his handling of expressive device it will be seen everywhere that though not proleptically gifted he always knew how to conform to enlightened usage of his own epoch.

Perhaps without the necessity of further analysis our point has been made. In the same decade Palestrina was writing his Magnificats (1575–85) Franco was writing his; a comparison of their Magnificats by no means throws discredit upon the Neo-Hispanist. One discovers instead that Franco had mastered the craft of his age, and that he transported to New Spain a type of liturgical music that compares favorably with what was being heard in the more pretentious European chapel establishments.

The rules formulated by the Third Mexican Provincial Council (1585) for the administration of archdiocesan choirs show the advanced stage of musical discipline in Franco's organization. From a purely musical point of view no other Mexican church council has at any time passed legislation so conducive to superior performance standards as did the 1585 council. Franco had the pleasure of seeing the assembled Mexican hierarchy—six bishops and an archbishop—pass a written rule to the effect that in the chapelmaster was vested absolute control over all musical forces in the cathedral—including not only his own choristers who would naturally obey him, but also including the clergy whose business it was to sing during the service. Furthermore all instrumentalists in the cathedral orchestra were by statute subjected to the control of the chapelmaster.

> Instrumentalists, choristers, as well as clergy who participate in the choral service, must reverently heed the instructions of the chapelmaster. . . . If he directs them to sing with organ accompaniment they shall obey; if he prescribes a descant above the cantus firmus they must likewise obey without excuse or delay. [23]

Further regulations passed in 1585 concerning *fa bordon*, alternation of organ and choir in psalm verses, singing of *cantus figuratus*, and like technical matters, enable us to reconstruct Franco's procedures with unusual precision, despite the lapse of centuries.[24]

NAHUATL HYMNS

Two hymns honoring the Virgin, both with Aztecan (Nahuatl) texts, and both attributed to Franco, deserve attention along with his more pretentious music.

First Nahuatl Hymn

* In the manuscript the tenor reads E instead of F.

** In the manuscript the tenor reads G instead of A.

Second Nahuatl Hymn

Valdés Codex, pages 244-5

Hernando Franco

[Moderato] ♩ in original = ♩ in transcription

The text of both foregoing hymns has been translated by the learned Nahuatl scholar, D. Mariano Rojas. The words of the first hymn say: "Celestial Queen, Mother of God, Our Advocate, pray for us." The words of the second say: "O Lady, beloved Mother of God, always virgin, intercede for us with Thy beloved Son, Jesu Christ, Thou most beloved of the Most High!" The actual text of both hymns in Nahuatl may prove interesting:

1. In ilhuicac cihuapille tenantzin Dios in titotepantlahtohcatzin. Mahuel tehuatzin topan xinotlahtolti in titlahtlacoanime.

2. Dios itlazo nantzine cemihcac ichpochtli cenca timitztotlatlauhtilia matopan ximotlatolti ixpantzinco in motlazo conetzin Jesu Cristo. Ca ompa timoyestica in inahuactzinco.

As can readily be seen, these hymns differ pronouncedly in style from Franco's liturgical music with Latin text. The traits which noticeably differ from his ecclesiastical manner include: (1) an abundance of parallel fifths, octaves, and other forbidden consecutives, (2) the use of unprepared and unresolved dissonance, (3) a constant reliance on accentual rather than agogic rhythm. In actual performance these two hymns seem much nearer to us than does the liturgical music; the jauntiness and carefreeness of the music exerts an immediate appeal. Such devices for the securing of rhythmic vitality as the hemiola at the beginning of the repeated section in the first hymn, and the obtrusive syncopations and frequent repeated notes in the second hymn, are all sufficiently obvious to make telling impressions at first hearing.

Both hymns are important in Mexican music history simply because they alone remain among the vast store of polyphonic compositions with Indian language text that must have once existed. If they are correctly attributed to Franco, then he showed when he wrote them an uncanny ability to doff the learned sock and sport it on the green. They show him in an unexpected mood, and prove he knew perfectly well how to act the *villano* with the blithest of the frottola composers.

THE PUEBLA SCHOOL OF COMPOSERS

Although Mexico City provides an example to the contrary, Spanish colonial policy did not dedicate itself simply to the planting of Spanish enclaves in populous Indian centers. The more typical Spanish colonial procedure involved the selection of an entirely new site such as Lima, where a new city with a completely Spanish background might grow up. In New Spain two important towns were founded soon after the Conquest with the express purpose of developing in them a pure Spanish tradition. One was Puebla de los Angeles, the other Guadalajara. In Puebla was constructed within a decade of its founding by the audiencia in 1531, a church so imposing that Motolinía called it handsomer than any other yet built in New Spain; he particularly praised its three imposing entrances with elaborate carvings, and the separation of the interior three aisles by black porphyry columns.[25] Charles V raised his church to a cathedral in 1550, granting it rich privileges with the intention of elevating it to equal dignity with the Toledo Cathedral.[26] During the next century royal benefactions lavished on the Puebla Cathedral made it the peer of the metropolitan cathedral itself.

The first composer of note at Puebla was Pedro Bermúdez. His music is the most rhythmically vital of any yet discovered by a Neo-Hispanic composer. As an example of his style we subjoin an excerpt from Psalm 69 (Vulgate), *Domine ad adjuvandum me festina.*

Domine ad adjuvandum

Puebla Choirbook No. 2, folios 54-5

Pedro Bermúdez

[Moderato]

Do - mi - ne ad ad-ju-van - dum me fes - ti - na.....

The powerful rhythmic drive in each individual voice part adds immeasurably to the virility of Bermúdez's superb setting. Just the rhythmic pattern of the upper voice alone, for instance, reading thus:

is sufficiently endowed with a life of its own to carry the listener's interest constantly forward. The other four voices have been assigned equally propulsive patterns.

In his four Salves he spoke in more passionate accents than Franco had permitted himself.[27] Active a generation after Franco, Bermúdez spoke with an enlarged harmonic vocabulary. His chord of suffering was the Italian augmented sixth. In his first *Salve Regina* for four voices he begins the phrase, "to thee we cry, weeping," with this melodic inflection:

Immediately thereafter occurs this passage:

Phrases like *lacrimum valle* ("vale of tears") are wrung dry of sentiment in Bermúdez's Salves. Without actually writing chromaticisms he did his utmost to imply them. He showed a fine sensitivity to the emotional impact of cross relations.[28]

Already before Bermúdez's time (c. 1605) the Puebla choir had achieved a reputation not only in New Spain but also in the homeland as well. Diego de Basalenque, born at Salamanca in 1577, was sent from Spain as a youth to study among other subjects music at Puebla; later when he came to write a chronicle of his order he said he learned music in the diatonic and chromatic kinds to perfection while a student at Puebla.[29] What Basalenque meant by diatonic genus music is clear; what he meant by chromatic genus music may be discovered by reading Juan Bermudo's explanation in his 1555 *Declaración de instrumentos* (Bk. V, ch. 32). Bermudo said (f. 138ᵛ): "What we now universally play and sing [though the accidentals are not written] is a mixture of the diatonic and chromatic kinds of music." The obligatory use of organ accompaniment for "chromatic genus" music was mentioned in a tract by the later theorist, Eximeno.[30]

The crowning epoch in Puebla's musical history was the fourteen-year period during which Bishop Juan de Palafox y Mendoza ruled the see. Himself an intimate of the Spanish royal house, a scion of nobility, and a devotee of the fine arts, he rose to be viceroy of New Spain for a brief time. His tastes were always patrician, and his learning immense. He spared no effort to make the consecration of the Puebla Cathedral on April 18, 1649, the most brilliant of its kind ever celebrated in the New World. In the official account, *Relación y descripción del Templo Real de la civdad de la Puebla de los Angeles . . . , y sv Catedral. Qve de orden de Sv Magestad acabò, y consagro a 18. de Abril de 1649,* constant mention is made of a double choir. His appropriations for music reached the unprecedented sum of 14,000 pesos annually, a sum considerably in excess of that spent anywhere in the New World during his particular epoch.[31]

Because his lavish spending made possible a double choir of "diestros" —skilled singers—the repertory at Puebla was enlarged to include music for two and three choirs by Bernardo de Peralta and Juan de Padilla. The sonorous ideal in the Puebla Cathedral approximated that of Giovanni Gabrieli's *Sacrae Symphoniae;* such a work as Peralta's twelve-voice Magnificat, thought to have been sung at the 1649 dedication ceremonies, while not of as Gargantuan dimension as Orazio Benevoli's festival Mass for the consecration of the Salzburg Cathedral (1628), is nevertheless a work of tremendous scope. Foreshadowing Bach in one detail, Peralta withholds his first vocal tutti until the "omnes" of *beatam me dicent omnes generationes.* The expressive devices furthermore are typically early baroque. *Et sanctum nomen* is answered back and forth in typical sequence pattern with this rhythmic pattern [musical notation]. Verse 5 of the Magnificat ("misericordia") is assigned the first choir—composed of light, high voices. *Fecit potentiam* is hurled between the choirs in an effective sequence involving this pattern: [musical notation]. *Dispersit superbos* is assigned this characteristic lashing rhythm: [musical notation]

[musical notation] . The Gloria moves up tier on tier to a resonant climax of really striking magnificence. The changes from duple to triple and from triple to duple meter throughout the work provide dramatic relief. On occasion Peralta does not scruple to write one melodic line in duple meter and another simultaneously in triple.

In 1649 at Palafox's behest there was printed at Puebla a 24-page book of choir regulations: *Reglas y ordenanzas del Coro desta Santa Iglesia Cathedral de la Puebla de los Angeles.* It was during Palafox's regime that Juan Gutierrez de Padilla was secured as Puebla chapelmaster; undoubtedly Padilla was a talent whom Palafox had personally observed in Spain or else was a rising light recommended to Palafox by one of his deputies in Spain (Palafox came over in 1639). Padilla's musical achievement has not yet been fully canvassed, but it is known that his extant repertory is larger than that of any other sixteenth or seventeenth century composer in Mexico. The first printed allusion to his Puebla activities occurs in the already cited *Relación y descripción* in which he is several times mentioned by name,[32] and his compositions lauded as the wonder of their time. His successor as chapelmaster was Licenciado Miguel Mateo

Dallo y Lana, who is now principally remembered for his part in setting Sor Juana Inés de la Cruz's *Villancicos* (printed at Puebla in 1690).[33] Padilla himself wrote numerous villancicos in the vernacular, in addition to liturgical compositions with Latin text, but he did not have the good fortune to conjoin any of his villancico-music with words by as famous a figure in Mexican letters as Sor Juana.

The first work of Padilla transcribed into modern score was a *Passion According to St. Matthew* (Steven Barwick: "Sacred Vocal Polyphony in Early Colonial Mexico," 1949). More recently Alice Ray's transcriptions of the Padilla Masses have extended our acquaintance with this fecund composer. The University of Southern California Madrigal Choir pioneered with the first performances of any Padilla music in this country. Their renditions were received with warmth, and the immediate impression left by the music was entirely positive. The singers themselves heartily applauded the music; Padilla's "orchestration" for voices avoids the tendency to thickness that so much double choir music shows. More than the sixteenth century music of Franco it commands the sympathy of modern audiences because a clear striving for climax inhabits all the larger vocal movements.

The use of accidentals for the most part adheres to normal early baroque practice; José de Torres's 1703 *Missarum Liber* printed at Madrid (a book now in the Puebla archives) shows a similar stage of advance in the use of accidentals. But Padilla sometimes intruded accidentals which call for a succession of diminished and augmented intervals that do not fit his normal practice. It is known that on occasion he parodied his own motets in his Masses.[34] Whether his more adventurous moments in the use of accidentals point to some unknown—possibly indigenous composition—which he was at the moment parodying, remains an open question. Such an explanation has been suggested, but the thesis yet lacks confirmation.

His *St. Matthew Passion* was not a continuous composition, but rather provided choral music for only the turba parts—that is to say the parts of the passion narrative in which the Jewish or heathen crowd speaks. In actual date of composition Padilla's probably was written about the same time as Heinrich Schütz's *Matthäus-Passion* (1666). The plan of both is analogous; both open with a choral section declaiming the title of the scripture selection about to be read. The number of choral sections in Padilla's Latin passion is 20; in Schütz's vernacular passion the number is

23. The choral sections in both are of about equal length, and they are both interspersed with monodic declamation of the remaining scriptural narrative. Three short excerpts are given below, the first in each case from Padilla, the second from Schütz. In general it will be seen that Padilla resorts to chromaticism to express emotion, whereas Schütz resorts to rhythmic oppositions. Padilla's would engender perhaps a more abstract reaction, and Schütz's a more personal. Padilla's is the more contemplative, Schütz's the more participative. In conformity with his liturgical purpose Padilla does not allow himself the dramatic assistance of repeating scriptural words. Schütz does, however, and his brief vignettes no doubt gain in sharpness because he repeats words and phrases, thus etching them in the hearer's imagination.

Padilla's passion was written for Palm Sunday, the traditional day for the reading of the Matthew narrative; Schütz's, on the other hand, was presumably intended for Good Friday, as was Bach's.

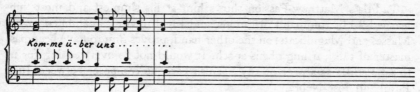

Let us see if Elias will save Him
Padilla [19.]

Padilla's Matthew-Passion shows him at his simplest and most "un-learned." His command of canonic and fugal device as exhibited in the Masses and Magnificats, on the other hand, proves him to have been past master of the learning of his epoch. It would not be overweening for us to set Padilla as a peer of any Spanish baroque composer between Juan Pujol and José Nebra.

The existence of a highly developed school of composers but accords with other evidences showing a high concentration of cultural activity in colonial Puebla. The cathedral grew ever more sumptuous with the passing of years. At a time when the Mexico City Cathedral was begin-ning to house expensive adornments brought from such distant places as Macao, Puebla Cathedral was being enriched at equally lavish expense. Her chroniclers were fond of listing the proofs that "this incomparable cathedral" took second place to none; "its like cannot be found elsewhere in America, not even at Mexico City." [35] The most significant single cul-tural asset in Puebla was the cathedral, no doubt, but from our viewpoint equally noteworthy was the magnificent Palafoxian Library—probably the most important single library in all colonial America during the eighteenth century.[36]

MUSIC IN MICHOACÁN

If Puebla developed a school of composers whose music compares favorably with the best homeland product of the epoch, one finds evidence that in Michoacán an important center of cultural activity sprang up also. The most notable epoch in the history of Michoacán music would seem to be the eighteenth century, during which a school of composers (whose works were preserved at the former convent of Santa Rosa de Santa María de Valladolid) was active. The beginnings of Michoacán music can, however, be traced back to the sixteenth century.

In 1572, as has already been shown in the discussion of music books printed in New Spain during the sixteenth century, Pedro Ocharte—the Frenchman from Rouen—ordered a hundred *Pasioneros* from his press delivered to the Tarasco linguist, Juan Diego de Rincón, then bishop of Michoacán. These *Passionarios* included music for the last three days of Holy Week, and therefore included music only for the passion narrative in the Fourth Gospel. In order to supply music for the other days of Holy Week when the other passion narratives were read, a Franciscan residing in the diocese of Michoacán conceived the idea of creating his own pseudo-plainsong setting of the other passion narratives. In order to make his projected book as usable as possible he set it up to include not only all four passions but also certain scripture selections read on Holy Saturday, namely parts of Lamentations and the so-called Prayer of Jeremy.

Juan Navarro, the Franciscan in question, was originally a native of Cádiz, but he claimed in his preface to the printed book that his music was written in the New World. It would therefore qualify as the oldest printed music actually composed in America. The style of the music is indistinguishable from conventional plainsong, but he stated in his introduction that he had actually made up the music himself. His book containing monodic settings of all four passions was entitled *Liber in quo quatuor passiones Christi Domini continentur,* and was published at Mexico City by the printer Didacus López Davalos in 1604. Consisting of 105 numbered leaves, the book is further distinguished as the only Neo-Hispanic imprint exclusively devoted to music. The first 89 folios contain the passions, and the remainder the Lamentations and Prayer of Jeremy.

Because the book was expressly designed to fulfill the needs of ordinary churches, the music enables us accurately to gauge the level of music ability among priests and deacons in the common-garden-variety church. That Navarro was intensely concerned over the financial success of the book is proved by his insertion of commendatory letters from Dominican and Augustinian authorities at the beginning of the book.[37] As a Franciscan he knew the importance of securing approbation not only from his own commissary general, from the archbishop, and from the viceroy. Without these three licences his book could never have gone to bed; but the approbations of the Dominican and Augustinian vicars choral were clearly inserted to help the sale of the book among clergy of those orders. It is obvious, therefore, that Navarro's *Quatuor Passiones* containing music of only moderate difficulty was a book which he hoped priests and deacons everywhere would use, even if they belonged to rival orders.

The book was ready for the printer in 1601; in that year the viceroy gave Navarro "copyright" privileges for twelve years, and declared a fine of 1,000 Castile ducats against anyone who presumed to break the copyright on it. In Navarro's letter dedicating the book to his provincial superior, he avowed he took no time from his major enterprise in order to compose the chants, but rather did them as a "nocturnal exercise." In the

preface to the reader (which follows the dedication) he wrote an interesting essay on the history of music in the Western Church; his frequent
and on the whole apt quotation from Scripture and from patristic authorities [38] indicates either his own extensive reading, or the easy availability
of a catena of well selected passages. In order to justify the time he had
spent composing music (an expense of time his fellow-friars had evidently
criticized) he reminded them that according to Revelation their chief occupation in heaven would be musical exercise. He then continued with the
following apologia pro vita sua:

> I have as a man endeavored to devote all my time to a heavenly work.
> . . . Whether I have excelled in that work or not, let others judge.
> . . . Those who always disparage the labors of others which they cannot
> duplicate, and those who clamor against the unceasing nightly toil of
> others, are but asked to recall the story of Michal, daughter of King Saul,
> and wife of David. She despised David for his playing and dancing before
> the Ark of the Covenant, and for her gesture of contempt she was pun-
> ished with sterility. Those who deride the conscientious endeavor of those
> who devote themselves to music, and who rail at the nightly labor of others
> while giving themselves to rest, relaxation, and leisurely living, we say are
> deprived of sweetness of disposition towards God or man, and are in reality
> dropping insidious poison. But just as David was not at all impaired in his
> joyful praise despite Michal's derision (for he said: "I shall go on playing
> before the Lord, and I shall yet be more shameless than I was hitherto,
> and will be base in mine own sight," 2 Reg. 6) so in like manner I shall
> also delight in the Lord and praise Him for His kindness. In His praise
> I shall spend my time with carefree mind, overlooking the assembly of
> those who unfeelingly mock and carp at my endeavor.[39]

Juan Navarro, the author of the work now under consideration,
Quatuor Passiones, was formerly confused with another Juan Navarro,
a Spanish polyphonist who died several years before the New World
book was published. Eitner's *Quellen-Lexicon* and *Grove's Dictionary* are
but two of the more available authorities which confused the two men.
Gilbert Chase, however, in an article entitled "Juan Navarro Hispalensis
and Juan Navarro Gaditanus" (*The Musical Quarterly*, April, 1945),
disentangled the two men. The mistake was a natural one to make; Juan
Navarro Hispalensis ("of Seville") published *Psalmi, Hymni, ac Magnificat totius anni* at Rome in 1590. A copy of this very 1590 book was
preserved in the Puebla cathedral archive; why should not Navarro His-

palensis have emigrated to Mexico? Rafael Mitjana, who first confused the two, did not know Juan Navarro Hispalensis was old enough in 1553 to compete for the Málaga chapelmastership left vacant in that year by Morales's death.

The temptation to carry over famous figures from the Old to the New World still persists, however, even if the Navarros have been forcibly separated into two distinct personalities. The most tantalizing identification now before the Latin American world takes Domenico Zipoli, the great Italian organist who became organist of the Jesuit church at Rome in 1696, to the Paraguay Jesuit mission in 1716.[40] But Adolfo Salazar, the Spanish musicographer, thinks it unlikely that so adept a musician as Zipoli ended his life in Argentinian obscurity.[41] Do we have here another case of homonymns? And was the José de Torres who succeeded Zumaya as chapelmaster at Mexico City in 1732 the same José de Torres who had already published a book of Masses in Spain and whose *Arte de canto llano nuevamente corr. y aora aument. por J. de Torres* was published at Madrid in 1734? [42] The breakdown of the Navarro identification has put everyone on guard, and no similar identification in the future is likely to be accepted without ironclad proof.

But even if denied the privilege of attributing *Quatuor Passiones* to an already renowned European figure, we still have before us a book worthy of inspection. Navarro though claiming as his model the Roman chant, presented his book as an original creation. It should be compared with an English redaction of plainsong by John Marbeck, *The Booke of Common Praier noted* (1550). The music in both books is closely patterned on traditional plainchant, but there is enough of the individual creator in both to justify calling them original products. Any melody which confines itself to those intervals found in Gregorian chant, which adheres to the same system of dominants and finals, and which does not flagrantly divide itself into rhythmic sequences, will seem to many in our own day scarcely distinguishable from authentic chant of the Middle Ages; nonetheless Navarro's music has an individual profile of its own and he therefore deserves to be classed as a creator. If Navarro in *Quatuor Passiones*, Marbeck in *The Booke of Common Praier noted,* and Luther in *Deudsche Messe,* all wrote melodies that sound alike, the reason is sufficiently obvious: despite their denominational differences, they all cobbled on the same musical last.

Navarro's music is all in the Dorian. The chants are predominantly syllabic, with only an occasional eruption into melisma. Melismas are reserved for words or expressions of dramatic intensity (such as, "My God, My God, why hast Thou forsaken Me?"). The punctum is used for unaccented syllables in the text, the virga for accented syllables. The neumes of two or more notes used are the podatus, clivis, scandicus, climacus, and porrectus. The neumes are printed in black over a red five-line staff, and the registration is often faulty; certainly it is poorer than in the sixteenth century Espinosa and Ocharte liturgical books. The F-clef on the middle line is the most common. B-flats and b-naturals are the only accidentals used. The four passions are written throughout in dialogue form, with the priest's voice as the higher. Modulation, in the plainsong sense, is conspicuously missing. The following example illustrates Navarro's style in one of his more expansive moments [43] (notes with dashes over them are virgas in the original):

("What, could ye not watch with me one hour? Watch and pray that ye enter not into temptation: the spirit indeed is willing, but the flesh is weak." Matt. 26:40b–41)

Torquemada (1615) noted the flourishing state of church music in Michoacán, and it therefore appears likely that enough sales of Navarro's book were made in his own territory to return him the costs of printing it. Throughout the seventeenth century we continue to encounter sporadic notices of musical life in Michoacán. It seems evident that Indian musical talent was for a longer time encouraged in such outlying centers as

Valladolid [now Morelia] than was the case at Mexico City. Diego de Basalenque, whose early studies at Puebla we have already mentioned, wrote a chronicle of Michoacán in which he told of two exceptionally talented Indians, father and son: the father brilliantly competed with the best Spanish organist of his time, and the son occupied the organist's bench in the Valladolid Cathedral.[44]

The eighteenth century school of composers devoted themselves largely to instrumental works, according to the catalogue supplied by Miguel Bernal Jiménez in his 1939 publication, *El Archivo Musical del Colegio de Santa Rosa de Santa María de Valladolid*. He presented in this monograph several excerpts in illustration of their achievements,[45] and he has promised us a fuller discussion of these eighteenth century composers in a later publication. Whether it later develops that all the listed composers in the Santa Rosa archive were Michoacán residents or not, at least the presence of their works in the archive denotes an advanced musical taste. A colonial orchestra capable of playing these works could hardly have existed in Valladolid unless some especially wealthy magnate with the generosity and artistic taste of a José de la Borda defrayed the expense. According to Bernal Jiménez a school of music was founded in Valladolid (Morelia) as early as 1743. It is significant that the first important republican composer in Mexico was a Morelian—José Mariano Elízaga. A major figure in nineteenth century Mexican music, Elízaga could hardly have outdistanced all his contemporaries in Mexico City unless his own background training (in Morelia) had been of quite a substantial kind.

MUSIC IN OTHER PROVINCIAL CENTERS

Oaxaca was another center whose records—scanty though they be—show that music of a pretentious kind was cultivated at the cathedral during colonial times. The best known of the Oaxaqueña chapelmasters was Juan Matías, an Indian from the Zapotec village of Zaapeche.[46] At the age of twenty he displayed such phenomenal ability both as a singer and as an organist that the then chapelmaster proposed to export him to Spain as a notable rarity for Spanish royalty to gape at; this plan was frustrated, however, because shipping at the moment was impossible to obtain and the chapelmaster himself died soon thereafter. During the competition for the post that shortly ensued, Matías successfully competed against "able

and illustrious competitors from both the capital city and from Puebla"
who offered themselves. Elected by common acclamation, Matías occupied the chapelmastership with distinction for a space of fifteen years. His
achievement was discussed by Guillermo A. Esteva in a short bulletin,
La Música Oaxaqueña, published at Oaxaca in 1931. Esteva concluded
that though Matías was a seventeenth century composer, his one surviving composition, a *Stabat Mater* [47] fragment, showed him to have been
but slightly interested in the contrapuntal exercises still popular among
Spanish choral composers of his epoch. Instead he wrote for voices with
organ accompaniment in a homophonic style. The following somewhat
trivial excerpt shows him in search of chromatic color; this kind of passage
need not indicate, however, that the best he was capable of elsewhere was
simply a succession of clichés.

Sporadic notices concerning certain other seventeenth and eighteenth century chapelmasters at Oaxaca are recoverable. A chapelmaster named Matheo Vallados, for instance, in 1691 set several villancicos of Sor Juana Inés de la Cruz which were sung with great success on the morning of November 25 in the Oaxaca Cathedral.[48] Notices of the kind that can be obtained, however, all point to the fact that in Oaxaca, in Querétaro, in Guadalajara, and elsewhere, the more influential posts during the seventeenth and eighteenth centuries were reserved for either foreigners, or in lieu of them, for creoles. Certainly no attempt was made during the middle and later portions of the colonial period to integrate Indians into the musical life of the church, as there had been during the missionary period. Had not the filling of an important post by an Indian grown to be a great rarity during the second century after Cortés's conquest, neither Basalenque nor Francisco Burgoa would have made so much of a few isolated cases when exceptional Indians did cross the rigid lines drawn between them and the master class.

The more typical mention of Indian participation in church music was not Burgoa's mention of Matías at Oaxaca, but Don Carlos de Sigüenza y Góngora's mention of the Indian outdoor dances and musical concert on native instruments which he saw when he visited Querétaro in 1675. Invited to help dedicate a church, Sigüenza y Góngora, professor of mathematics in the University of Mexico, made a trip up to Querétaro in that year, and left a minute description in his *Glorias de Querétaro*. What he saw the Indians doing was dancing their famous *toncontín* during the fourth part of an elaborate masquerade in honor of the Virgin.[49] Sigüenza y Góngora, who was himself profoundly learned in Nahuatl, said they played the tlapanhuehuetl, the teponaztli, the omichicahuaztli, the ayacaztli, the cuauhtlapitzalli, "and other similar instruments suitable to the Mexican nation." With these "they praised the Virgin in holy songs conceived in a most elegant style." The Spaniards, on the other hand, had their own orchestra of "suavissimos instrumentos"[50] that played indoors during interludes between readings in a poetical tourney. Inside the church Sigüenza y Góngora himself sung one Mass and assisted at another one sung by Padre Juan de Robles.[51] He obviously considered the Indians had a distinct contribution to make—their own music sung and danced in their own way—but just as obviously he thought the music for the "main events" should be music played on European instruments by musicians of European stock. Don Carlos's attitude represented the enlightened attitude of a colonial who while a friend of the Indian, did not favor cultural integration.[52]

THE VILLANCICO IN NEW SPAIN

The Neo-Hispanic compositions thus far alluded to in this chapter use Latin texts in nearly every instance. During the seventeenth and eighteenth centuries, however, a large literature of villancicos sprang up, all using Spanish texts. According to dictionary definition a villancico is a Christmas carol or a metric composition sung in church on certain other festival occasions. Perhaps a third of the preserved Neo-Hispanic villancicos were intended for use at Christmas; the other two-thirds were written for other festivals in the church year. In all of them a note of intense happiness is found; words and music alike breathe an atmosphere of exuberance and exhilaration.

In New Spain all the villancicos thus far encountered were intended for church usage. The villancico originated, however, not as a type of sacred song, but rather as a type of secular song. The earliest printed villancicos —Juan Vásquez's *Villancicos* (Osuna, 1551) and his *Recopilación de sonetos y villancicos a quatro y a cinco* (Seville, 1560); and the anonymous villancicos in the so-called *Cancionero de Upsala* (Venice, 1556)—treated sacred themes only in the rarest instances. Almost invariably they had to do with the pangs of love, the joys of love, the awakening of love, or "the spring time, the only pretty ring time, when birds do sing, hey ding a ding, ding." The melodies "had a simple folk-like quality, even when associated with a sophisticated text; the meaning of the text was translated into simple musical terms, and the expressive effect never disregarded." [53]

Because of the secular origin of the villancico, and also because its text even when pertaining to a religious subject remained in the vernacular, the use of the villancico in churches was discouraged during the sixteenth century. Philip II (whose religious austerity is well known) would have none of it.[54] But with his passing in 1598, the villancico gradually intruded itself, and during the seventeenth and eighteenth centuries usurped first place in the affections of the broader public. In New Spain the publication of villancicos (text only) became an endemic disease. Every saint's day was celebrated with new villancicos; these were sung at matins, usually, but during the latter part of the sixteenth century even so proper a poetess as the Jeronymite nun, Sor Juana, wrote villancicos which troped the Mass. As examples of her interpolated tropes we point to her expansion of the Gloria in excelsis (St. Peter Nolasco villancicos, 1677) and of the Ite missa est (St. Catharine villancicos, 1691). Because the prevailing mood in the villancico was always that of happiness, she abstained from troping the sober sections in the Mass such as the Kyrie and Agnus Dei. However since the Gloria and Ite both express triumph and exaltation she did not hesitate to provide Spanish tropes for these particularly joyous sections. It must be confessed her villancicos are charming beyond all expectation, and it is not to be wondered at that in her lifetime during one fourteen-year period (1677–91) demand was so great she published fifteen collections. She, moreover, was but one of a flourishing school of villancico writers in New Spain. At a time the paper shortage was so drastic that no one could publish a scholarly work in New Spain—not even the illustrious Sigüenza y Góngora [55]—these villancico writers, many of them mere hacks, were able to get their ephemeral jottings into print. That such a number of villancico collections could have reached print is proof irrefutable of their enormous popularity.

Because of Sor Juana's acknowledged literary supremacy—she is acknowledged to have been the most brilliant literary light in New Spain during the entire colonial period—her villancico collections will here be examined briefly. As a literary type it is known that the villancico conventionally began with a refrain [*estribillo*] sung by a chorus, then proceeded to a bipartite stanza [*coplas*] sung by a soloist or soloists, then to the refrain again by the chorus, then to a new stanza but sung to the same music as the first stanza, then to the refrain, then to a third stanza if desired, then to the refrain, and so on and on, always ending at the last with the refrain. Sor Juana's villancicos usually follow the conventional estribillo-coplas-estribillo-coplas-estribillo pattern. But she imposed upon her villancicos a larger literary unity by gathering them almost invariably into villancico-sequences. Everyone knows what is meant by a sonnet-sequence; Sor Juana did not try to gather as many villancicos into a sequence as most sonneteers do, but usually gathered only eight or nine into a particular sequence. Each sequence honored some chosen saint. The villancicos in a particular sequence were usually distributed with three sung at the first nocturn of matins, two or three at the next nocturn, and one or two at the third nocturn. If villancicos to be sung at Mass were included, their position in the villancico-sequence was at the end. The latter villancicos in a series were the longest. Often one of the villancicos for the second nocturn would be called a *jácara*. Often the final villancico in the entire sequence if it were not a villancico for Mass would be called an *ensalada*.

Her villancico-sequences are really best described as playlets, with each villancico fulfilling the function of a separate scene speeding forward the action. The first two or three villancicos in a particular sequence set the stage by telling whose day is being celebrated. The *jácara*, which she explains as meaning the same thing as a *corrido*,[56] tells in jaunty ballad fashion the story of an exploit or group of exploits by the saint being honored. The only pronounced difference between a seventeenth century jácara honoring Nolasco and a twentieth century corrido memorializing Zapata is that one is a ballad concerning the exploits of a religious figure and the other is a ballad concerning the exploits of a political figure. The ensalada at the end of Sor Juana's villancico-sequences are medleys in which a host of comic characters are pushed out on the stage, as it were, to delight the audience with a little buffoonery. In the ensalada Sor Juana and her other contemporary villancico-writers often indulged in slang, colloquialisms, and dialect. A Negro with a James Whitcomb Riley accent, an Indian with half his vocabulary composed of Nahuatl words, or a university student who spouts Latin at every opportunity, were stock figures in Sor Juana's ensaladas.

Addressing ourselves now to the Nolasco villancicos, sung at the Mexico City Cathedral on January 31, 1677, with words by Sor Juana and music by Joseph de Agurto y Loaysa, chapelmaster of the cathedral, we discover that there were in this sequence ten villancicos. Three were allotted the first nocturn, three the second, two the third, and two were inserted in Mass. The opening villancico sets the stage by telling us Nolasco was a Frenchman who spent his life ransoming Christian captives from the Moors. The second and third in the first nocturn describe his apotheosis. The first and second for the second nocturn continue in the lyric vein, but the third—a jácara—changes to the narrative mood. "Listen," Sor Juana says, "while I sing his valiant deeds." Then she tells how he came to Barcelona, how he formed a project for ransoming captives, and how his exertions were rewarded. The second villancico for the third nocturn introduces in an *ensaladilla*—a little medley—first a Negro who sings a dance song while shaking a gourd. In it he sadly reflects that if only he were white he would be better treated. He confesses that the other night while he was at his conga,[57] he had some wicked thoughts, but he hopes his good angel will pardon him now. Then he sings the estribillo again: Tumba, la, la, la, tumba, la, le, le. This particular Negro song receives as its title, *Porto Rico;* the porto rico was an extremely popular negroid dance introduced from the West Indies. After this porto rico a young university student spouting Latin phrases honoring Nolasco steps forward. Everything he say in Latin sounds like something entirely different and irrelevant in Spanish. His next door neighbor, a simple man, thinks the university fop is saying some highly ridiculous things, such as, how do you like your liquor, where did you learn to be a warlock, and so on. Sor Juana carries off this little repartee between the fop and the simpleton with real éclat. Then she brings on an Indian who is a baker. He sings a tocotín (the same thing as a toncontín).[58] In it he plays a bit of a braggart, says if he had been Nolasco he wouldn't have paid ransom to a Moorish dog, no, he would have killed him with his bare fists. After the ensaladilla Sor Juana finally brings her Nolasco villancico-sequence to a conclusion with two of them designed for the Mass that followed matins. Of the pair of concluding villancicos the first expands the Gloria in excelsis, but the other has no obvious relation to the liturgy.

Her other villancico-sequences are equally fresh and delightful. Her subject matter varied; one was for Christmas, others were for such saints as Peter, Joseph, and Catharine; she also wrote several for special events in the life of the Virgin Mary. In one of her Virgin Mary sequences she introduced a truly virtuostic villancico founded on musical puns.[59] The Virgin is represented as the teacher of a singing class who instructs her pupils to raise their voices by successive degrees until they reach the celestial. Juana's puns can hardly be translated, but are of this order: b flat is the earthly sound, but the Virgin raises the pitch to b natural, the heavenly sound. The Virgin shows how to make a perfect counterpoint with the Three Persons in the Trinity, and shows how to lift the imperfect duple, two-dimensioned, earthbound rhythm, to the perfect triple, three-dimensioned, heavenly rhythm. Man's phrygian mode (the Spanish word *frigio* is a pun for *frio*)—that is to say, his frigid mode—aroused justly the wrath of God, but as Mary teaches him to sing in a dorian mode (a dorian punning with adoring) the divine wrath is mollified.

Her musical knowledge was gained from *El Melopeo y Maestro* by Pedro Cerone,[60] an invaluable work published at Naples in 1613, but written in Spanish. Her own annotated copy of Cerone still survives.[61] She may possibly have known other musical treatises. The leading book shop in Mexico City in 1683 was that of Paula Benavides; [62] an inventory of the stock preserved from that year shows two other titles: *El Porqué de la música* by Andrés Lorente (published at Alcalá de Henares in 1672) and *Arte de canto llano* by Francisco de Montanos (published at Madrid in 1648). Both these other books are now recognized as superior books of their kind; Lorente's book has been characterized as "one of the best planned and intelligently executed didactic books published during the baroque epoch." [63] The accessibility of these books in Mexico City during the latter part of the seventeenth century proves a certain diffusion of music knowledge in the colony; had there not been a rather persistent demand for serious theoretical treatises no commercial seller would have stocked such books. Professor I. A. Leonard, an authority on colonial culture of the middle period, has reminded us that "colonial readers were able to acquire a wide variety of the books that their relatives enjoyed in Spain, and . . . their opportunities for stimulation in this respect were hardly less than those of the Spaniards who remained in the homeland." The most convincing proof of the rather widespread diffusion of musical knowledge during Juana's time, however, comes from an analysis of her own allusions to music, and not from a study of booksellers' lists.

Of the four composers' names associated with her villancicos, two were provincial chapelmasters and two chapelmasters at the Mexico City Cathedral. Joseph de Agurto y Loaysa, Mexico City chapelmaster, wrote the music for her villancico-sequences published at the capital city between 1677 and 1686, and Antonio de Salazar, Agurto y Loaysa's successor, provided the music for her villancico publications at the capital between 1689 and 1691. Salazar, whose music for two villancicos honoring Ildephonsus is transcribed below, was probably her only worthy collaborator. His Latin hymns are superb, and show him to have been a master contrapuntalist in an epoch when the art of vocal polyphony was decaying.

His name is a common one in Spanish, but it has been suggested that he came from Seville, since certain Salazar compositions are preserved in the Seville cathedral archive.[64] He came at a time the Cabildo was more than ordinarily eager to secure a competent composer. In 1682 the Cathedral Cabildo invited applications for a chapelmaster to succeed Agurto y Loaysa, who was then presumably near the retirement age. Three competitors appeared for the post, one of whom, a Juan Coronado, was forced to withdraw since he was adjudged an incompetent as a composer. A Nicolas Marín was chosen, but seems not to have actually entered upon the exercise of chapelmaster duties; [65] in any event Salazar became the chapelmaster in 1687 or 1688, occupying the post as Agurto y Loaysa's immediate successor. Salazar remained for almost a quarter century; he was followed by Manuel Zumaya, thought to have been his pupil. Zumaya, who remained until 1732, in which year he removed to Oaxaca, was the first Mexico City chapelmaster who we are certain was a creole.[66] Like Loaysa and Salazar, Zumaya continued to compose villancicos, but during his epoch the villancico developed into a cantata, with an opening chorus, interspersed arias, and a choral finale.

The villancicos of Salazar and Zumaya both presuppose an orchestral accompaniment, and the vocal parts therefore represent only a skeleton. Figured bass was utilized in eighteenth century music composed in Mexico,[67] but no indication remains that it was used during the seventeenth; this generalization may later prove ill-founded, but seems accurate now. The two villancicos with Salazar music printed below were written for a celebration on January 23, 1691, honoring Ildephonsus, an ecclesiastic of the seventh century who wrote in behalf of the perpetual virginity. His cult was extremely popular in Mexico. The sense of the first one runs thus:

Estribillo   Listen to our taunt hurled at the heretic, Helvidius. May his life be a thousand times embittered. Listen while everyone derides him; listen while the heavens, on the other hand, rejoice at his discomfiture.

Coplas   If he thinks we are going to trade insult for insult this time he is mistaken; we are going to hit back three times for his every two times, because we already know he is a blasphemer and a scoundrel.

The sense of the second runs as follows:

Estribillo   Take care against the wild beast who stamps the ground on the fertile banks of the Tagus hoping he will consume the flock on the other side. But his evil designs are known, and will be frustrated. Ildephonsus will rescue his favorite flock.

Coplas   1. The lurking figure of Helvidius can be discerned in the darkness of the night. He wants to play the wolf and carry off his victims, but like a booby he gives himself away with his wolf howls.

2. Although the French beast rages at the flock, Ildephonsus, shepherd

of the sheep, will whirl around and protect them so that not even the purity of their wool will be soiled.

3. Let the wild beast who comes raging from abroad deceitfully wrapped in a ewe's skin realize his evil designs are known; he cannot spread his plague in Spanish dominions.

The meaning of these two villancicos seems at first somewhat abstruse, but the political situation in 1691 makes clear their true significance. Helvidius, who lived sometime before 383, is only a straw man set up to be knocked down. Nothing is known of Helvidius's nationality, and there is no reason to believe he was French.[68] But for the purposes of the villancicos at hand, Helvidius had to be a French heretic, and Ildephonsus had to be a Spanish hero protecting the flock against the base intruder. The Tagus river is mentioned because on its banks Ildephonsus set up shop, as it were, while he was writing his theological treatises. Helvidius and Ildephonsus were merely convenient prototypes. Spain and France were at war in 1691, and for propaganda purposes the signatories of the League of Augsburg (to which Charles II adhered) labeled their opponent, Louis XIV as insufficiently firm in the faith. It mattered not for the propaganda purposes in hand that Louis XIV was at the particular moment (1691) thoroughly under the dominance of a Jesuit confessor.

These villancicos carry therefore a double meaning. The well-known Neo-Hispanist, Alfonso Méndez Plancarte, thinks these Ildephonsus verses were written by a peninsular poet.[69]

— por tres   por blas-fe—mo por   so-ez   que sus a-po—

—dos pre—vie—ne. —

Villancico (4 voices)
Guarda la fiera

Antonio de Salazar, 1691

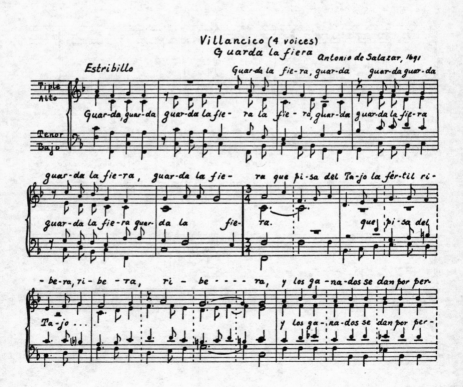

Estribillo

Guar-da la fie-ra, guar-da   guar-da guar-da

Tiple / Alto: Guar-da, guar-da guar-da la fie — ra la fie — ra, guar-da guar-da la fie-ra

Tenor / Bajo:

guar-da la fie-ra,   guar-da la fie — ra que pi-sa del Ta-jo la fér-til ri-

guar-da la fie-ra guar-da la   fie—ra.   que pi-sa del

Ta-jo...

—be-ra, ri-be — ra,   ri — be · · · · ra, y los ga-na-dos se dan por per-

y los ga — na-dos se dan por per-

MUSIC AT THE MEXICO CITY CATHEDRAL (SALAZAR TO ALDANA)

A list is fortunately still extant in which are given the names of fifteen different instruments used in the cathedral orchestra during 1691.[70] It is also known that these instruments were used conjointly as a group accompanying the Salazar villancicos sung on June 29 of that year. Presumably the same instruments were used in accompanying the two villancicos honoring Ildephonsus which were sung earlier that same year (January 23), and whose vocal parts in condensed score have been shown above. This June 29 list has been found particularly helpful because it names specific instruments; this list was the first which specifically named the violin; it also mentioned the treble viol, the tenor viol, and the rebeck. The other chordophones named in the list were the bandore, the cittern, the marine trumpet, and the harp. The brass instruments used were the clarion, the trumpet, and the trombone. The only two woodwinds mentioned in the list were the double-reed chirimía, for which instrument the violin is spoken of as providing a suitable obbligato, and the bassoon. Flutes did not appear in the 1691 list, although it is conjectured recorders were still used in the cathedral orchestra. The organ is mentioned, but its function seems to have been relatively unimportant as far as the effect of the total ensemble was concerned.

The interior of the Mexico City Cathedral—and now we speak of the present structure—had only recently been finished when Salazar became chapelmaster. The second solemn dedication of the cathedral had occurred in 1667 when the interior was completed.[71] Three years before the solemn act a campanile had been erected containing twenty bells.[72] These were not a tuned carillon, but simply rang peals. When they started ringing while the cathedral orchestra and choir were performing, Sor Juana exclaimed, "Jesus! what confusion!" (¡Jesús, y que confusión!) [73] Any mental picture which can be conjured up of the flickering lights illuminating this vast cathedral, of the altars served by richly vested clergy, of the fine canvases by such capable Neo-Hispanic painters as the two Echaves, the two Juarezes, and Juan Correa, hung everywhere, will probably still fall short of the actual panoply and display during Salazar's incumbency. When one sets his surging hymns or his bright and gaudy villancicos in their proper environment, calling up in imagination the sharply differentiated tone colors in his orchestra, one then catches some notion of the potent synoptic experience which the Neo-Hispanic church specialized in providing. The humbler folk in the city might want food; in 1692, for instance, a great corn-riot broke out in the Mexico City market. But Mexico has always specialized in dramatic contrast. The poor Indian woman who was pressed to death in the riot on June 8 while the tintinnabulation of the bells, bells, bells, at the cathedral blended with a gay villancico was but the ancestor of a hundred others who have perished while the band played on.

Salazar's hymns are hymns in the Palestrina or Victoria sense of the word *hymn*—that is to say, polyphonic settings of certain texts that in Latin usage are classified as hymns. From a musical standpoint the word *motet* would more aptly describe a Salazar hymn as far as English readers are concerned. His hymns were not at all intended for congregations, but for his professionalized choir members to sing. Perhaps the most important of his hymns preserved in the Puebla archive is the St. James hymn (St. James is the patron saint of Spain).[74] His other hymns preserved at Puebla include two for the Assumption and one each for SS. Peter and Paul and for St. Joseph. In addition, two Salazar hymns are preserved at the Mexico City Cathedral *tesoro artístico*.

Manuel Zumaya, Salazar's successor, was the first chapelmaster at Mexico City who can definitely be identified as a creole. Beristaín y Souza tells us that Zumaya was born in Mexico, that he became a priest, and that he acquired fluency in Italian.[75] Zumaya's musical importance rests not so much, however, on the fact he was the first Mexico City chapelmaster who can be proved to have been born in Mexico. Rather it rests on the fact he was the composer of the first opera produced in the New World, *La Parténope,* given at the viceregal palace on May 1, 1711. The libretto was by Silvio Stampiglia, and another opera using the same libretto had been produced at Naples in 1699 with music by the obscure Neapolitan composer, Luigi Manzo.[76] Since it is difficult to account for Zumaya's acquaintance with this particular libretto unless he himself had lived in Italy, and more particularly in Naples, it has been postulated that in early youth he studied in Italy. Wherever he may have acquired his musical knowledge, he still is distinguished as the first American composer of opera, and his *La Parténope* is still distinguished as the first opera of any sort produced on American soil.

Before the production of *La Parténope* he had already published an original play, *El Rodrigo,* printed in 1708. After the arrival of a new viceroy, the Duke of Linares, Don Fernando de Alencastre Noroña y Silva, on January 15, 1711, Zumaya was immediately pressed into the duke's musical service. Beristaín y Souza tells us that the duke was a devotee of Italian opera. Zumaya was commissioned to translate Italian libretti, and to write new music for these libretti. Beristaín y Souza adds that his music thoroughly pleased the duke. Zumaya if not in Italy at least somewhere had learned how to please him. The libretto of *La Parténope* was printed with text in both Spanish and Italian, and although the music has not survived it must have been thoroughly Italianate. Like the prevailing baroque plots, that of *La Parténope* was intricate in the extreme. Two of the seven characters were rival leading ladies—princesses. Their roles were in all probability sung by cathedral choir boys. The continued production of operas in the Italian manner was inhibited in Mexico largely through lack of a troupe. The first Italian troupe settled in Madrid in 1703, but the viceregal court could not independently support a troupe.

Zumaya's term as chapelmaster lasted until 1732; in that year he went to Oaxaca with Tomás Montaño, dean of the Mexico Cathedral who was elevated to the bishopric of Oaxaca. In Oaxaca Zumaya devoted himself entirely to religious duties. He translated a biography of Sertorio Caputo, a Jesuit, from Italian into Spanish, and cultivated "the sacred sciences." There he died "much lamented by his parishioners." Zumaya's Magnificats and villancicos surviving in the Mexico City *tesoro artístico* have not yet been examined minutely, but Estrada, present organist at the cathedral, thinks him to have been the finest Mexican composer of the eighteenth century. A villancico transcribed by Saldívar, if it may be taken as representative of Zumaya's style, shows him to have conceived of the form not in terms of a refrain-stanza-refrain pattern, but rather as a miniature cantata. After the opening tenor solo, in the example Saldívar transcribed, the estribillo required an eight-part double chorus. Throughout the double chorus the interior voice parts seem more often designed as mere harmonic padding than as independent vocal lines. The ten measures between the one numbered 24 and the one numbered 34 in the Alto I part (estribillo) provide an excellent example of an instrumentally conceived inner part, for instance. But there are also imitations, and in total effect—even if the separate vocal parts often lack a rhythmic vitality of their own—the villancico in question undoubtedly conveyed an

impression of garish brilliancy. The contrast between the opening tenor
solo (an introduction) and the estribillo is well handled; the tenor solo,
with its supple ternary flow, gives no hint of the hammering force in the
estribillo to follow.

The whole of the Zumaya villancico is too lengthy to set out here.
Simply as a sample we have therefore chosen the opening tenor solo, following it with several bars of the estribillo. It should be noted that the
two choirs in the estribillo are throughout handled in antiphonal style.
The words laud Peter, as would befit his day in the church calendar. The
text is probably Pedro Muñoz de Castro's; he is known to have been
supplying Zumaya with villancico-texts. But Castro's lack the inimitable
swing of Sor Juana's. He left out the low comedy characters which she
was so fond of introducing in her ensaladas at the end of her villancico-
sequences, and instead wrote "glosas," smelling of the lamp.

Zumaya's music, like that of several other Neo-Hispanic compeers, seems worthy of protracted study. For the music of some of his later eighteenth century successors in the Mexico City chapelmastership less favorable representations can be made, however. His immediate successor was José de Torres (1732), during whose regime a new organ of monumental size was installed at the cathedral.

Puebla had in 1695 secured a new organ built by the brothers Tiburcio and Felix Sans of Aragon, both of whom had been expressly imported for the purpose of building Puebla an organ suitable for its musical pretensions.[77] Guadalajara at a cost of 20,000 pesos—an enormous figure in that day—had secured in 1730 a handsomely cased instrument built by the famous maestro, José Nazarre, containing 2,226 pipes.[78] Mexico City, not to be outdistanced by any provincial center, commissioned a new instrument of even larger size. At the dedication on August 15, 1735, "several thousand" persons saw Don Juan de Vizarrón y Eguiarreta, who was at the moment both archbishop and viceroy, cooperate with the audiencia in staging a solemn "act." If Guadalajara's had 2,226 pipes, Mexico's had to have more, and the total number was therefore 3,350. The number of mixture stops alone reached 86. Five hidden bellows supplied the necessary wind.

Manuel de San Vicente, whose *Exacta Descripción de la Magnífica Corte Mexicana* was published at Cádiz, Spain, in 1768, listed this organ, built in Mexico City but under European supervision, as one of the wonders of the New World. At the time he visited Mexico the organ was one of the principal daily attractions; visitors today can still see the tremendous rows of pipes, and although the organ is now no longer usable because it has fallen completely into disrepair, it takes no great stretch of the imagination to appreciate San Vincente's glowing account. As he described it, the organ was divided: what amounted to a completely individualized instrument was placed on each side of the nave. The two antiphonal choirs were therefore each supported by two antiphonal organs. The pipes of each of the antiphonal organs were again subdivided and housed in four separate chambers. The ideal of a unified instrument which many organ builders today follow was completely absent from the minds of Neo-Hispanic builders. Theirs had no swell shutters, and whatever effects of loudness and softness were procured on their organs were more the result of nearness or distance of the pipes rather than of voicing of individual ranks. The names of stops cannot be readily translated into modern terms. We have no exact record of the stops on the Mexico organ when it was dedicated but the *Gazeta de México* carried a list of the Guadalajara stops at the time of the Guadalajara dedication ceremony. The list included "octavas, dozenas, quinzenas, decisetenas, decinovenas, cimbales, ventidocenas, nazardos, cornetas, trompeta real, bajoncillos, clarines, trompeta magna, chirimía, oboe, voces naturales y sictas." [79] Our understanding of the Spanish organ ideal during the Cabanillas period is still in such a primitive state that we have no exact means of equating the practice of the early eighteenth century with our own. It does seem obvious, however, that the Neo-Hispanic organ contained several stops imitating instruments in common use; mixtures, moreover, were as important (proportionately speaking) as they were in Bach's Leipzig organ of the same period. The pedals extending through only one octave (from C to B♮) were not disposed, however, as a keyboard for the feet in Neo-Hispanic organs.[80] Independent parts were not written for the pedals, which were actually short knobs. These knobs though horizontally laid out did not admit of any rapid foot-work, since they could be played only with the toes. Obviously legato in any kind of moving passage was out of the question.

The organ cases were of incomparable richness. In San Vicente's opinion—and he had seen the best in Spain—the costliness of the Mexico City organ was unparalleled. The top level of the pipes stood 47 feet above the floor of the choir. In conformity with the usual Spanish practice of the time, the lips of the Mexico pipes were surrounded with brightly painted faces representing angels. With his mouth wide open each angel looked as if any instant he were ready to blow. Pál Kelemen, noted art historian of our own time, in 1942 wrote an interesting study of "Church Organs in Colonial Mexico"; while he ignored musical technicalities, which were not germane to his purpose in writing the article, he nevertheless did us a service by calling attention to the superb craftsmanship of these eighteenth century organs. He praised "these majestic instruments . . . built by inspired artists and devoted artisans," which though now silenced "are monuments of hope for a brighter future in which mankind will recover its love for the arts and for humanitarian values." [81]

If the organ dedication was the most spectacular event during his incumbency, Torres deserves mention also as a creditable composer if not an inspired one. Masses of his are preserved at Morelia as well as at Mexico. He favored the music of the Italianized Spaniard, Domingo Terradellas (1713–51), and acquired a 5-part Mass with orchestral accompaniment by him; as is the case with certain works by Galuppi and Jommelli,[82] the only known score of the Terradellas Mass is today preserved in Mexico. Whether a unique copy in Mexico means the work was especially procured for performance in Mexico, we are not prepared to say. What these scores do indicate with certainty, however, is the active participation of the colony in the musical life of the home country until the very end of the colonial epoch. The weaknesses that beset Spanish music during the eighteenth century were precisely those which beset Mexico—the influx of second-rate Italian musicians exercising the most deleterious influence. Ignacio Jerusalem, who became chapelmaster at Mexico City in 1764, provides but one especially conspicuous example of a second-rate Italian who, graduating from the orchestra pit at the Coliseo de México, carried into the cathedral the vapid inanities of Italian opera at its worst. He did further harm by selfishly opposing the University rector who wanted an independent university *capilla de música* [83] (singing traditional polyphony).

In contrast with the insipidities of Jerusalem and Antonio Juanas, José María Aldana sounded a somewhat fresher note; he also was essentially a theater musician, beginning his metropolitan career as a second violinist in the Coliseo de México orchestra in 1786. During the 1790–1 season he was advanced to the directorship of the Coliseo orchestra.[84] His playing was combined with teaching in the Colegio de Infantes, and like many of his musical colleagues during the latter days of the viceregal period, his income was meager. He is alleged to have been chapelmaster in the cathedral, but if so his dates would overlap with those of Juanas. He undoubtedly played in the cathedral orchestra, however. His *Mass in D*, revived for the Museum of Modern Art concerts in 1940, follows the pattern of the usual Italian Mass of the late eighteenth century. A succession of short choruses with little or no contrapuntal writing was interspersed with solos and duets. Aldana's Mass started with an instrumental introduction, *allegro*, followed by a choral Kyrie, *largo*. The Christe eleison— andante, G major, ¾—contrasted neatly with the first Kyrie. The second Kyrie ran no slightest risk of tiring the audience, comprising as it did only two measures. The Gloria, a fast ⅝ *allegro*, was succeeded by a Laudamus te, *andante* in b minor, sung as a solo, but with no indication of voice except range (a mezzo's range). The Gratias agimus, of which we present a few sample measures, called for only three voice parts, two trebles and a bass. The remaining short sections need not be described. The Sanctus and Agnus were combined in a single skeleton movement, in accordance with the musically indefensible practice of the time. In this example, as in others of its immediate epoch, the *largo* should doubtless be understood more in our present sense of *moderato*. The popularity of this Mass obviously extended beyond Aldana's own immediate epoch. A copy of the manuscript

made about 1850 is on display in the library of the Conservatorio Nacional
at Mexico City. The copy was made for an actual performance of the work.
The style of the work can be taken to have appealed more to nineteenth
century Mexicans than the style of anterior colonial composers such as
López y Capilla and Padilla.

Aldana has the distinction of having been the only known colonial composer who paid a musical tribute to San Felipe de Jesús.[85] The Virgin of
Guadalupe inspired numerous tributes, but San Felipe—the only canonized Mexican—next to none. The first performance of Aldana's San Felipe
hymn occurred by a coincidence the very day of his death, February 7,

1810. He had lived through an epoch when bad taste prevailed everywhere in Spanish and Neo-Hispanic music. Although he adapted himself
perforce to the shallow taste of his epoch, his own musical instincts were
healthier than those of his audiences.

REASONS FOR THE DECLINE OF NEO-HISPANIC MUSIC

New Spain during three centuries was essentially a cultural outpost of
the homeland. During Spain's heroic period, music in the colony pros-
pered. Not only were works of Morales, Guerrero, and Cabezón [86] immediately imported and performed, but also excellently trained musicians
from such universities as Salamanca implanted a living tradition in the
New World. Furthermore the musical standards of the Mexico and
Puebla cathedrals were deliberately set with the purpose of rivaling the
highest standards in any Spanish cathedral.

The colony developed always as a branch growing out of the Spanish
trunk. When sap rose in the trunk, leaves appeared in the Neo-Hispanic
branch. But when the sap in the home trunk dried up, the musical life of
the colony lacking any rootage of its own necessarily withered also.

No really effective schools for imparting music instruction on a broad
professional level developed in Mexico, and the lack of schools, rather
than the lack of musicians, proved ultimately the most harmful result of
homeland domination. Although choir-schools such as those at Mexico
City, Puebla, and Morelia continued to train adequate cathedral singers,
and although certain convent music schools prepared efficient female teachers of music, schools that could give sufficiently broad preparation for such
responsibilities as those of a chapelmaster were lacking. There is sufficient
presumptive evidence to show that when at last the Mexico City Cathedral
did engage a chapelmaster of New World birth—Zumaya—his musical
credentials had been gained not in Mexico but rather in Italy. Conservatories of the kind Dr. Burney saw during his visit to Naples, "three . . . for
the education of boys who are intended for the profession of music"
(1773), nowhere existed in eighteenth century Mexico.

There was a convent music school founded in 1740 at the San Miguel
de Belén Convent in the capital; [87] there were also two convent music
schools outside Mexico City. Bernal Jiménez has offered evidence showing that the Colegio de Santa Rosa María founded at Morelia in 1743 was
called a conservatory.[88] He also has shown that the short-lived Colegio

de San Nicolás founded at San Luis Potosí in 1760 was primarily a music school. These three institutions, however excellent they may have been, only partially fulfilled a need since they trained feminine talent. Boys could only have secured professional training by going abroad.

But even, however, had conservatories for men as well as women existed, and had opportunities for advanced professional training been freely available, it is doubtful that creoles would often have successfully competed for chapelmasterships in the most prestigious locations. With chapelmasterships in colonial Mexico, as with conductorships in present-day America, the prizes were usually bestowed upon Europeans.

Neo-Hispanic music insofar as it was "high art" was certainly not Mexican music, if by Mexican is meant non-European. Even the Indians who were trained to compose reaped praise only when their Masses and villancicos sounded acceptable to the European ears of the friar-chroniclers. True, for conversion purposes, the friars encouraged Indian music, and as Sigüenza y Góngora in 1675 observed at Querétaro, the Indian musical contribution continued to be welcomed at church feasts. But in the sense of "high art" any Indian contribution—such as that of Juan Matías during his exceptional years of service in the Oaxaca Cathedral—had to conform to the European ideal.

Perhaps when the repertory of Neo-Hispanic music has been studied more minutely it will be possible to isolate in the works of Bermúdez, Salazar, and Zumaya traces of Indian influence. Perhaps Padilla used Indian themes; but even if these traces are found it seems categorically certain the Indian element was never intruded for its own sake. On the title page of the 1556 *Constituciones del arçobispado . . . de Tenuxtitlan Mexico,* if we look attentively, we can see at the bottom of the page some nopal cactus incongruously shooting up its stems. Not unless a person looks attentively does he see the nopal cactus. So it will probably be with Neo-Hispanic music. An attentive student may find a non-European theme here or there, but his finding of it will be the reward of close study.

The more Indian a present-day Mexican feels himself to be the less interested is he likely to be in the remains of colonial music. If the Mexican, who is first an Indian, pays Neo-Hispanic music any attention at all, he is likelier to disparage than praise it. It is a well known fact that one of the first acts of the Mexican Congress after Independence was to propose that Cortés's bones be dug up and burnt. When any mind at all has been paid the Neo-Hispanic composers, the spirited approach of many a Mexican

Indian has been to dig it all out of its present resting-places in cathedrals and burn it, "as Cortés's bones should have been burnt." Outsiders who are emotionally uninvolved can admire a Miguel Cabrera painting or a Francisco Tresguerras church without bothering mentally to count the number of dead bodies taken up out of a Zacatecas silver mine every time a new artistic masterpiece was created in New Spain, but the literate Mexican who prides himself on being an Indian remembers.

The outsider admiring the Tasco or the Celaya churches often does not know how few the Europeans actually were who dominated Mexico for three hundred years. The total number of Spaniards who came during three centuries has by informed historians been estimated at only 300,000. All the vast panoply of New Spain was created primarily to glorify the urges of the few. How few they were may be judged by Mexico City alone, which contained the largest concentration of Europeans. Here in 1680 in a population of 400,000 there were only 22,000 Spaniards who effectively controlled the city, and therefore the colony.[89] Another 50,000 in the city were creoles of unmixed European blood. Skipping over a century one finds that in 1790 the population of Mexico City was estimated at only 113,000, with 2,000 Europeans and 65,000 pure blooded creoles.[90] If these were the population figures in the capital where the greatest concentration of Europeans and creoles was to be found, the percentages over the colony generally were much smaller. The Spaniard in Mexico, riding as he did on the backs of the Indian, the mestizo, and the Negro, lived the life of a patrician. With their manual assistance he reared to himself such enduring and pretentious monuments that even today the ruins excite wonder and admiration. But the Mexican who feels the throbbing of his Indian blood within him cannot forget that these monuments sepulcher his ancestors' blood, sweat, and tears.

SECULAR MUSIC DURING THE SEVENTEENTH AND EIGHTEENTH CENTURIES

Where the musical remains have themselves perished, it is still often possible to reconstruct the story of Mexican colonial church music simply from reading the ecclesiastical records that survive. But with colonial secular music no such copious "literary" aids are available to the historian, who must instead rely exclusively on the music itself which survives. Three tablatures may be instanced as examples of what remains. The first tablature was described in the July 21, 1942, issue of *Revista Musical Mexicana*, and in three successive issues of that magazine photographic reproductions were given. The tablature in question exists today only in a fragmentary condition, but can be dated at about 1620. The tablature is in tetragram for organ, and follows the same system of tablature encountered in Francisco Correa's *Facultad Organica* published at Alcalá de Henares in 1626. On page 5 of the tablature occurs this indication: "Tiento de quarto tono, medio Registro, tiple del Maestro Fran.co correa y son muy elegantes sus obras de este Maestro." It has thus far proved impossible to collate the top part of the particular tiento in the Mexican tablature with any one of the fourth tone compositions (listed as such) in the Correa *Libro de tientos*, recently published in modern transcription. However, a comparison of the facsimile page in the Correa volume [91] with the facsimile pages in the *Revista Musical Mexicana* [92] clearly proves that the Mexican tablature follows the same system of organ tablature. In present-day terminology the title would mean a "tiento in the fourth tone, played on an 8-foot stop, with the soprano part by Maestro Francisco Correa, whose works are extremely elegant." An overly precise definition of the term *tiento* cannot be given, but it was a contrapuntal form similar to the ricercar. Cabezón's and Correa's are the best known tientos. The Correa reference in the Mexican tablature establishes but another link with peninsular musical culture. Correa, thought to have had Portuguese antecedents, was organist at the Seville Cathedral—parent of the Mexico City Cathedral. Correa's tientos are indeed "elegant," as anyone who has studied their style in the new edition issued by the Instituto Español de Musicología must agree. The enthusiasm of the unknown tablaturist in Mexico who wrote "son muy elegantes sus obras de este Maestro" proves more than amply justifiable.

This particular organ tablature contains another interesting notation (on page 1): "Esta fanfarria sse llama scala celite, puso el apellido el Maestro Antonio carrasio, porque es muy bueno tiento de octavo tono. tiple de cabrera. en el peru fue Maestro." I follow Saldívar, possessor of this tablature, in the punctuation of this sentence. The same sentence can clearly be read in the photostatic reproduction of this particular page in *Revista Musical Mexicana*. The reference to a *fanfarria* composed by a Peruvian master, dating as it does from the early years of the seventeenth century, provides an interesting musical link between the two colonies at a very early date. Transcriptions of this piece and of the several others in this particular organ tablature have been promised by Saldívar.

The second tablature deserving of mention is also in Gabriel Saldívar's possession. The title of this second tablature, *Método de Citara*, indicates its original purpose as an instruction book for the cittern. The author was one Sebastián de Aguirre, and his tablature has been dated c. 1650. His book primarily contained dances, among them the following: *pavana, pasacalle, gallarda, branle, panamá, zarabanda, minuete, puertorrico de la Puebla, paso de fantasía, portuguesa, francés, balona de bailar,* and *morisca.* Aguirre also included a *tocotín,* referred to as a "pole dance around a hungry tree." This Indian tocotín, according to Saldívar, is almost exclusively pentatonic throughout. In Aguirre's tablature what is probably the oldest Negro dance also occurs, labeled a *portorrico de los negros.* Lastly there is a *corrido,* which also takes priority as the oldest musical example in its class. The contents of this book, as briefly listed, show its value, and when a transcription of it appears the musical world will better be able to appreciate its debt to Dr. Saldívar for his discovery of it. Since he is its possessor, any anticipation of his results would be inopportune.

The third tablature is in the manuscript division of the Biblioteca Nacional.[93] A *Tablatura de vihuela* dated approximately 1740, it contains fifty types of dance music. These dances occur: *jota, fandango, folias españolas, folias italianas, sarabanda, paspied, coranta, cotillón, rigaudon, rondeau, alemanda, burro, tarantela, valona,* and *seguidillas.* The most unusual type listed is titled *cumbees o cantos negros.* Here again in this tablature the powerful impress of the Negro in colonial dance types is clearly discernible. The cumbees are subtitled *cantos en idioma guinea.* In playing the cumbees the player is directed to hit his vihuela with a thump at certain odd moments. In this vihuela tablature occurs also a *zarambeques;* this name was applied to a five-string variant of the guitar much favored by the Negroes in the hot country.

Attempts at reducing this Biblioteca Nacional tablature to modern notation for a long time proved futile until it was discovered that an unusual accordatura had been used in tuning this particular *vihuela de mano.* The five open strings sounded these notes: F (below the bass clef)—C—A flat —E flat—B flat. Because of the Negro music which it contains, a publication of this vihuela tablature in modern notation will be particularly welcomed. Certain other features in the book enhance its value. Seventeen movements from Corelli chamber sonatas in vihuela-transcription are contained in it, and in addition a complete *Sonata de Samuel Trent*. Samuel Trent's sonata, comprising a "preludio, largo, giga, and alegro," may be an original sonata, or it may be a transcription. Since Samuel Trent is a figure in music history thus far completely "desconocido," we have no slightest means of guessing how his music got into a colonial tablature in Mexico.

NEO-HISPANIC FOLK-MUSIC

The Spaniards dispersed throughout Mexico carried Andalusian, Castilian, Galician, Extremaduran, and Aragonese folk-songs with them into the remotest corners of the colony. The colonizers were not simply "peninsulars" but on the contrary represented a variety of national traditions in the peninsula; Aragon and Castile, for instance, were not united until the end of the fifteenth century when Ferdinand and Isabella in marrying united the crowns. An amazing diversity of local traditions from the peninsula was introduced into the New World colonies, and any attempt to pigeon-hole colonial folk-song into such and such neat categories does violence to the richness and diversity of it. The Mexican scholar, Vicente T. Mendoza, brought out in 1939 an historical study of the type of folksong now known as *corrido*. In the space of 833 pages he laboriously discussed the different types of *corrido* that have been sung at various times in Mexico; he also discussed the Spanish *romance*, or ballad, which he defined as the ancestor of the Mexican *corrido*. He found ample proof that the Spaniards long after their departure from Spain still continued in their romances to keep alive the local history of the homeland region from which they originally came.

The conquistadores sang folk-songs; Bernal Díaz mentioned several of these by name, such as those beginning,[94]

        Mira Nero de Tarpeya/a Roma como se ardia . . .

and

        Cata Francia, Montesinos,/cata Paris, la ciudad . . .

and

        Denos Dios ventura en armas/como al Paladín Roldán . . .

Francisco de Salinas's *De musica libri septem* (1577) provided a printed source of folk-song melody, enabling one to judge the musical characteristics of the sixteenth century folk repertory. Collections of Spanish folk-poetry (without music) are to be found in such publications as the *Cancionero de Romances* (Antwerp, 1548), the *Silva de Romances* (Zaragoza, 1550), and other *romanceros* of slightly later date; all this balladry has been enthusiastically lauded by Ramon Menéndez Pidal, and several prominent students of Spanish literature following his lead have devoted themselves to an exhaustive investigation of the ballad cycles. The first *romance* known to have been published at Mexico City appeared in 1658 (words only); others appeared in 1709, 1717, 1724, 1734, 1764, and 1779.[95] These were fugitive publications, usually comprising only a few pages, and the list of dates gives no true idea, perhaps, of the numbers printed in Mexico. The wide diffusion of them is instanced by the number that survived in peripheral New Mexico. Professor Aurelio Espinosa at the time he published his *Romancero Nuevo Mexicano* (1915) had succeeded in locating ten traditional ballads which had been sung in New Mexico probably since the time Juan de Oñate, or at least since the reconquest under de Vargas (1692). Subsequent investigation brought the number of New Mexican romances to forty, of which "thirty-two are found in Spain and Spanish America as well as in the Sephardic colonies of America." [96] This wide diffusion of traditional ballads is the more remarkable because very often in the remotest spots are preserved today the purest and most uncorrupted versions.

The same situation exists in the case of English ballads yet preserved by the mountaineers in the Appalachians, where until the juke-box epoch, the ballads with their modal tunes were still sung as they were two hundred or more years ago in England when the mountaineers' ancestors first emigrated. In the Appalachians an uncorrupted *Barbara Allen* would, however, be less remarkable than would an uncorrupted *Gerineldo* in New Mexico, simply because in one place the English tradition once established remained dominant, whereas in the other a Spanish tradition has given way to a bilingual culture. For lovers of folk-poetry and folk-music a study of variants in the words and melodies of the romances known as *Delgadina* (the *Cenci* theme), *La esposa infiel* (unfaithful wife), *Bernal Francés* (mistaken identity of the paramour), *Don Gato* (a romantic cat), *Gerineldo* (page's love for a princess), *Mambrú* (arms and the man), and so on, has provided an interesting exercise. The oldest of these such as *Gerineldo* and *La batalla de Roncesvalles* concern incidents that happened in Charlemagne's time. Obviously the music cannot be uncorrupted after a thousand years, but if the words have not changed significantly during several centuries, it is also probable that the tunes are substantially the same as those sung hundreds of years ago. In a history of Mexican music we mention these Spanish ballads merely to emphasize again the persistence of Spanish cultural elements among the descendants of the invaders. As one historian said recently: "Where there is a group of Spaniards, there are *coplas;* wherever there is a Spanish community, even at the Antipodes, there spring up *romances.*" [97]

Since *romances* and their Mexican successors, *corridos* and *décimas,* were folk-expressions we should not expect to find *romance*-music or *corrido*-music "high art." The single melodic line was accompanied oftenest by some such folk-instrument as the hurdy-gurdy (*vihuela de rueda*); [98] for each successive stanza the same tune was repeated. The range of the melodies scarcely ever exceeded a sixth. Closely allied with the romances were their religious counterparts, the *alabados.* They, too, preserved the folk-elements—strong accentual rhythms, melodies cast in sequence patterns, implied tonic-dominant harmony everywhere. The *alabados* in New Spain stood in relation to the liturgical music of the day as gospel songs of the Homer Rodeheaver type stand today in relation to Randall Thompson's *Alleluia.*

If in a discussion of music in the United States slightly more time were spent discussing Copland's *In the Beginning* than some such hymn as *In the Garden,* no one would therefore have the right to infer that *In the Beginning* touches the lives of as many as *In the Garden.* Charles Seeger has pleaded eloquently that students of Latin American music spend more time with those types of music that touch the lives of many, than those types that touch the lives of only a few. Mr. Seeger, one of the most sympathetic students of folk-music in our time, wrote in 1943:

> To an understanding of contemporary music activity and to history, due regard for the mediocre, especially when functioning upon a very large scale is essential. The contemporary popular commercial idiom holds the public attention and interest of uncounted millions. [99]

Applying ourselves to the "mediocre" in colonial music, such as the *alabados* with their constant doubling of the melody in thirds, we may be able to reach nearer to the souls of the commonalty. The "popular commercial idiom" of any day will always be that idiom which reaches the greatest number. Mr. Seeger has therefore spoken justly in recalling historians from the ivory tower of "high art" to the more important business of everyday music as it has touched the lives of the many rather than the few.

Because essentially the music of Franco, Bermúdez, Padilla, and the rest, glorified the privileged few, it lost relevance when the old order gave way to the new. The musicians of the new era after 1821 ostentatiously discarded the past with all its "outworn" theories, and instead announced their intention of building a musical culture on an entirely new foundation.

NOTES

1. Manuel Sánchez, *Regla de N.P.S. Francisco y breve declaración de sus preceptos para su mejor observancia y facil inteligencia con una instrucción para los Novicios . . . y breve explicación del canto llano con advertencias* (México: Bernardo de Hogal, 1725). Breathing a visible sigh of relief at the conclusion of the section on plainchant, Sánchez wrote (p. 53): "The teaching of plainchant is not my profession and the writing of this guide to plainchant has cost me such effort that only the precept of obedience has sustained me until I reached a conclusion." Of interest in this 78-page book are the Guidonian hands on pp. 52 and 58.
2. Francisco Lorenzana, *Missa Gothica* . . . (Puebla: Typis Seminarii Palafoxiani, 1770). Lorenzana, who became a cardinal after his return to Europe, was interested in the Mozarabic rite. On pp. 69–72 Mozarabic neumes are transcribed into their supposed modern equivalencies. Between pp. 73 and 137 a lengthy disquisition on Mozarabic usages is inserted. Mitjana believed the transliterations of Mozarabic neumes in this missal might afford a clue to their correct interpretation; no agreement has yet been reached, however, on the exact significance of Mozarabic neumes despite much patient research.
3. Jesús Bal y Gay, editor of the *Cancionero de Upsala,* co-editor of the indispensable quarterly, *Nuestra Música,* and chief of the research section at Bellas Artes, has been entrusted with this important editorial task involving the complete known works of Juan de Lienas. Bal y Gay came to Mexico during the Spanish Revolution. He was the focus of a controversy during the summer of 1950 provoked by his forthright newspaper criticism of a Mexican performing artist who failed to reach a high professional standard. His influence has doubtless been salutary.
4. This list represents only those works whose presence in the *tesoros artísticos* of the Mexico City and Puebla cathedrals was verifiable in 1950.
5. Lota M. Spell, "Music in the Cathedral of Mexico in the Sixteenth Century," *The Hispanic American Review,* August, 1946, p. 313.
6. Cristóbal Bermúdez Plata (ed.), *Catálogo de Pasajeros a Indias* . . . (Sevilla, Imp. de la Gavidia, 1946), III, 147 (2192).

7. Spell, *op. cit.*, p. 311 (note 90), adequately documents this amusing transaction.

8. Jesús Estrada, "Clásicos de Nueva España: Ensayo histórico sobre los Maestros de Capilla de la Catedral de México," *Schola Cantorum* (Morelia), July, 1945, p. 101.

9. Steven Barwick, "Sacred Vocal Polyphony . . . ," p. 114.

10. This habit persisted as an abuse throughout the colonial epoch: "de otra parte del elemento religioso . . . produce graves escándalos por la frequencia con que era notada su presencia en las casas de juego" (Cayetano Alcázar Molina, *Los Virreinatos en el Siglo XVIII*, Barcelona, 1945, p. 13).

11. Saldívar, *op. cit.*, p. 123.

12. Estrada, *op. cit.*, p. 101.

13. *La Catedral y el Sagrario de México* (México: Departamento Editorial de la Dirección General de las Bellas Artes, 1917), p. xxv.

14. *Ibid.*, p. xxvi.

15. *Ibid.*, p. xxiv.

16. Palestrina, *Opere Complete*, XVI (1943), p. 323. Concerning Lassus's unique continuous setting of all the verses, see Charles Van den Borren, *Orlande de Lassus* (Paris: Librairie Felix Alcan, 1920), p. 152.

17. Henry Coates, *Palestrina* (London: J. M. Dent, 1938), p. 184.

18. *Ibid.*, p. 186.

19. For modern reprints see Philippi de Monte, *Canticum Magnificat* (Bruges: Desclée de Brouwer et Socios, 1930); and R. J. van Maldeghem, *Trésor Musical* . . . (Brussels: C. Muquardt, 1893), pp. 23 ff. (de la Rue).

20. Barwick, *Supplement*, p. 62. See also p. 100.

21. *Ibid.*, p. 44. See other examples on pp. 64, 84, 101, 120.

22. *Ibid.*, pp. 71 and 72. The contrasts between "Esurientes" and "Fecit potentiam" in the other Magnificats are all splendidly conceived, and deserve study.

23. Lorenzana, *Concilium Mexicanum Provinciale III* (México: Joseph de Hogal, 1770), Statuta Ordinata, p. 68.

24. *Ibid.*, pp. 66–70 (especially p. 70).

25. García Icazbalceta, *Colección de Documentos para la Historia de México* (1858), p. 242.

26. Nicolás León, *Bibliografía Mexicana del Siglo XVIII* (1908), pp. 199–200 (quoting Diego Antonio de Castro's *Historia de la ciudad de la Puebla*, Puebla, 1746).

27. Barwick, *Supplement*, pp. 184–216.

28. Bermúdez read a maximum meaning into every exceptional procedure; see the nota cambiata, p. 185 (meas. 16); the augmented sixths on pp. 198 and 208; the diminished interval in the penultimate measure of p. 190; see also p. 189 (meas. 6).

29. Saldívar, *op. cit.*, p. 107.

30. *Duda de D. Antonio Eximeno sobre el Ensayo fundamental practico de contrapunto del M.R.P.M. Fray Juan Bautista Martini* . . . (Madrid: Imp. Real, 1797), p. 55.

31. Antonio Tamariz de Carmona, *Relación y descripción* . . . (Puebla, 1649),

fol. 31ʳ. In 1647, a year for which exact sums spent on music in the Mexico City Cathedral are recorded, only 5,500 pesos were spent. (See Isabel Pope's figures in *Nuestra Música*, Iᵉʳ Trimestre 1951, p. 23.)

32. Tamariz de Carmona, fols. 20ʳ and 31ʳ. Padilla is called "insigne Maestro." His peninsular antecedents before his arrival in New Spain can only be guessed at. His later Spanish career was a fitting fulfillment after his distinguished service at Puebla. He was successively chapelmaster at the Zamora Convent of San Pablo, Zamora Cathedral (7 May 1661–27 Jan 1663) and Toledo Cathedral (7 Sep 1663–16 Dec 1673). An eight voice Magnificat is preserved in the Valladolid archive.

33. J. T. Medina, *La Imprenta en Puebla* (Santiago de Chile: Imp. Cervantes, 1908), pp. 84–5.

34. Miss Alice Ray has found two examples of parodyings.

35. León, *op. cit.* (1908), p. 206.

36. Juan B. Iguíniz, "La Biblioteca Palafoxiana de Puebla," *Anales del Museo Nacional de Arqueología, Historia y Etnología*, 1913, p. 293.

37. The letters of commendation are dated November 24, 1601 (Dominican) and November 28, 1601 (Augustinian); publication of *Quatuor Passiones* was, however, for some reason held up three years after all the necessary approvals.

38. The authority of Ambrose, Augustine, Gregory, Isidore, and Rabanus Maurus is invoked; Navarro also plentifully quotes Scripture.

39. Last page (unnumbered) in *Preface to the Reader*.

40. Guillermo Furlong, *Músicos Argentinos* (Buenos Aires: Editorial Huarpes, 1945), p. 115. The first disclosure was made by Lauro Ayesterán in *Zipoli, el gran compositor y organista romano del 1700 en el Rio de La Plata* (Montevideo: Imp. Uruguaya, s.a., 1941). Zipoli, born in Tuscany in 1688, supposedly sailed from Cádiz in the company of 72 Jesuits (1717), and spent the years, 1718–26, in Córdoba, Argentina.

41. Adolfo Salazar, "El Caso de Domenico Zipoli," *Nuestra Música* (Mexico), May, 1946, pp. 80–3.

42. A re-issue of Francisco de Montanos's *Arte de canto llano* (Salamanca, 1610), with editorial additions by José de Torres. The Torres identification is, however, completely untenable.

43. Navarro, *Quatuor Passiones*, folio 8ᵛ.

44. Diego Basalenque, *Historia de la provincia . . . de Michoacán, del orden de n.p.s. Agustín* (México: Barbedillo y comp., 1886), I, 124.

45. The three otherwise unknown composers whose works seem the most substantial were (1) Francisco Moratilla (active as a villancico-composer during the 1720's), (2) Antonio Rodil (composer of an *Obertura con Violini, Viola, Oboe, Trompe Obligatti e Basso* constructed on the Scarlatti-overture pattern: *allegro-grave-presto*, (3) Antonio Sarrier (composer of an *Obertura con Violini, Viola, Oboe, Trompas e Basso* divided into the following three movements: *allegro-andante-fuga*). For further details see Miguel Bernal Jiménez, *Morelia Colonial: El Archivo Musical Del Colegio de Santa Rosa . . .* (Morelia: Ediciones de la Universidad Michoacana, 1939), pp. 19–29.

46. Francisco de Burgoa, *Geográphica Descripción de la Parte Septentrional, del Polo Artico de la América* (México: Publicaciones del Archivo General de la Nación, 1934), I, 416. Burgoa's two-volume description, originally published at Mexico City in 1674, contained several invaluable musical references. See Tomo II (1934 edition), p. 422.

47. Guillermo A. Esteva, *La música Oaxaqueña* (Oaxaca, 1931), pp. 9–10. According to Esteva Matías was born at Coyotepec *c.* 1635, but he has no exact date. The authenticity of the *Stabat Mater* fragment must rest on Esteva's own voucher.

48. J. T. Medina, *op. cit.*, pp. 91–2.

49. Carlos de Sigüenza y Góngora, *Glorias de Querétaro* (Mexico, 1680), p. 51. For explanation of these instruments see our Chapter I, "Early Aboriginal Music."

50. Sigüenza y Góngora, *op. cit.*, p. 60.

51. *Ibid.*, p. 56. Sigüenza y Góngora said de Robles "sang like a swan."

52. While the friars were still making conversions, music as a tool was eagerly seized upon, but after the zeal for conversions cooled, no one in authority among the Spaniards favored teaching them music. The Indians during the eighteenth century were actually much worse off musically than during the sixteenth. For the low estate to which music declined among them, see the request for the reestablishment of the Indian school, the Colegio de Santiago Tlaltelolco; this request in the form of a memorial signed by eight Indian chiefs was presented to one of the archepiscopal supervisors in 1728. In part it read: "The singers whose duty among us it is to sing at Mass and at the daily office are [so badly trained] that they cause laughter and contempt for the divine mysteries, rather than true devotion and contrite meditation." (Reprinted in *Boletín del Archivo de la Nación*, January–February, 1935, p. 31.)

53. Isabel Pope, "The Musical Development and Form of the Spanish *Villancico*," *Papers of the American Musicological Society* (*1940*), p. 15.

54. Higinio Anglés, *La Música Española* . . . (Barcelona: Biblioteca Central, 1941), p. 41. "El villancico religioso que se había practicado en el siglo XVI, no obstante la prohibición de Felipe II . . ."

55. Irving A. Leonard, *Don Carlos de Sigüenza y Góngora: A Mexican Savant of the Seventeenth Century* (Berkeley: University of California Press, 1929), p. 17.

56. Sor Juana Inés de la Cruz, *Poemas de la Unica Poetisa Americana, Musa Dezima* (Madrid: Juan Garcia Infançon, 1690), p. 271. "Un corrido es lo mismo q̃ una Xacara."

57. *Ibid.*, p. 266. (*Coplas,* line 9.)

58. Another tocotín, even more astounding than the Nolasco tocotín because written throughout in Nahuatl, was inserted in the second nocturn of the 1687 Villancicos for August 15 (Assumption). The metrical scheme in the Nolasco tocotín differs from the scheme of the Assumption tocotín. See *Poemas* (1690), p. 274.

59. *Ibid.*, pp. 275–6.

60. For a discussion of Cerone's continuing relevance, see Ruth Hannas, "Cerone's Approach to the Teaching of Counterpoint," *Papers of the American Musicological Society* (*1937*), pp. 75–80.

61. Two facsimile pages showing her annotations appear in E. Abreu Gómez, *Sor*

Juana Inés de la Cruz: Bibliografía y Biblioteca (México: Monografias Bibliograficas, 1934), pp. 448–9.

62. I. A. Leonard, "On the Mexican Book Trade, 1683," *The Hispanic American Historical Review*, August, 1947, p. 419.

63. *Enciclopedia Universal Ilustrada* (Barcelona: J. Espasa), XXXI, 221.

64. Henri Collet, *Le Mysticisme Musical Espagnol* (Paris: Librairie Félix Alcan, 1913), p. 248. The inventory at the Seville Cathedral listing Salazar's name was made in 1721.

65. Jesús Estrada, "Clásicos de la Nueva España," June, 1945, p. 90.

66. José Mariano Beristaín y Souza, *Biblioteca Hispano Americana Setentrional* (Amecameca: Colegio Católico, 1883), III, 325.

67. For a facsimile reproduction of an eighteenth century Mexican manuscript with figured bass, see Saldívar, pp. 133–4.

68. Jerome in his diatribe against Helvidius gave no hint of the latter's being anything else than Roman. It is possible the writer of this villancico confused Helvidius with another of Jerome's enemies, namely, Vigilantius. Vigilantius was a Gaul.

69. Méndez Plancarte, *Poetas Novohispanos: Segundo Siglo, Parte Segunda* (México: Universidad Nacional Autonoma, 1945), p. 136.

70. *Ibid.*, p. 113.

71. Francisco Sedano, *Noticias de México. . . .* (Mexico, 1880), p. 83.

72. *Ibid.*, p. 83.

73. For attribution of the 1691 San Pedro Villancicos to Sor Juana, see Gómez, *op. cit.*, p. 445.

74. The Salazar hymns are on ff. 129, 131, 149, 150, and 151 of *Libro de Coro V* at Puebla.

75. Beristaín y Souza said that for the Duke of Linares's amusement Zumaya translated various Italian libretti and wrote music for them. Opera as such gained a tardy foothold in Spain; for a discussion of Spanish antecedents see Gilbert Chase, "Origins of the Lyric Theater in Spain," *The Musical Quarterly*, July, 1939.

76. Francesco Florimo, *La Scuola Musicale di Napoli e i suoi Conservatorii* (Naples: Vinc. Morano, 1881), IV, 8.

77. Saldívar, p. 189.

78. N. León, *Bibliografía Mexicana del Siglo XVIII* (1903), p. 223. León reprinted the *Gazeta de México*; the account of the Guadalajara organ appeared in the December, 1730, issue of the *Gazeta*.

79. *Ibid.*, p. 223.

80. English organs during this period lacked pedals; many Spanish organs also lacked them. The Seville organ had them, however; for an authoritative description of Spanish organs during the baroque era see Albert Merklin, *Aus Spaniens altem Orgelbau* (Mainz: Rheingold-Verlag, 1939), especially pp. 61–2.

81. Pál Kelemen, "Church Organs in Colonial Mexico," *Bulletin of the Pan American Union*, March, 1942, p. 132.

82. Bernal Jiménez, *op. cit.*, pp. 44–5.

83. For details of the dispute between university and cathedral authorities, see

Isabel Pope, "Documentos Relacionados con la Historia de la Música en México," *Nuestra Música*, Ier Trimestre, 1951; Jerusalem carried the dispute to Spain.

84. Weinstock, *Mexican Music* (1940), p. 9.

85. San Felipe was canonized in 1862.

86. Furlong, *op. cit.*, p. 19. In 1586 three Cabezón volumes were sent to Mexico, according to a booklist printed by Leonard.

87. Saldívar, p. 145.

88. Miguel Bernal Jiménez, "La Música en Valladolid de Michoacán," *Nuestra Música*, 3er Trimestre, 1951, p. 163. In a brief dated February 12, 1746, Pope Benedict XIV called the Morelia Colegio de Santa Rosa María a "conservatorium mulierum et puellarum."

89. I. A. Leonard, *op. cit.*, p. 404.

90. H. R. Wagner, *The Rise of Fernando Cortés* (The Cortés Society, 1944), p. 498, n. 16.

91. Francisco Correa de Arauxo, *Libro de tientos* . . . (Barcelona: Instituto Español de Musicología, 1948), facing p. 33.

92. *Revista Musical Mexicana*, July–August–September, 1942, pp. 37–8, 65–6, 110–1.

93. Collocation number: 15–4–152. This tablature is in pentagram.

94. Vicente T. Mendoza, *El Romance Español y El Corrido Mexicano* (México, Imp. Universitaria, 1939), p. 125.

95. *Ibid.*, pp. 783–5.

96. Arthur L. Campa, *Spanish Folk-Poetry in New Mexico* (Albuquerque: University of New Mexico Press, 1946), p. 29.

97. E. Allison Peers, *A Critical Anthology of Spanish Verse* (University of California Press, 1949), p. xxxix.

98. Mendoza, *op. cit.*, p. 28. The picture on this page should be noted.

99. *Handbook of Latin American Studies* (Cambridge: Harvard University Press, 1943), p. 446.

THE OPERATIC NINETEENTH
CENTURY

Since most of the Spanish colonies in the New World revolted during the
same decade, 1810–1820, it has often been assumed that culturally as well
as politically the colonies had all reached approximately the same stage in
their development around 1810. This is an untenable assumption, however. Other colonies were at the crest of their wave, musically speaking.
Mexico was in a trough.

Among the colonies which were at their crest were Cuba and Venezuela.
In Cuba, Esteban Salas, chapelmaster at Santiago from 1764 until his
death in 1803, remained continuously productive throughout the forty-
year period of his service, turning out a succession of Masses and other
sacred works whose quality was noteworthy.[1] In Venezuela a whole school
of composers in Caracas, including one or two such as José Lamas and
Cayetano Carreño whose worth has not been matched at any other period
in Venezuelan history, made the capital a respected music center during
the immediate pre-independence epoch.[2]

But in other Hispanic countries, musical life was at low ebb. In Argentina the posts of distinction were all occupied by foreigners of dubious
merit.[3] In Peru musical life in 1800 had entered a purely reproductive
phase. Columbia was actually worse off (musically) in the latter part of
the eighteenth century than she had been a century earlier. For that matter
it could almost be said Columbia was less advanced musically in 1800 than
in 1550—if we think for a moment of what had happened in once proud
Cartagena. The Cartagena Cathedral precentor, Juan Pérez Materano,

distinguished himself by being the first in the Americas to finish a book, *Canto de órgano y canto llano,* which he craved Charles V's permission to have printed in 1554.[4] Some of his admirers even called him a second "Josquin." No one of equivalent distinction appeared in Columbian musical annals during the entire colonial period.

MEXICAN MUSIC DURING THE LAST YEARS OF THE VICEROYALTY

Mexican music was unfortunately in a depressed state at the end of the colonial period for the same reasons apparently that Argentinian, Peruvian, and Columbian music were depressed at the same time. Here are the inadequacies that may be noted in Mexico City around 1800: (1) Even the more ambitious composers such as Manuel Arenzana, Soto Carrillo, Luis Medina, and others mentioned as outstanding in the columns of the *Diario de México,* devoted themselves not to the larger forms of musical composition but entirely to journeyman work on theatrical farces, interludes, and "comedies with music." (2) Performance standards had notoriously declined. (3) Better off economically than such a poor colony as Venezuela, Mexico attracted foreign talent, but in so doing lost a chance to exploit her native-born talents needing encouragement.

Documentation in support of these generalizations will be offered, first in respect to the operatic situation. The first opera was produced at the viceregal palace in 1711—the very year Handel's first opera in England, *Rinaldo,* was produced. But the lack of an Italian troupe and of a suitable playhouse inhibited further operatic experiment after the Duke of Linares withdrew his powerful patronage. The ventures in the direction of "opera" during the last years of the century were commercialistic efforts, all designed to pay their way at the playhouse, the Coliseo Nuevo,[5] and where possible to reap a profit for the impresario. It is a truism in opera history that provincial houses run on a commercial basis never have encouraged high standards, and the Coliseo Nuevo, insofar as can now be ascertained, did not provide an exception to the rule.

The musical fare at the Coliseo during the sample seasons of 1805–6, and 1806–7, included predominantly zarzuelas of the bufa type, tonadillas, and sainetes. Zarzuelas, an idiomatic type in the Spanish theater, were produced in Spain as early as Lope de Vega's time (1629);[6] they differ from operas in that spoken dialogue is the rule. The zarzuela was usually short—an hour in length perhaps—and other theatrical fare went

into a single evening's entertainment. The tonadilla was a short skit originally intended as an entr'acte; [7] its purpose was oftenest sharply satirical,
and two characters were usually sufficient. The sainete was a farce, placed
at the tail-end of a theatrical evening as a rule; almost invariably it emphasized the lewd for the benefit of the groundlings.[8] The evening's entertainment was therefore highly diverse, constituting not an artistic unity
but an olla-podrida.

The more substantial offerings of the 1805 season included Cimarosa's
El Filósofo Burlado, billed as a "zarzuela bufa," [9] Manuel Arenzana's
El Extrangero, billed as a comedy in two acts with music,[10] Arenzana's
Los Dos Ribales en amor, billed as a "new duo," [11] and Luis Medina's
Siana y Silvio, billed as a "bailete," [12] but with singing as well as dancing.
Cimarosa was, of course, an international figure, but his opera in Mexico
became a zarzuela, with numerous topical spoken asides. Arenzana was
chapelmaster at the Puebla Cathedral in 1805–6. Medina (1751–1806),
also from Puebla, had come to Mexico City in 1770, acquiring in the capital a post as accountant in the Royal Court of Justice.[13] His two daughters
sang in *Siana y Silvio*, and he himself played their guitar accompaniment.

The most notable event in 1806 was the Mexican première of Paisiello's
Il barbiere di Siviglia, translated however into Spanish and presented as
an "opera bufa en cuatro actos." On December 4, 1806, the première date,
the *Diario de México* carried the following notice:

> The orchestra will be considerably enlarged in order to meet the instru-
> mental specifications in this opera. The interludes will consist of short
> Mexican dances [bailes del país] in order not to lengthen unduly the whole
> evening's presentation. The admission price will be double the ordinary
> price in order to pay for the heavy expenses of this production.

Five days later a repeat performance was staged, with interludes again
consisting of popular Mexican songs [sonecitos del país]. The two foreign
composers whose operas were played during the early years of the nineteenth century (before independence was achieved) were Cimarosa and
Paisiello.

The star system with the usual inequities in pay ruled in the Coliseo
opera troupe. The principal singers during the 1806–7 season were
Dolores Munguía (1,600 pesos), Josefa Cardenas (1,000 pesos), Andrés
Castillo (1,500 pesos), Victorio Rocamora (1,050 pesos), and Antonio
Bemasconi (600 pesos). Luciano Cortés, also an author, earned more than
any of the other singers simply because he wrote plays as well as sang;

his combined earnings were 3,000 pesos.[14] Ten years later Munguía was still singing (2,700 pesos), as was Andrés Castillo (4,380).[15] These salaries individually mean little unless we compare them with those of the orchestral players, who received salaries averaging a third of the singers' salaries,[16] and unless we take into consideration the purchasing power of the peso. The singers all received salaries in excess of the top salaries in colonial government bureaus.

But in return for the large investment which drove the Coliseo management to financial ruin in 1816,[17] it can hardly be said that the Mexican public received a high standard of performance from singers or orchestra. The orchestra comprised in 1813 when prices were at a peak, sixteen players. Concerning their quality, a correspondent of the *Diario de México* wrote in the February 25 and 26 (1813) issues the following statement:

> The chief defect is the instability of the beat throughout the whole orchestra. . . . The trumpets . . . the kettledrums . . . and the double basses . . . sound miserably. We must confess, however, that their thin rasping tone and the poverty of the whole orchestra is not entirely the fault of the players, but is partly due to the location of the orchestra. The pit is entirely too small, squeezed between the stage and the front rows. Moreover the acoustical effect is further hampered by the absorption of sound in the alleys running beneath the stage. . . . And if the flute, the bassoon, and the clarinet discharge their duties intelligently and artistically, we might bespeak greater attention to the written notes by the flutist and the bassoonist, and less attempt to add capricious adornments. The first violinist should play more decisively and vigorously. He is the rudder of the orchestra, and fewer violent pitchings occur when the first violinist from time to time indicates the beat; . . . mistakes would moreover be considerably reduced if more rehearsing were done.

None of the singers was noted as a vocalist. Under the system then prevailing the singer's principal asset was his or her acting ability, not vocalism. If frequent objections were made by the discerning to the vocalism of the singers, even more inept was their musicianship considered to be.

The rank favoritism bestowed upon imported players, singers, and composers, was also a subject for comment. Manuel Corral, a sycophantic Spaniard whose musical merits were negligible, forced performances of his theatrical pieces because he stood high in the favor of Viceroy Apodaca.[18] An Italian, Esteban Cristiani, a teacher of piano, succeeded in having his jottings taken seriously enough to reach performance.[19] Andrés Castillo, a member of the imported troupe, further augmented his income by composing lurid sainetes, completely devoid of artistic purpose.

When José Aldana ventured a different type of entertainment he was petulantly thrust aside. Aldana was a Mexican, and when a concerto he offered was badly received, an anonymous letter, signed only, "A Lover of Music," appeared in the *Diario de México* (October 13, 1805):

> Please tell D. José Aldana, first violinist in the theater orchestra, that he should change his name to Aldani or Mr. Aldam, and act like a foreigner, if he wants to gain the applause that he deserves. . . . Or he might consider impersonating a woman. . . .
>
> Those who know something of the art of music, and have heard him, know his merits; but the greater part of his audience has ears but no musical understanding, and so responded coldly to the refinements of the violin concerto he played yesterday.

MUSIC AT THE SCHOOL OF MINES IN MEXICO CITY

If the Coliseo de México provided no arena for regular performances of first-class music, the newly opened School of Mines, built under the superintendence of the renowned neo-classicist, Manuel Tolsa, did. In a "large and well-lighted hall of the new school, an orchestra of uncommon merit" gave concerts which were called "academies of music." [20] The mine-owners as a class were not only the wealthiest, but also the most enlightened musically of the colonial aristocracy, if one can judge from their patronage of these academies. Aldana played in this orchestra, as did also two other violinists remembered as better-than-average performers, Vicente Castro and Manuel Delgado. The School of Mines orchestra was not, however, organized on the Mannheim pattern, and still depended upon a concertmaster instead of a conductor for the beat. A mandolin player and a guitar player were regularly enrolled in the orchestra; but Haydn appears to have been a composer much favored in the academies. Amateurs as well as professional performed, and Otto Mayer-Serra, historian of Mexican music during the nineteenth century, points to the preponderancy of female amateurs as an ominous sign.

The individual performer who won the most liberal praise was the pianist, Soto Carrillo. His polished performances of Haydn sonatas were admired, and he was considered an excellent extemporizer. [21] As a composer he had made a name with his "boleros, polonaises, and tonadillas." A trait in his playing which won praise was his firm "command of rhythm." Along with another pianist, Horcasitas by name, [22] he helped to popularize the piano as the coming instrument in Mexico. Before long everyone with pretensions to culture owned an instrument of a kind. Pianos were not only imported from Spain during the early 1800's but were also manufactured in Mexico, both at Durango and at Mexico City. Notices in the *Gazeta de México* as early as 1793 [23] confirm our assertion of piano-manufacture in Durango and as early as 1796 [24] of piano-manufacture in Mexico City.

At the academies in the School of Mines music history for the first time in Mexico formed a topic for learned discussion. A *Discurso sobre la música* published in the October 24, 1807, issue of the *Diario de México* sums up the ideas on music history that were then entertained among the well-informed. The anonymous author of this "discourse" delighted in quoting Aristotle and Pindar, as if Aristotelian music theory were still a living reality. The Spanish author most reverentially referred to was Tomás de Iriarte (1750–91); Iriarte's didactic poem, *La Música*, provided the author of the *Diario de México* discourse with a rich lode of factual information. On Iriarte's authority, *canto llano* was defined as monodic music with each note in the chant occupying a beat of equal length; *canto figurado* as homophonic music; and *canto de órgano* as polyphonic or contrapuntal music. Boethius's classification of modes was believed still valid. Guido d'Arezzo was listed as the "inventor of notation in 1025."

The author of the *Discurso* was interested in the marimba, which he considered a Guatemalan instrument. A characteristic feature of the marimba in his opinion was the placing of gourds under the wooden keys to enforce resonance. He was interested also in Franklin's harmonica exhibited in Paris "in 1765." But he was patently in error in ascribing the invention of the trumpet to one Denner, a flute-maker of Nuremberg, in 1690. Like too many successor music historians in Mexico, the *Discurso* author interested himself primarily in European music, which he could know about only at second hand, and neglected his own country. The only bit of information he gave that interests us now was his statement that the marimba was an instrument indigenous to Guatemala.

INSTRUMENTS AND INSTRUMENT TUNING

The first notice of the tuning of keyed instruments in equal temperament appears in a *Gazeta de México* announcement, November 21, 1786. On that date Manuel Duarte y Dávila, organ-builder, and caretaker of

organs in the Puebla Cathedral, announced he had introduced at Puebla
a new system of tuning invented by Don Félix Falco a century earlier
and successfully tested in the royal chapel of Charles II. Falco, according
to Duarte y Dávila, was a Valencian, but other information than his natal
city and approximate date is not given in the *Gazeta* announcement.

The supplying of small organs with only eight or ten ranks kept Duarte
busy; he built on a cost plus percentage basis.[25] Mariano Placeres at
Durango did the same thing. Manuel Pérez, with a shop at Monterilla
No. 8 in the capital, frequently advertised small organs of his own fabrica-
tion for sale (1796–8). After 1800 advertisements of imported pianos
began to appear. The first pianos actually constructed in Mexico were
probably those made by a German who chose Adán Miller as a trade
name. Inquisition records reveal him to have been active as an instrument
maker at Mexico City between 1790 and 1795.[26]

In 1799 the price asked for pianos in Mexico City was 400 pesos; the
same year the annual rental of a house near the zócalo—which would have
been considered then the best location—cost between 500 and 600 pesos.
Although it has not been possible to find any advertisement listing English pianos before 1821, pianos made in Cartagena (Spain) "imitando á
los Ingleses" were offered as the most desirable purchases in 1804.[27] It
is a well known fact that English pianos were preferred on the continent
during the first decades of the nineteenth century; Beethoven, for instance, preferred a Broadwood. After Mexico gained her independence
and no longer had to import via Spain, English pianos were always the
preferred purchases of the Mexican upper classes until near the close of
the nineteenth century.

DANCE TYPES POPULAR AT THE END OF THE VICEREGAL PERIOD

All the dance types popular at the close of the viceregal period—except
the jarabe—have now become obsolete. In the dance music which still
survives from the opening years of the nineteenth century no style traits
that later became identified as peculiarly Mexican intruded themselves.
As examples of late colonial dances we offer first a *contradanza* printed in
the *Diario de México* (July 3, 1809), but without ascription to a named
composer; then a *Minuet with Variations* by Aldana; and finally a *Polaca*.
Though all exceedingly charming, not one of these three can truthfully
be said to exhibit even idiomatic Spanish traits, much less traits identifiable

as precursor Mexican. The contradanza seems more akin to certain German *contratanzen* of the late eighteenth century than to the contradanzas so highly popular in the West Indies during the nineteenth century.[28] The squareness of the division into precise eight-bar periods, each repeated, is notable in this *Diario de México* contradanza.

Contradanza (1809)

Diario de México (Vol. II, p. 11)[29]

In Aldana's *Minuet with Variations* one encounters Mozartian naïveté. Surely no one without autograph proof would ever suspect this music of having been written in Mexico, so alien is its spirit to the stereotype of what Spanish or Mexican music should be. The Teutonic influence may have reached Mexico in any of several ways. Certain direct contacts existed between Germany and Mexico during the late eighteenth century; the earliest piano manufacturer, as we already have seen, was a German immigrant; German instruments "made in Augsburg" somehow found their way to the port of Veracruz and were publicly offered for sale in 1794. In addition to occasional direct contacts, a number of opportunities existed for indirect contacts. Iriarte, the most admired Spanish writer on music (*La Música*, 1769, 1784), classified Gluck, Haydn, as Jommelli as his favorite composers; his recommendation as far as Haydn's music was concerned bore fruit in Mexico—Haydn piano sonatas were played by Soto Carrillo at the School of Mines academies. It is, of course, a well known fact that late eighteenth century Spain was passionately addicted to Haydn (Haydn wrote the *Seven Last Words* specifically for Cádiz cathedral).[30]

Aldana's minuet bespeaks Mozart more than Haydn in our opinion, but whatever the influence, the music carries itself with an aristocratic elegance not lightly tossed aside. No Mexican pianist up to the present moment seems to have interested himself in playing it, but the music is distinctly worthy of re-hearing. In the manuscript copy there are no marks of expression. The tempo indication is given as "despacio," which may be interpreted "leisurely," or "gently." It is a notorious fact that the average player of today faced with an urtext assumes all refinements of expression must be excluded; but the success of Aldana's minuet depends as surely on refinements in performance as does Mozart's *Minuet in D*, K. 355.

Minuet with Variations

[Andante]   José Aldana (1800?)

If a contredanse and a minuet seem strangely incongruous in early nine-teenth century Mexico, even stranger seems a polonaise. Possibly the *polaca* given below was written during the 1790's—so thinks Saldívar. Whatever its exact date, it departs widely from any authentic Polish type known to us. This particular *polaca* remains anonymous, but Soto Carrillo is known to have composed polonaises, and may be offered as a candidate for authorship.

Polaca

While no one of these three examples of late viceregal music can lay any claim to greatness, nevertheless each has been worth listing if only to reinforce this important principle: no literate composer of the late colonial period wrote dances classifiable as "Mexican" dances. True, "bailes del país" were called for in the theater, and some of the aristocracy fancied the native tunes of Mexico sufficiently to pay clock-makers the price of cutting "sonecitos del país" on the musical clocks fashionable in Mexico as in Europe around 1800.[31] But composers who possessed enough technical skill to note down their own inspirations—whether their music was difficult or easy—disdained the writing of native-type tunes or dances. They preferred to cultivate some international dance type, such as the contredanse, the minuet, or the polonaise, rather than to write a jarabe in a local idiom. Only after independence does one find "name" composers signing their names to such distinctively Mexican dance types as the jarabe.

Certainly the jarabe existed as a dance type before independence, but every allusion to it during the late colonial period was clearly a disparaging allusion. The Inquisition authorities took an exceedingly dim view of it, condemning it at first on moral grounds. During the struggle for independence the jarabe earned the reputation of being insurrectionary music, and was therefore banned for political reasons. The first dated mention of the jarabe occurred in 1789.[32] A dance tune called a *pan de jarabe* was denounced in that year to the Inquisition authorities in the Puebla diocese. The words of the song were submitted for examination, and ran like this: Hell no longer exists; the demons have ceased to be; come then, my dear, no one will damn us.[33] In 1796 another *pan de xarabe* was denounced to the Inquisition because its words were considered salacious and the dance gestures used while singing it considered lewd. In 1802 the Inquisition in Mexico City forbade the dancing of the jarabe, and issued a statement of reasons which read in part:

> Latterly there has been introduced amongst us another type of dance called the *jarabe gatuno* so indecent, lewd, disgraceful, and provocative, that words cannot encompass the evil of it. The verses and the accompanying actions, movements, and gestures, shoot the poison of lust directly into the eyes, ears, and senses. That lascivious demon, Asmodeus himself [Tobit 3.8], has certainly inspired this dance, so destructive is it of all Christian morals; but not only of religious virtue, even of the most elementary decencies. Its obscenity would shock even the most debased Sybarite. . . . We are obliged by the character of our sacred office, which pledges us to the salvation of souls by the blood of Jesus Christ, to prohibit, banish, and extirpate this dance. . . .[34]

Though prohibited in 1802, the jarabe continued to be sung and danced. The word "jarabe" actually means syrup. "Pan de jarabe" would mean, "syrupy bread." Faced with the same kind of stopper on direct sexual language now encountered with radio, songsters in viceregal Mexico with a legion of decency at their throats used certain substitute words. The phenomenon of substitute words is of course familiar in many hits of our own epoch, and their meanings were surely understood then as now without benefit of diagrams.

Not only did the jarabe ordinarily have devious sexual meanings, but also the jarabe with its ambiguous language became a favorite dance and song of the incipient revolutionaries. In the November 12, 1813, deposition taken under Inquisition authority at Valladolid—the testimony being that of Joaquín Ponce, cathedral precentor—it was noted by the examining officials that the secret revolutionary song sung at the conspiratorial meetings in the house of a certain García was a jarabe.[35]

After 1813 the jarabe was adopted as the song and dance of the revolutionaries everywhere throughout Mexico. The oldest surviving jarabes were written down during the flush of the revolutionary enthusiasm. The few surviving exemplars that can tentatively be dated before the final achievement of independence in 1821 lack words. Perhaps the oldest is one for guitar. Another composed around 1820 was written for piano. The time signature in both reads ¾. Though neither the guitar nor piano jarabes to which we are at the moment referring included a tempo mark, both were obviously intended to be played fast. The movement of sixteenths in both is almost uninterrupted. The piano jarabe indeed looks on the page like a Czerny exercise. The harmonic scheme of both calls for notice: both in C major, they tirelessly repeat the same harmonies forever and a day—C chord, G chord, D dominant seventh, G dominant seventh, then C again, and the same pattern of chord change repeated. The busyness of the sixteenth notes and the tedium of the repetitive harmonies militates against artistic success in either exemplar. The piano jarabe in particular includes so much ding-dong repetition that no musically sensitive person could sincerely praise it as a work of art. But if neither were works of art, at least they were historical landmarks, for later during the century the jarabe was taken to the bosom of every true Mexican composer; jarabes by J. Antonio Gómez (1841) or by Julio Ituarte (in *Ecos de México*, c. 1885) are perhaps not unworthy of comparison with Slavonic Dances by Dvořák or Norwegian Dances by Grieg.

JOSÉ MARIANO ELÍZAGA: A PIONEER DURING THE REVOLUTIONARY EPOCH

The composers in Mexico who most successfully met the challenge of changed conditions after independence were those like Elízaga who gladly accepted the new order, and ceased to hanker after the vanished stability of the viceregal epoch. It was typical of Elízaga that he should have been one of the first to drop the title "Don"—mark of a Spanish gentleman—and adopt the title "Citizen" instead.

But he had profited from the advantages of the old order. Born in 1786 at Morelia,[36] from infancy he was ushered into a musical atmosphere. His father, a music teacher, noticed his phenomenal ear when he was only five. The news that he could toddle to the keyboard and there imitate successfully the best efforts of his father's students was not slow in circulating. A long descriptive article telling of the lad's precocity appeared in the

Gazeta de México, October 2, 1792. With a father as persistent as Leopold Mozart in advertising his genius, the child began to be talked about in the viceroy's presence. The Conde de Revillagigedo, 51st Viceroy, a man of extraordinary sensitivity, immediately wanted to hear the wonder child. Sent for, the child with his parents made the toilsome journey to the capital. The gifts of the *wunderkind* exceeded every expectation, and the viceroy offered to pay the family expenses if the father would permit the child's enrolment at the choirschool for boys attached to the metropolitan cathedral.

This choirschool, known as the Colegio de Infantes de Coro de la Santa Iglesia Catedral, existed for the purpose of preparing its students for service as acolytes and as singers. Its curriculum included languages as well as music. The Elízagas stayed in the capital, however, only a year, and then returned to Morelia (then known as Valladolid). There he came under the tuition of José María Carrasco, organist of Morelia Cathedral, and a musician of unusual worth. The cabildo, recognizing the further growth of the young musician could best be promoted by another year at the capital, sent him back at the age of twelve for a year's study with Soto Carrillo, who had been Carrasco's own teacher.

Upon his return home after the year with Soto Carrillo the cabildo voted the purchase of the best available piano in Mexico City so their youthful prodigy might pass on the benefits of his newly gained knowledge. After Carrasco won the principal organistship at Puebla, a higher paying post than the Morelia first organistship, the second Morelia organist became first, and the third second, leaving the third vacant. This third organistship fell to Elízaga, who when he began occupying it was thirteen. The next five years were spent in broadening his general education. He studied Latin with a teacher at the Valladolid Seminary. Torpid as one might today suppose the atmosphere of a late colonial seminary to have been, the more probable truth is that the atmosphere of this particular one was charged with electricity. Hidalgo, the George Washington of Mexico, was rector of the Valladolid seminary when Elízaga was still in swaddling clothes, and Morelos, the other principal figure in Mexico's fight for independence, was a fellow-townsman of Elízaga's and had gone to school under Hidalgo.

Elízaga did not himself take a gun, as did the priests, Hidalgo and Morelos, who were leaders in the revolt. But when the latter in 1813 was riding high on the crest of the revolutionary movement, Elízaga, fired with enthusiasm, set a poem eulogizing the insurrectionary Morelos to music. Contact with another revolutionary leader resulted from his engagement as piano tutor for a girl in one of the leading families of the town, Ana María Huarte. Doña Ana María became the wife of General Iturbide who after the expulsion of the last viceroy contrived to have himself named first emperor of Mexico. During his year of rule—1822—he brought Elízaga to Mexico City and installed him as imperial chapelmaster. During that year Elízaga finished preparing for the press a theoretical treatise, *Elementos de Música*. Though actual publication did not occur until after Iturbide's abdication, nevertheless Iturbide had made possible its publication.

Elementos de Música, a didactic work, was but the first of Elízaga's contributions to music life in the infant nation. A second valuable contribution was his leadership in a philharmonic society founded in 1824; this society's announced objectives were the patronage of orchestral concerts and the support of a conservatory. The conservatory came into being the next year with a "grand" opening exercise on Sunday morning, April 17, attended by the president of the republic and other notables. Elízaga's support for his excellent schemes failed him, however, and after two years of financial struggle he removed to Guadalajara where the chapelmastership promised security. There he remained for three years (1827–30), significantly bettering the music standards at the cathedral.

Hoping against hope for a better turn in the capital, he abandoned Guadalajara and returned to Mexico City in 1830. Private lessons supported him for eight years, and though he lacked the kind of powerful support Iturbide had given he was able to publish at his own expense another didactic work of capital value, *Principios de la Armonía y Melodía* (1835). In 1838 he accepted a position as tutor to the sons of a wealthy landowner, Echaiz by name, whose properties had swollen at the time of the Spanish expulsion. This tutorship occupied Elízaga two years, after which his journeying ended with a return to his natal city, now re-named Morelia in honor of the patriot Morelos whom Elízaga had eulogized in 1813. Elízaga's last years were spent as chapelmaster in the Morelia Cathedral. He died in 1842, aged fifty-six.

His surviving compositions were all destined for church usage. Two Masses, one for Guadalajara and another for Morelia, a *Miserere*, a set of Lamentations, a set of Responses, and music for the Matins of Transfiguration survive. His music, though far removed from the austere ideal of Pius X's *Motu Proprio*, nevertheless deserves performance; if the liturgical improprieties prevent its being heard in a Roman Catholic church today, still a Mass of his (only one is complete) might effectively be presented in a concert hall. All of it calls for orchestral accompaniment. Present-day realities militate against revival of his music; the assembling of a chorus and orchestra is difficult enough today even for the best-known choral masterpieces. But a recorded performance making known his music to a wide public would establish him as one of the indubitably important New World composers of the nineteenth century.

ELÍZAGA'S PRINTED WORKS

The need for a music press was insistently felt in late viceregal Mexico. As a substitute for staff notation the *Diario de México* published in 1809 an article proposing music printing by means of cipher.[37] But 1809 was too late a date to propose any cipher scheme or any return to tablature systems of notation. A music press capable of executing music in the conventional staff system was imperatively needed. Not the least of Elízaga's achievements was his partnership in the founding of such a press. He told the story of its foundation in the February 2, 1826 issue of *El Águila Mexicana*:

> Citizen Mariano Elízaga has the honor to announce to the public and more especially to lovers of music that in partnership with Citizen Manuel Rionda he has established a music press—the first and at present the only enterprise of its kind in the Republic. It is not easy to understand the difficulties and anxieties this project has cost us unless one pauses to consider just what is involved in undertaking a completely new enterprise of any kind. Without expert guidance and without even occasional advice from an experienced individual, we have undertaken a project whose difficulties we have been able to surmount only by repeated trial and error. . . . Although we have not yet been able to achieve perfection, at least the results satisfy our expectations for a first venture. In token of the publisher's interest in the furtherance of art, we offer our fellow citizens an original *Valse with Variations* as the first printed work from our recently founded press. [Citizen Elízaga composed this *Valse* himself.] . . . We have chosen a small piece in the hope an inexpensive composition reproduced on Mexican paper made here at San Angel would circulate widely, and publicize not only its composer, but also provide an earnest of the later work we plan to accomplish. . . . If this advertisement of the

founding of a press meets with a favorable reception, we plan also the establishment of a music periodical, in which we will publish keyboard pieces and guitar pieces; in it we may include also songs and duos with keyboard and guitar accompaniments. We plan certainly to include the best selections from the current European repertory. . . . The *Valse with Variations* we are now announcing, and other music which will later be published, may be purchased at Escalerillas No. 12, the address at which the Philharmonic Society is presently located.[38]

Elízaga's energetic efforts as a music educator can fittingly be compared with those of Lowell Mason, pioneer music educator in the United States. Both men realized that any permanent success depended upon raising the general level of music sensitivity in a young republic. Both were intensely interested in pedagogy; both adopted their churches as foci for their professional activities in music. Elízaga was born only six years before Mason, but died thirty years before Mason. Nevertheless their epochs of productivity overlapped. Both men contributed immensely to the advance of music in their respective countries by publishing music textbooks. Mason's singing instructors sold thousands of copies, and were used everywhere. Elízaga's two texts, *Elementos de Música* (1823) and *Principios de la Armonía . . .* (1835), although not the best-sellers Mason's books became, missed wide popularity only because he addressed a more advanced student than did Mason.

Books of a pedagogical nature lack glamor, but after surveying Elízaga's one can hardly fail to praise him unstintingly for their merits. Elízaga began his *Elementos* (1823) with a preface calling attention to the musical resources of the young nation. "We have talents in our very midst who ought to develop into Jommellis, Tartinis, Dusseks, and Haydns, if proper opportunities for self-development were afforded," he pointed out.[39] But he went on to observe that "unfortunately our music has sunk to a disgracefully low level, both in church and in chamber music." He saw the standards of the late viceregal period pitched at too low a level to inspire youth. The root of the evil as he saw it lay in bad teaching. To remedy the evils first a blow for freedom from antiquated music theories must be struck.[40] The advance of art he felt stifled as long as the authority of outdated theorists such as Kircher continued to be invoked. The day of the Guidonian hand must end.

Elízaga's remarks on fledgling composers of his epoch make interesting reading:

The bad taste and the wilderness of unprofitable notes in so much of our own product distresses me. . . . Why are we unable to find Mexicans whose works deserve comparison with those of Mozart and Beethoven? Surely the reason stems largely from our improper methods of music instruction. Music has not been studied from a properly systematic point of view, but has been instead encrusted with a thick overlay of unprofitable Gothic ornaments.[41]

The respite from an everlasting round of daily duties at the organ bench in his home town and his appointment to the chapelmastership of Iturbide's short-lived imperial chapel gave him leisure, he said, to examine several systems of music theory then before the public. "By chance I came upon a book by the Abbé D. Antonio Eximeno on the *Origin, Progress, Decadence, and Restoration of Music* which utterly differed from all the others. Here at last was a book in which I encountered that which I have always desired: a clear, comprehensive system, a method, a penetrating analysis of the various different aspects of musical science."

Eximeno's *Del Origen y Reglas,* the book to which Elízaga referred, was of course one of the most stimulating treatments of music theory by any eighteenth century author, not even excepting Rameau, whom Elízaga knew and admired. A member of the same company as Kircher, Eximeno had been forced to flee to Italy, where his book had first appeared in Italian (1774); Elízaga knew the Spanish translation. In our own century Pedrell has devoted an entire book to Eximeno,[42] so important does he seem even now after a long lapse of time. Eximeno was preeminently an empiric. "May God in His mercy relieve us," he wrote, "from the continued cleavage between practice and theory which defaces the art of music." A sample of Eximeno's vigorous and trenchant style may be gathered from the following typical quotation from him: "The vain expenditure of time and effort on writing music that conforms to the theories of word-spinning 'authorities' is a catastrophe; all music study should be founded directly on the models of practicing musicians, not on the fancies of theorists whose favorite exercise is the concatenation of precepts fastened in the chains of a Gothic vocabulary."[43]

Eximeno stimulated Elízaga in much the same fashion Pestalozzi stimulated Lowell Mason. Although Elízaga did not share Mason's opportunities to test his educational philosophy on a grand scale, still he did found a conservatory—the first in the new republic—and did write two useful texts. The harmony text, which appeared twelve years after the

Elementos, covers much the same territory a first-year college text in harmony covers today. Dressed up in an attractive format, enlivened with examples from composers of a later day, and provided with exercises to test the student's progress at the end of each unit, the *Principios* could even today serve as a useful beginning text in conventional four-part harmony.

ELÍZAGA'S SUCCESSORS

Although inaugurated amid considerable pomp and ceremony, Elízaga's 1825 conservatory lacked stable support, and therefore did not last. Several other conservatories were attempted in Mexico City before one which succeeded in outliving violent political changes was finally founded (1866). Elízaga's most important immediate successor was José Antonio Gómez, whose Academia de Música (1839) flourished for several years. Gómez issued two didactic works, *Gramática Razonada Musical* (1840) and *Instructor Filarmónico* (1843), both of which were designed for immediate use with his own pupils. During 1853 "His Most Serene Highness," General Santa Anna, conceived the plan of a government supported conservatory, and chose the famous double-bassist, Giovanni Bottesini (1821–89), then resident in Mexico, as organizer of the faculty.[44] Santa Anna, however, did not have time to consummate his national conservatory, and only after the Maximilian episode did one actually come into being.

The conservatory founded under the auspices of a reorganized Sociedad Filarmónica Mexicana in 1866 was the first which offered free instruction.[45] The Sociedad contributed to the support of the conservatory during the first two seasons, and by governmental consent the sequestrated buildings formerly belonging to the University of Mexico (founded in 1553) were used for classes. The first director of the 1866 conservatory, Agustín Caballero, a priest, resigned after the government assumed full responsibility for the support of the conservatory in 1877. In the latter year the name was changed to Conservatorio Nacional de Música, and under this name the conservatory has continued to function during the last seventy-five years.

The curriculum of the 1866 conservatory was for forty years modeled on that of Italian conservatories. The programs of the conservatory founded by Gómez in 1839 and the conservatory founded by the Sociedad Filarmónica in 1866 followed the same pattern—operatic arias, duos, and piano transcriptions of operatic excerpts dominated all student and faculty programs. The subjects of instruction in 1866 were: solfège, piano, strings, woodwinds, harmony, instrumentation and orchestration, composition, Spanish language, French, music history and biography, acoustics, physiology of voice, history of instruments, esthetics.[46] At the first public concert given by the students in 1866 (for which there was an admission charge) selections from four different operas by Verdi were performed: *Nabucodonosor*, *Giovanna d'Arco*, *Macbeth*, and *La forza del destino*. No German music of any description was offered. On the other hand, a *Sinfonia*, previously unheard, by the precocious Mexican, Joaquín Beristaín (1817–39), whose untimely death at twenty-two was one of the tragic losses of the nineteenth century, was resurrected and played. The orchestra for the occasion was composed of students, but augmented by experienced professionals from the opera orchestra.

Any scrutiny of curricula at later stages during the nineteenth century, or any look at later student programs, leads to but one conclusion: the Mexican musical horizon between independence and the close of the Porfirian epoch (1911) was narrowly confined within the world of Italian opera. Rossini, Bellini, Donizetti, and Verdi were the uncontested gods of nineteenth century Mexican music.

THE MANUEL GARCÍA EPISODE

The singing of opera in Italian did not begin in Mexico until after independence. Cimarosa and Paisiello were sung in Spanish during the late viceregal period. It remained for Manuel García, himself a native of Seville, to popularize Italian opera in Italian. García, fifty-two years of age when he reached Mexico, had triumphed everywhere in Europe, and came fresh from successes in New York; as an international figure he had adopted Italian exclusively. His presentation of Rossini's *Il barbieri* created a sensation, and his Italian was accepted naturally, but when he turned to a work of his own—*El Abufar*, variously styled a tonadilla or a zarzuela in the newspapers of the period—the public complained they could not understand him. In *El Águila Mexicana* appeared this comment on *El Abufar* (July 13, 1827):

> The number of persons who understand Italian or who are content simply to enjoy the singing and the music without knowing what is going

on, cannot be as large in. Mexico as in Paris or London—certainly the number is not large enough to pay the costs of grand opera here. If Señor García and his family were Italians, there might be legitimate reason for their singing in Italian, but their native language is Spanish.

Despite this commonsense reproach, Italian became during the 1830's the only language in which opera was sung in Mexico. Beginning in 1831 the Teatro Principal, newly refurbished, housed a regular annual season of Italian opera, with Rossini dominating the bills. Filippo Galli (born Rome, 1783) was the acknowledged singing star in Mexico, and Lauro Rossi (born Macerata, Italy, 1810) was imported to write operas suitable for the Italian troupe.[47] The Italians naturally banded together in a clique while in Mexico, much to the detriment of native Mexicans.

FOREIGN OPINION ON MUSIC IN THE YOUNG REPUBLIC

The Spanish policy of exclusion discouraged foreigners from casual traveling in Hispanic America during the late colonial period. Only exceptional individual scientists such as Alexander von Humboldt, or members of accredited teams, were permitted to observe life in the colonies at first hand. After independence, however, a number of observers swarmed into the young republics, leaving often engaging accounts of cultural life in the nations they visited. One of the earliest in Mexico was a Britisher, Bullock by name, whose *Six Months' Residence and Travels in Mexico* appeared at London in 1824. According to Bullock, musical life suffered intensely in Mexico during the revolutionary epoch. His pejorative comments ran like these:

> Mexico has but one place of dramatic exhibition; it is a building of considerable size, . . . [but] the orchestra is indifferent, and the performers in general below mediocrity. . . . During the time of Gálvez [1785–6] the Coliseo was much more splendid.[48]

Mme. Calderón de la Barca, wife of the first Spanish envoy (but herself of distinguished Scots lineage), was among the most perceptive visitors in the early years of the republic. Her entrée as wife of a ranking diplomat enabled her to satisfy her lively curiosity, and her *Life in Mexico*, an extraordinarily informative book, was the result. Because she herself knew enough music to play Mozart piano sonatas her musical comments represented enlightened opinion. Music in Mexico, she said, was a sixth sense. After hearing the band at a village fiesta, she remarked, "The music was good, which would hardly be the case in any but a Mexican village." [49] In 1841 she was struck by the large number of pianos everywhere. "In every part of Mexico, town or country, there is a piano (*tal cual*) in every house, . . . [and] there is evidently a great deal of musical taste." However, she went on to remark: "But most of those who play are self-taught, and naturally abandon it very soon, for want of encouragement or instruction." [50]

She accounted for the high mortality rate of musical talent as "the melancholy effect produced by years of civil war and unsettled government." She admitted that the finest performances in Mexico were staged by the Italian troupe "brought by Señor Roca to the Teatro des Gallos," but she was none too happy over the fact the same theater was used at one moment for a cock-fight and at the next for a gala performance of *Lucia di Lammermoor.* Her opinion of the Italian opera she heard in Mexico was distinctly enthusiastic in comparison with the opinions on an Italian troupe appearing in Peru at the identical moment of her writing (1841). Here are the remarks of a traveler in Peru during that year:

> For some years past a company of Italians, settled in Lima, have given operatic performances on a small scale. One of them, Signora Pantanelli, is an excellent singer . . . but the rest are decidedly bad. The operas performed are *Giulietta y Romeo, Lucia di Lammermoor, La Somnambula,* and *Il barbiere di Siviglia;* . . . a mutilated *Norma* and a much curtailed *Semiramide.* Want of stage room is an obstacle to the representation of operas. . . . The orchestra is defective, and ought to be much improved, to give satisfaction to a public passionately fond of music.[51]

But if Mme. Calderón de la Barca entertained a better opinion of the troupe playing in Mexico than did the commentator on Peruvian opera, the repertory at both Lima and Mexico City consisted of the same monotonously recurring items. The Italian troupes in neither city were interested in encouraging talent in the countries where they made their livings.

Mme. Calderón de la Barca complained that opera invaded even the sanctuary in Mexico. Concerning the Good Friday music at the Mexico City cathedral she wrote:

As the *Miserere* was to be performed in the cathedral late in the evening, we went there, though with small hopes of making our way through the tremendous crowd. The music began with a crash . . . and such discordance of instruments and voices, such confusion worse confounded, such inharmonious harmony, never before deafened mortal ears. The very spheres seemed out of tune and rolling and crashing over each other. I could have cried *Miserere!* with the loudest; and in the midst of all the undrilled band was a *music-master* with violin stick uplifted, rushing desperately from one to the other, in vain endeavoring to keep time, and frightened at the clamour he himself had been instrumental in raising. . . . The noise was so great as to be really alarming. . . . The calm face of the Virgin seemed to look reproachfully down.[52]

She remarked that during an outdoor procession on Good Friday night "the Host moved by, and then a military band struck up an air from *Semiramide*." [53] At a ceremony she later attended during which a young girl took the veil at the fabulously endowed Convent of the Incarnation, "the church was very brilliantly illuminated, and as we entered, the band was playing one of Strauss's waltzes!" [54] At a Mass "where only well dressed people were admitted [Santo Domingo Church], the music was beautiful, but too gay for a church. There were violins and wind instruments, and several amateur players." [55]

The mania for Italian opera among the rich and well-born in Mexico produced these deleterious results during the nineteenth century: (1) Second-rate Italians siphoned off performance fees. (2) Conservatories prepared everyone either to sing in opera, accompany opera, or write opera. (3) All other musical types were syncretized with Italian opera. After surveying the baneful effects of the opera craze in Mexico Mme. Calderón de la Barca turned with a hopeful sigh of relief to the native dances of Mexico. In 1840 she noted the following types of dances: jarabes, aforrados, enanos, palomos, and zapateros.[56]

MEXICAN OPERA COMPOSERS OF THE MID-CENTURY

Luis Baca (1826-55), originally from Durango, was the first native composer of operas after independence. Neither his *Leonor* nor *Giovanna di Castiglia* was produced, however. Scion of a distinguished provincial family, he enjoyed exceptional advantages in his music study. He passed from the tuition of the Durango chapelmaster to José Antonio Gómez's newly founded conservatory in Mexico City. His parents wished him a more stable career than that of a musician, and sent him in 1844 to study medicine in Europe, but in Paris he established contact with Donizetti, then a visitor at the French capital, and was by Donizetti encouraged to continue in music.

An *Ave Maria* of Baca's published in a sumptuous edition at Paris (1850), with a decorative cover showing the Mexico City Cathedral and beneath it a flowery dedication to Gómez (then chapelmaster), earned Baca favorable publicity at home, especially after a leading female opera star premiered it in Paris and the critics there spoke of it favorably. Baca was but one of many during his century—both in Mexico and the United States—who found a quicker road to homeland fame through European successes than through any possible American exertions. Upon Baca's return to Mexico he was palpably lauded beyond his deserts, and had he lived beyond his thirtieth year his European operas would no doubt have been granted a Mexican hearing. He died, however, before Mexican performances could be pressurized from the Italian troupe.

Cenobio Paniagua (1821–82) [57] was the more fortunate Mexican who finally succeeded in having an opera of his, *Catalina di Guisa,* given a Mexican hearing. Like William Henry Fry who had the distinction of being the first United States composer to gain an opera performance, Paniagua discovered that the Italian troupe would sing his opera only on condition the libretto were in Italian. Every possible concession was made the performing whims of the Italian troupers, and Paniagua's opera therefore came dangerously near being a mere carbon copy of a Donizetti opera. Paniagua did not have Fry's personal wealth and was not able to mount his *Catalina di Guisa* at his own charges; its first production therefore had to wait fourteen years after its composition.

Paniagua started as a violinist in the Morelia Cathedral where his uncle conducted the orchestra. When his uncle removed to Mexico City he was taken along. The "music-master" whose direction of the cathedral orchestra so offended Mme. Calderón de la Barca, Ignacio Triujeque, took an instant liking to the young player, and offered him a place in the cathedral orchestra. If the orchestra was indeed as bad as she thought, then his years in it were valueless musically. But he made contacts with such famous individuals as Bottesini while playing in it. His *Catalina di Guisa,* composed in 1845, reached the boards largely because Paniagua tirelessly cultivated his Italian colleagues in the music profession during the next several years after its completion. *Catalina's* success was enormous, and Paniagua was repaid his years of waiting by a fond adulation no other Mexican operatist of the nineteenth century perhaps duplicated. Around him drew a group of young composers all hoping to share the limelight with him. His success with *Catalina* was not, however, duplicated when he proceeded to mount his second opera, *Pietro d'Abano*, in 1863. By this time he had organized his own Mexican troupe. Eager to cash in on his *Catalina* success, he very unwisely intruded his own daughter into principal roles in his Mexican troupe. What he started as a patriotic venture degenerated into a mere family matter. Paniagua's reputation also declined when the Mexican public discovered notable similarities between *Catalina*, revived in 1863, and an Italian opera, *Marcos Visconti*, which had been mounted in Mexico the same year, but had been composed in 1855. Forgetting that Paniagua had composed his *Catalina* in 1845, the critics began to call Paniagua a plagiarist. What they failed to recognize sufficiently, of course, was the fact that all second-rate Italian opera tended to duplicate itself.

With his reputation in the capital on the skids, Paniagua decided to leave and in 1868 removed to the small town of Córdoba. His energies were there deflected into religious composition, but his *Siete Palabras* (1869), his *Tobias* (1870), and his later Masses added nothing to his reputation. His last composition was a requiem, finished a few days before his death on November 2, 1882. The many gestures of appreciation after his passing hardly obscured the fact his had been a progressively deteriorating career after the first triumphal production of *Catalina* in 1859. The last production of this opera occurring in 1872 at the provincial theater in Orizaba was a sad anticlimax to the history of an opera that began with the reputation of being the Mexican masterwork of the century.

Paniagua's most important pupil was Melesio Morales (1838–1908). Like his master, Melesio Morales enjoyed for a brief hour a resounding success. His *Ildegonda*, produced at Mexico City in 1866 and three years later at Florence, Italy, won him almost as extravagant tributes as Paniagua received with *Catalina*. But everything he attempted in the operatic line after *Ildegonda* sent his reputation tobogganing downhill, and when he died at seventy he was a musical nonentity. Once the cock of the walk, musically speaking, at the end he died as unloved and unwanted as did

General Santa Anna, another cock whose comb no one wanted to see shaken when he grew old.

Born in Mexico City of middleclass parents,[58] he showed musical aptitude as a child, and composed several small pieces when he was only twelve. He palmed off one of his own compositions as a mazurka by Thalberg, having learned already as an adolescent that a famous composer's work commanded respect not accorded a beginner's. When he revealed his deception, the Mexican music public began to take serious notice of his work. Before he reached twenty, he sketched out his first big work, the opera *Romeo y Julieta*.

Morales after re-doing the orchestration three times, offered it to the Maretzek opera troupe, which had premiered *Catalina*. Unable to impress the impresario, Morales turned to the municipal government for financial backing. After several vain promises, the municipal government officials who had halfheartedly promised their backing withdrew. Only by the slenderest thread was it finally presented at the end of January in 1863. During his frenetic search for a patron, or better, an angel, Morales found only one secure friend, the singer, Roncari. And Roncari told him he never could hope for a great success as long as he stayed in Mexico. "You must go to Europe. A prophet is not without honor, except in his own country."

The European trip was not to materialize until later, but Morales for the next several years prepared for it. *Ildegonda* was his second opera produced in Mexico. The story of its presentation reads like a saga. An insolent Italian impresario, Biacchi by name, refused even to consider it unless Morales personally deposited enough money to defray the entire cost of production. Desperately eager to bring it to a hearing, Morales through an intermediary reached Maximilian and received a guaranty from him. On January 27, 1866, it was performed. Three months later he left for Europe, where he remained three years. When he returned again home he came as a conquering hero, because he had succeeded in the meantime accomplishing the supposedly impossible—his *Ildegonda* had been performed at Florence (1869). The glory that supposedly shone on Mexico because *Ildegonda* was successfully presented at Florence floated over his head when he returned, and during the remainder of his life he fancied himself surrounded by a halo. Looking back over the years, Morales in 1907 said that "his own triumph was a great victory for Mexican art." Though undoubtedly the three performances in Florence were enthusiastically received, still Morales's dinning the press notices into the ears of his Mexican confrères after thirty years alienated even the ones who had borne him home in triumph when he first returned.

Even as late as 1907 Morales was still carrying dogeared copies of the notices that had read: "In resumé, the opera of Morales was received with enthusiasm. The composer was recalled eighteen times in order to acknowledge applause." [59] Morales never let the Mexican public forget that the Florentines had recalled him eighteen times. As he told his own story:

> Upon my return I founded a school of composition based on the Neapolitan model. Among my students have been some who accepted my assistance gladly, but later proved themselves Judases. . . . I have taught over three hundred students during the past thirty-six years, among them Ricardo Castro and Julián Carrillo.[60]

But after calling the roll of his "famous" pupils he concluded that like the ten lepers, only one had returned to give thanks to the physician who had healed them.

Morales wrote five other operas, but only one, *Cleopatra,* won a hearty reception (Teatro Nacional, November 14, 1891). Like Paniagua he became interested in founding a musical dynasty, and after heroic efforts gained a performance for his son's opera, *Colón en Santo Domingo* (Teatro Nacional, October 21, 1892). His own final effort was a one-act opera, *Anita,* which told a rather interesting and compact story of the famous 1867 siege of Puebla.

MELESIO MORALES'S ONE "MEXICAN" OPERA

Anita, the libretto of which (by Enrique Golisciani) was printed in 1903,[61] has never been produced, and yet because of its brevity and meatier musical substance might yet be successfully presented. According to Morales's younger colleagues, the old maestro was a Bourbon at heart —he never learned anything new, despite change, and never forgot anything. But *Anita* proves he lent *verismo* a willing ear. The instrumental interludes may not pack the emotional punch of Puccini's, but they are by no means undistinguished. The choral music would be stirring in the best *Simon Boccanegra* fashion, and the solos and concerted numbers are all extremely well written for voice. The high notes would give the principal singers every opportunity to tear a passion to tatters, to very rags, to split

the ears of the groundlings. And in the very torrent, tempest, and whirl-
wind of passion, grand pauses in the best melodramatic manner would chill
the marrow.[62]

The plot centers around the eternal conflict between love and duty. The
four principal characters are Manuel, captain of a band of Mexican soldiers
fighting Maximilian; Anita, his sister; Rodrigo, a Mexican soldier in
love with her; and Gaston, son of the French colonel, D'Auvray. The
opera, which is in one act, with two scenes, opens with a symphonic prelude,
a "sinfonia," depicting the melancholy of a deserted battlefield at sunset.
The curtain rises, discovering a well-appointed room in a Puebla mansion.
Rodrigo (baritone) enters, and calls for Captain Manuel. Battle music is
heard outside the window. Anita (lyric soprano) enters, singing of the
protector who once saved her and Manuel, her brother, from being mis-
treated by a band of ruffian insurgents during French hostilities. While
she sings of him, Gaston, wounded, knocks asking succor. Gaston (tenor),
though son of the French colonel now driven in defeat, has not made
known his identity to Anita. She only recognizes him for a protector wearing the officer uniform of the French army. Anita gives him asylum. A
little later the Mexican soldiers return victorious from the battle against
the French, and Rodrigo boasts of having himself killed Colonel D'Auvray. Gaston, hiding in the next room, hears his boast, and indiscreetly
rushes out. He is immediately seized and escorted to prison.

The second scene discovers Gaston in prison, guarded by a henchman
of Manuel's. He sings an affecting romanza telling his love for Anita,
and conjuring her in a vision. Anita, materializing, comes carrying her
brother's cloak and cap as disguise. After a declaration of undying love,
Gaston accepts the disguise. Anita assures him she can mollify her
brother, Manuel. Gaston then leaves in the disguise, but hard on his
heels Rodrigo, himself in love with Anita, bursts in. Finding Anita but
no Gaston, he immediately apprehends the worst, and grows insane with
jealous fury. Outside a shot is heard. Gaston has been detected in the
very act of escaping, and the disguise is pulled off him. Furious at learning
at last how Anita loved Gaston, Rodrigo pulls his trigger and shoots her.
Manuel rushes in from the eaves and bends prostrate over her body as
the curtain falls. Then trumpets blare forth the Mexican national anthem.
Duty has conquered.

Gaston during his prison romanza had sung: "Glory, what is glory? An
illusion, a trap! The most winsome and inspiring realities of life are re-

jected, while everything is sacrificed to this vain illusion of 'glory'." But Gaston is proved wrong. In the end the lesson is brought strongly home. Glory and honor are everything.

Morales, having offended all the musical powers-that-be in Mexico by his lofty egotism, never succeeded in having his one opera that might have remained in the repertory produced. But long before he was pushed off into a corner to die unloved, the official opinion of the younger generation had been expressed by Gustavo E. Campa, a director of the Conservatorio Nacional. Campa, whose personal feelings Morales had ruthlessly trampled upon, wrote:

> Morales was not and could not be a revolutionary in art. Educated in a school which in his epoch preserved an intransigently conservative attitude, he himself adopted the conservative attitude as a matter of principle, and adhered to it with all his soul. His conservatism was the root of his controversy with the younger generation, and was the cause of those frequent violent encounters with those who professed different artistic ideals. His conservatism provoked those bitter efforts of his to denigrate every new artistic idea. But he attempted the impossible.[63]

And so the career of the one Mexican operatist of the century with four successfully produced operas in Mexico and one successfully produced in Italy ended with a fizzle instead of a grand finale. At his peak lauded by the great Ignacio Altamirano (a man whose literary stature almost equaled Juárez's political stature), Morales at the end won accolades from nobody, and crept off into a hole where he could only sit by the wall and tell sad tales.

ANGELA PERALTA: "THE MEXICAN NIGHTINGALE" (1845–83)

The most spectacular performing artist perhaps ever developed in Mexico was the magnificent soprano, Angela Peralta. She starred not only in the first performances of Melesio Morales's *Ildegonda* (January 27, 1866) and his *Gino Corsini* (July 14, 1877), but also in the first performance of Aniceto Ortega's *Guatimotzín* (September 13, 1871). The very least of her activities were, however, her creations of the leading roles in Mexican operas.

Her parents were impoverished folk from Puebla,[64] and her musical advancement entirely resulted from her own amazing musical gifts. She sang a cavatina from Bellini's now forgotten opera, *Belisarius,* so expertly when she was auditioned by the visiting German celebrity, Henriette Sontag, that the latter rapturously threw her arms about her and prophesied an international future for her. Tutored by Agustín Balderas, Angela made huge strides, and was ready for a debut in *Il trovatore* at the Gran Teatro Nacional when she was but fifteen. So brilliant was her success that funds were given for a European study period. She went to Spain, was dubbed "The Mexican Nightingale" straight off; then traveled on to Milan where after a short period of study she appeared in May, 1862, as Lucia in Donizetti's opera. She next sang in *Somnambula* at a highly successful Turin debut. She then went as far afield as Egypt, carrying all before her. Upon her return to Mexico in 1865 she was immediately taken up by the Italian impresario, Biacchi, and patronized liberally by the Maximilianists. So important was her appearance to the success of any opera she consented to play in that she was awarded a 20 percent of the gross for every performance.

After marrying a cousin, she set off on another foreign tour in 1867, which took her to Havana, then to New York, then to Madrid, and thence to several other capitals. Upon returning home after this particular tour she decided to form her own opera company in Mexico. She proceeded to barnstorm the entire republic, including in her repertory the following operas as mainstays: *Lucia di Lammermoor, La traviata, Lucrezia Borgia, Dinorah, La forza del destino, I puritani, Ruy Blas, Norma, Somnambula, Marta.* She played *Lucia* according to her count, 166 times, and *Somnambula,* 122 times.

Around her was pivoted the Mexican premiere of the Verdi Requiem, given October 12, 1877, "in memory of three noble liberators, Juárez, Lincoln, and Thiers." She premiered her last Mexican opera the same year, *Gino Corsini,* by Melesio Morales. Her last public appearance occurred at Mazatlán on the west coast of Mexico, where on August 23, 1883, she sang in *Il trovatore.* There she contracted yellow fever and died at the age of only thirty-eight. Playing in the orchestra accompanying her while she was on her last tour was a young violinist, Juventino Rosas (1868–94), who was later to compose a set of waltzes that has vied with the Blue Danube in international popularity—*Sobre las Olas.* At the very hour of her death she married a paramour who was but one of many sharing her affections after her husband's untimely death.

The scandal of her free and easy private life was, however, soon forgotten and only the memory of her astounding voice, her wide repertory, and her indefatigable energy remained. She was not only an executant; she was a composer besides. Her *Album Musical de Angela Peralta* (1875) contained nineteen piano pieces, all of the salon type. The titles betray them: *Loin de toi, El Deseo, Vuelta á la patria;* there are a schottisch, a polka-mazurka, a romanza, a valse, but no dances identifiably "Mexican."

OTHER MEXICAN OPERA COMPOSERS OF THE NINETEENTH CENTURY

Besides singing in the premieres of two Morales operas, Angela Peralta also took the part of the Aztec princess in Aniceto Ortega's "episodio musical," *Guatimotzín,* the first performance of which was given September 25, 1871. Ortega, a gifted amateur, pursued the career of an obstetrician and in addition taught medicine at the national school of medicine. But like Borodin, though he pursued science as a career and art as a sideline, his heart was in music.

Ortega first came before the public as a composer in 1867 when two of his marches, *Marcha Zaragoza* and *Marcha Republicana,* climaxed a patriotic program at the Gran Teatro under auspices of the Sociedad Filarmónica. Twenty pianists sitting two at a piano joined forces with a military band in both marches.[65] In October of the same year the *Marcha Zaragoza* was published with a picture of an eagle clutching victory in his talons and fiercely gazing upward at the words "Cinco de Mayo." [66] The Fifth of May was of course the day on which in 1862 General Ignacio Zaragoza had repulsed the French troops before Puebla, after which he reported to President Juárez: "The national arms have covered themselves with glory."

The choice of the last Aztec prince for protagonist in his short opera was undoubtedly well timed. At approximately the time Ortega's opera was premiered, Alfredo Chavero, a leading literary light of the period, was engaged in writing a tribute to the Aztecs, *Quetzalcoatl: Ensayo tragico en tres actos y en verso.* The salvation from the French had been achieved because a Zapotec Indian had willed victory, and a grateful Mexico looked to its Indian ancestry with renewed eyes of longing. The whole republic was astir with resurgent Indianism. In order to glorify Cuauhtémoc Ortega's librettist grossly distorted history; Cuauhtémoc did not "prefer death to dishonor" as the opera would have us believe, but instead survived three years after the fall of Mexico. But no matter—history or no history—the opera served a patriotic purpose, and achieved an enormous success.

Ortega was lauded to the skies; as Luis Castillo Ledón, the historian of Mexican opera, described his success:

> *Guatimotzin* created a furor; Ortega achieved a noisier, a more spontaneous, and a more complete triumph than any previous opera composer, not even excepting Paniagua. . . . The press glorified his achievement, heaping praises upon him for his "creation" of a national opera. . . . His work perfectly suited the requirements of his time; utilizing as had all its predecessors Mexican operas the whole apparatus of Italian opera, . . . yet at the same time it appealed to the patriotic ardor of the audience by romanticizing an Aztec theme.[67]

Whatever small flecks of technical incompetence were discerned in the score were hastily blown aside as of no importance; Ortega was spared criticism his technical inadequacies would surely have caused simply because he sheltered himself under the name of being an amateur.

The other opera composers who deserve at least brief mention because their works achieved performance may be summarily listed:[68] Miguel Meneses (*Agorante, Rey de la Nubia,* July 6, 1863); Octaviano Valle (*Clotilde de Coscena,* July 19, 1863); Torres Serratos (*Los dos Fóscari,* November 11, 1863); Leonardo Canales (*Pirro de Aragón,* July 12, 1864); Miguel Planas (*Don Quijote en la Ventana Encantada,* May 5, 1871), and Felipe Villanueva (*Keofar,* July 29, 1893). The operas of Ricardo Castro (1864–1907), Ernesto Elorduy (1853–1912), and Gustavo E. Campa (1863–1934), properly belong with the story of the twentieth century, but since all three were direct continuators of nineteenth century operatic traditions, their works may appropriately be classified in the same school; all three, Castro, Elorduy, and Campa, were fin-de-siècle Porfirians, rather than pathbreakers in a new epoch.

ASSESSMENT OF NINETEENTH CENTURY MEXICAN OPERA

Before attempting any overall assessment of their artistic merits, we may first count the number of composers of operas, and the number of operas presented. Paniagua with three, Melesio Morales with four, his son with one, and seven other operatists of the nineteenth century with one each, yields a total of ten opera composers with fifteen produced operas. To this might be added a lyric drama of the pianist, Julio Ituarte, *El Último Pensamiento de Weber*,[69] if one is willing to accept a loose definition of what constitutes opera. Adding the fin-de-siècle composers we have for the Mexican school thirteen composers of produced works and nineteen operas.

The number of additional composers who wrote opera, but had no luck at getting their work produced, must undoubtedly be large. The ultimate value of their efforts can be judged fairly perhaps only by a critic who sympathizes with the esthetics of Italian opera. In so-called informed circles in Mexico today the nineteenth century operatists are laughed out of court. But opera "dates" more quickly than any other type of music. Of all Verdi's own immediate contemporaries in Italy itself, not one opera composer is still remembered today. A convenient proof can be made by listing the composers whom Verdi called upon to assist him in writing a Requiem honoring Rossini; of the dozen he thought worthy of assisting him in his commemoration project—Buzzola, Bazzini, Pedrotti, Cagnoni, Ricci, Nini, Boucheron, Coccia, Gaspari, Platania, Petrella, and Mabellini —what one is so much as remembered today even by name? If in Italy, the home of opera, only one composer wrote who still commands respect, we should hardly expect a group of a dozen or more Mexican operatists active at the same period to be judged strictly on the lasting qualities of their music. Dead it may be now, but in their own day and time men like Paniagua, Melesio Morales, and Ortega, each in his own way helped solidify a cultural consciousness in the new republic without which Mexico would have been the poorer.

Their efforts were certainly the peers of any United States operas written during the same period, and if we question the taste of their music, at least they were making it and far more of it (proportionately) than was being made at the same time in this country.

SALON MUSIC

The amount of salon music published in Mexico between 1870 and 1900 was enormous. The catalogue of A. Wagner y Levien Sucs., for instance, contained works by 103 nineteenth century Mexican salon composers. This firm, which eventually became the most important actually engaged in the business of printing music in Mexico, had branch houses in Guadalajara, Puebla, Monterrey, Veracruz, Mérida, and Tampico,

during the late nineteenth century. Founded by Germans, the firm necessarily underwent reorganization after the 1910 Revolution. But this house
has been but one catering to the demand for salon pieces by Mexican composers.

At present the library of the Conservatorio Nacional contains salon
pieces, mostly in manuscript, of well over three hundred nineteenth century Mexican composers. The titles do not stimulate minute examination
—most of them sound like the pieces in Angela Peralta's 1875 Album.
But the mere listing of names shows how many would-be composers there
were in Mexico during the Porfirian epoch. They were, moreover, scattered over the entire republic. In a study of music in Guadalajara, Mexico's
second city, José G. Montes de Oca compiled a list of 45 musicians who
were active in that city alone during the last decade of the nineteenth century. Not all confined their efforts to mere salon pieces such as polkas,
valses, schottishes, mazurkas, marches, potpourris, boleros, pasodobles,
meditations, and caprices—although this class dominated. Some attempted
larger things,[70] but for every one concerto for piano there were hundreds
of ephemeral jottings. Justly to comprehend what was happening in
Guadalajara around 1900 we should need to compare it with a town in
the United States of comparable size at the turn of the century—Buffalo,
New York, for instance. If there were 45 persons in Buffalo in 1900 classifiable as "composers" no WPA history has brought together a record of
them. The composer in Buffalo during the latter years of the century who
is best remembered today was, interestingly enough, Jaime Nunó (1824–
1908),[71] the composer of the music for the Mexican national anthem.
Where records have been assembled of would-be composers in this country
between 1890 and 1900 almost invariably the names have belonged to
individuals such as Nunó, who had emigrated from elsewhere, Spain via
Mexico in Nunó's case.

The most conspicuous success among all the salon pieces composed in
Mexico during the nineteenth century was undoubtedly Rosas's *Sobre las
Olas.* Juventino Rosas,[72] who died in July, 1894, at the age of only twenty-
six, composed his internationally acclaimed set of waltzes in 1891 when
he was only twenty-three. Why this one particular set should have carried
his name around the world, while other sets, such as *Amelia, Dos Pensami-
entos, Flores de Maragarita,* or *Ilusiones Juveniles,*[73] though also published by Wagner and Levien and therefore equally accessible, should not
have aroused a ripple of international interest remains an unsolved mys-

tery. *Sobre las Olas*, moreover, remains perennially popular. As recently as 1951 when the moving picture, "The Great Caruso," was issued by Metro-Goldwyn-Mayer, Rosas's *Sobre las Olas* was made over into a song for Dorothy Caruso (Ann Blyth) to sing in the film, with the new title, "The Loveliest Night of the Year."

Rosas's own life has never been filmed, but since he lived a tempestuous one, the movie possibilities are great. A pure-blooded Otomí Indian,[74] he was born in the tiny village of Santa Cruz de Galeana in the state of Guanajuato. His father brought him to Mexico City before he was six, and set him to playing violin in a roaming family quartet, which consisted of father Jesús playing the harp, brother Patrocinio singing, and brother Manuel playing the guitar. This family combination broke up when Manuel was killed with a dagger thrust during a love-quarrel. Juventino then started playing the violin at San Sebastián Church where his was also the chore of bell-ringing. From bell-ringing he graduated to a first violinist's desk in the opera orchestra accompanying Angela Peralta during her last tour of the republic. He was with her at Mazatlán in 1883 when she was stricken with yellow fever; although but fifteen at the time, he was a mainstay of the orchestra.

After her death Juventino got back to Mexico City the best way he could, and arriving in the capital with no funds, his own father now dead, and all other resources gone, he enlisted in the army as a bandsman. Unable to endure the rigors of military life, he broke his enlistment before his term had expired. He found refuge in a friend's house, where he turned out an enormous number of salon pieces for immediate publication. He found casual employment as a violinist, and fell desperately in love. Rejected because of the instability of his fortunes, he took ship for Havana with a traveling zarzuela company. Soon after reaching Cuba, the company disbanded, and again he was left stranded. He fell ill, perhaps with typhoid, and died a short distance south of Havana at Batabanó.

If one were asked to define the particular qualities in *Sobre las Olas* which distinguish it from hundreds of Viennese waltzes, the task might prove difficult. Actually all five waltzes in the *Sobre las Olas* set are cast in four eight-bar phrases, with cadences of the most conventional variety occurring at the end of each phrase. Perhaps the secret of the popularity lies simply in the winsomeness of the tunes. The tunes in all five of the set show his fondness for skipping to and from the leading tone; but he never seems gauche doing it. Whatever the ultimate reason for *Sobre las*

Olas's popularity, Rosas deserves remembrance as a successful competitor on Johann Strauss's own stamping ground. Few of the many millions who saw "The Great Caruso" realized that the most sentimental moment in the film was a song with music by a nineteenth century Otomí Indian. Because his waltzes do not sound "Indian" Mexican music historians have treated them cavalierly. But he deserves better of them.

In Rubén M. Campos's *El Folklore Musical de las Ciudades* are printed 84 other popular salon type pieces along with *Sobre las Olas*. The enormous vogue of all this salon repertory in Mexico during the latter part of the nineteenth century proves how internationally minded the townspeople were. Their polkas, mazurkas, valses, and schottisches were all international dance types. It is no more possible to find a nationalist soul of the picturesque sombrero kind in Mexican music in salon genre (during the epoch of Porfirio Díaz) than it is to find such a Mexican soul in the music of Paniagua's or Melesio Morales's operas.

PIANO VIRTUOSI DURING THE LATTER HALF OF THE CENTURY

The first internationally renowned pianist to visit Mexico was Henri Herz, whose appearance occurred in 1849—the same year Vieuxtemps, the famous violinist, toured Mexico. With his ever watchful eye for publicity, Herz soon after his arrival announced in the newspapers his eagerness to compose a national anthem for Mexico, which still at that moment lacked one. During August of that year a committee of literary experts invited Mexican poets to submit lyrics; the words chosen were then put to music by Herz, but fortunately for Mexico, perhaps, his music failed to receive official endorsement. If his efforts at supplying music for a national anthem failed, his piano playing at least left a lasting impression.

One who profited most by his example was Tomás León (1826–93), who later became the first "professor of piano" in the 1866 Conservatorio. At his house, in fact, the idea of founding a new national conservatory was hatched. After the triumph of *Ildegonda* a group of friends met at León's house to congratulate Melesio Morales on his success; as Morales later told the story of that epochal meeting:

> One evening my friends were celebrating the triumph in León's house. . . . At an appropriate moment this speech was made: "Gentlemen,

the triumph of our friend Morales is a great victory for Mexican art. For his complete success, I congratulate the composer. . . . But in the midst of his good fortune, we must confess we have paid dearly for the satisfaction of having overcome the animosity and avarice of a foreign impresario. In order that the same difficulties may not be repeated, I propose, gentlemen, that we found a school where Mexican artists will have a chance to prepare themselves. . . . Only by training our own artists can we hope to create a truly elevated national art.[75]

León then became the first to propagandize extensively in behalf of Beethoven. He played his solo sonatas, and in conjunction with Agustín Balderas gave the first performance of Beethoven's *Symphony No. 7* (in four-hand arrangement) at a Sociedad Filarmónica concert on July 27, 1867.[76] If this should seem a rather late date for Beethoven to be driving an entering wedge in Mexico, it may be well for us to remember that not even in Rome was the Eroica Symphony heard nor the Emperor Concerto until the same decade when Sgambati premiered them at the *Sala Dante*. To León Aniceto Ortega dedicated his *Invocación á Beethoven, Opus 2,* one of the most serious Mexican piano pieces of the epoch (first performed in 1867).

León in 1871 played a Beethoven "Gran sonata" (opus number not designated) at the second of two concerts organized as part of the first Beethoven festival concerts in Mexico.[77] At these two festival concerts Morales conducted first performances of the second and fifth Symphonies with an orchestra of 86 players. The Beethoven Violin Concerto and Leonora No. 3 were also given first performances at these two concerts. León's own publications, brought out by the Mexican firm of H. Nagel, run mostly towards the salon type; but the memories of his pupils emphasize his predilection for the weightier German composers.

José Antonio Gómez, as has already been noted, brought out a series of bravura variations for piano using a jarabe for the theme. León was the second to do the same thing in an *Jarabe Nacional,* published by the firm of Bizet Hermanos. Julio Ituarte was the third to publish a series of variations on national airs in *Ecos de México.* The progress of nineteenth century virtuostic ideals is clearly apparent in these three—Gómez's in 1841 moved in Kalkbrenner's world; Ituarte's published by Nagel about 1885 in Liszt's.

Julio Ituarte (1845–1905)[78] was León's best pupil. He mastered the Thalberg-Gottschalk-Prudent vapidities current in his epoch with effortless ease and quickly became the idol of Mexican aristocracy. Although he lacked León's solid interest in Beethoven and Mozart, he soon became a more talked-of pianist simply because he catered to public taste instead of forming it. He composed a number of fantasias with such titles as these: *La Tempestad* ("The Tempest"), *La Aurora* ("The Dawn"), *El Artista muere* ("The Dying Artist"), *Las Golondrinas* ("The Swallows"). He also transcribed what was probably the first Mexican piece of program music, Beristaín's orchestral fantasy, *La Primavera* ("The Spring").

From 1868 until 1885 he taught piano at the conservatory. He gained some practical experience with stage work in 1877 when he prepared the choristers for the Peralta premiere of *Aïda*. The conductor of the orchestra at that premiere ostentatiously did without the score during the performance. Noting the tremendous impression this feat of memory produced, Ituarte resolved to be the first Mexican pianist to perform everything from memory.

After resigning his post at the conservatory to gain more time for composition he wrote a two-act zarzuela, *Sustos y Gustos,* produced in 1887 with enormous success. The music for this operetta whose action has to do with the adventures of an office worker playing truant on his pretended saint's day has unfortunately disappeared. A second zarzuela in three acts was less successful. In 1897 after tours throughout Mexico and Cuba he returned to piano teaching at the conservatory. His opinions concerning Paderewski's first appearances in Mexico (1900) make interesting reading. The audience at Paderewski's first concert was extremely slim, and he was criticized harshly in the Mexican journals for his excesses, and his failure to play the written notes and observe the written signs for expression. Ituarte said:

> Genius does not have to submit itself to the ferule of mediocrity. The majority of pianists should recite the music strictly adhering to the written notes and the written marks of expression. But the great artist makes his own laws. . . . The Polish pianist must be judged as a man apart.
> . . . Those critics who abuse him and deem his style of execution unpardonable . . . calling it blurred, indistinct, strident at times, and often abounding in wrong notes . . . are approaching his playing with the wrong attitude.[79]

After Ituarte the next virtuoso of distinction was Felipe Villanueva (1863–93) who like Rosas was a pure-blooded Indian. Villanueva's career was cut short in his thirtieth year, but not before he had written a copious amount of salon music. A specialty of his was cross rhythms, the left hand in ¾ while the right played in ¼, for instance. Several of his pieces printed in Campos's collection, *El Folklore de las Ciudades,* possess great charm.

Ricardo Castro (1864–1907) like Villanueva did not live to see the full fruition of his genius, dying in his forty-third year. But he became probably the best piano virtuoso Mexico possessed during the century.

RICARDO CASTRO: THE MOST "EUROPEIZANTE" NINETEENTH CENTURY COMPOSER

William Berrien in discussing "Latin American Music" once spoke of Castro as the most *europeizante* of the nineteenth century composers.[80] Castro undoubtedly possessed exceptional advantages for the acquiring of a Europeanized veneer. His father, a prominent man of affairs in Durango, where Castro was born February 7, 1864,[81] was elected to the Mexican Congress in 1877, and carried his family with him to the capital. The thirteen year old boy had already learned what there was to learn in Durango, and was therefore ready to study with the best teachers in the conservatory. In 1879 he began composition with Melesio Morales, and in 1881 piano with Ituarte. At the Querétaro Exposition in 1882 he won a prize and three years later he was sent to the New Orleans Cotton Exposition to represent his republic. While in the United States he traveled further north, giving recitals in Chicago, Philadelphia, and New York. When he returned to Mexico he joined with Gustavo E. Campa and Felipe Villanueva in a new *Instituto Musical,* a competing conservatory with the national. At the age of twenty-five he had made enough stir to win favorable mention in Felipe Pedrell's *Ilustración Musical Hispano Mexicana,* published at Barcelona.

He played the Grieg Concerto at the Teatro Nacional in a concert in June, 1892. Sensing the lack of any chamber music tradition in Mexico he assisted in organizing a new *Sociedad Filarmónica Mexicana,* which sponsored several notable chamber concerts late in the '90's. He played in the Schumann Piano Quintet, the A minor Tschaikowsky Piano Trio, and in the G minor Rubinstein Piano Trio, cooperating in first performances of these particular works in Mexico. In 1900 he won a post teaching composition in the Conservatorio Nacional. Morales, testy as an old eagle, venomously tried to have his former pupil ousted, but unsuccessfully.

On November 9, 1900, his opera *Atzimba,* whose libretto had to do with events during the Spanish conquest of Michoacán, was given its first performance.

In 1902 the Díaz government gave him a grant in the equivalency of 500 francs a month so he could study in Europe. A further 700 pesos for travel expenses was provided. In January, 1903, Castro arrived in Paris, where through his connections as a prizewinner from Mexico he secured a performance of his 'Cello Concerto on April 6. This particular concerto abounds in excellencies. The performer was M. Loevensohn, a Belgian, who premiered the work in Brussels shortly after giving it a Paris performance. A copy of it is to be seen in the Fleisher Collection at the Philadelphia Free Library, and a glance at it will dispel anyone's idea Castro was still unformed as a composer when he first went to Europe.

The first movement, an *allegro moderato* in C minor, contains inspired writing; the bridging of the first and second movement with a 'cello cadenza is a happy device. The *thème varié* (p. 39) which serves as a second movement modulates widely; the variations are in the manner of character variations such as Schumann tried in his *Études Symphoniques.* The third movement, a *vivo* in C major (p. 79), contains a reprise of the throbbing cantabile theme from the first movement. If there are reminiscences of Schumann or of Tschaikowsky in it, so are there reminiscences of other composers in the Elgar and in the Dvořák 'Cello Concertos. Castro's would make a welcome addition to the eternal small round of 'cello works; the orchestration is brilliant without being overbearing, and the 'cello is everywhere treated idiomatically. Castro was especially well advised in his use of register contrasts.

Two days after the 'Cello Concerto was premiered, Castro gave a piano recital at the Salle Erard. The newspaper reports of his Parisian performances, one appearing in the April 9, 1903, *Le Figaro* and the other in the April 15, 1903, *Le Monde Musical,*[82] extravagantly praised him both as a pianist and as a composer.

While he was in Paris Castro took some lessons with Eugen d'Albert, who had already done Mexican music a service by playing two of Villanueva's short pieces in his European concert programs. In May of 1904 Castro played several times in Belgium, appearing on the 17th in Brussels. He gave the first performance of his Piano Concerto, Op. 22, in Antwerp in a concert on December 28, 1904. Since the December concert included also the 'Cello Concerto again, and in addition excerpts from *Atzimba,*

Castro's three-act opera, we may profitably quote from the review which appeared in the January 1, 1905, *La Fédération Artistique:* [83]

> The composer gave a masterful performance of his Concerto for Piano, a dashing and effective work. . . . The Concerto for Violoncello contains themes of profound beauty; the orchestration, attractive in the introduction, reveals genuine mastery when the solo part begins. The level of workmanship is brilliantly sustained in the *andante* and in the *vivo.* . . . [The 'cellist] projected this well-contrived work with maximum effect. The orchestra also played Castro's *Marcha tarasca* from the lyric drama, *Atzimba;* the march is founded on popular Mexican themes picturesquely developed. . . . At the end of the concert the closing scene from *Atzimba* (for soloists, mixed chorus, and orchestra) proved a deeply moving experience. . . . In order to appreciate Castro's full worth, a review of other concertos for violoncello might prove a salutary discipline; certainly his shines out with peculiar worth above even some of the better known ones. . . .

During his European tour Castro visited Germany where he was deeply impressed by the Bayreuth festival performances. He also entered into a contract with the Leipzig firm of Friedrich Hofmeister for publication of his larger works. Hofmeister brought out the Piano Concerto, both in the conventional reduction for second piano of the orchestra part, and also in full score. Later the same firm issued his second opera, *La Légende de Rudel,* libretto in French. The Mexican firm of H. Nagel Sucesores published the piano score of *Atzimba.* Three of Castro's large works therefore became available shortly before his premature death.

Of the Piano Concerto it may be said that its merits approximate those of the First Piano Concerto by another American composer who was fortunate enough to establish a German publishing connection during his European sojourn, Edward MacDowell. The larger literature of the piano concerto has resulted in severer canons of criticism and Castro's today seems less worthy of being revived than does his 'Cello Concerto. The opening movement in A minor, *allegro moderato,* allows the piano a rather pompous entry with a dialogue between a thunderous octave bass and high chords in the treble. The cantabile duet between piano and clarinet (C major) strikes a better pose. At letter 5 in the score the diminished seventh chord receives a too thorough workout. The recapitulation proceeds conventionally with the second theme decoratively presented in A major. As in the 'Cello Concerto, the first and second movements are bridged with a cadenza; the piano cadenza, however, conspicuously lacks thematic significance. The second movement, a large ternary form, poises itself between a B Major *andante* and an A minor *allegro appassionato*. The last movement is a lively polonaise in A major. Its affinities lie not with Chopin but with the von Weber of the *Polacca brillante*. A *grandioso* at the close of the last movement recapitulates the second theme from the first movement.

From our present-day vantage point it seems the piano does too much in this concerto; the solo part too uniformly carries the musical substance. Though the orchestra, which is standard in size with an added flute and English Horn part but only two trumpets, seems always well enough treated when the piano ceases playing, its part otherwise than in interludes seems supplementary rather than complimentary. The modulations are often as abrupt as Liszt's, and the Lisztian technique betrays itself in the figuration. But if the technical difficulties are no greater than those encountered in other fin-de-siècle concertos, they do prove Castro had mastered the conventional pianism of his epoch. Even reasonably well played this concerto would as well split the ears of the groundlings as the next one.

In September, 1906, Castro returned to Mexico, having in Europe readied his opera, *La Légende de Rudel;* at the Mexican premiere the libretto had to be translated into Italian for the benefit of the everlasting Italians in Mexico. In January, 1907, he was named director of the Conservatorio Nacional, but unfortunately he died at the height of his powers in November of that same year. His death was interpreted as an occasion for national mourning, and during a three-day period all higher educational institutions observed commemorative exercises.

Despite Castro's acknowledged achievement in his own day, he is today regarded with the same polite indifference in sophisticated Mexican musical circles that MacDowell is greeted with in "advanced" circles of this country. Castro, like MacDowell, now has the reputation of having been somewhat dowdyish; the style of both composers has now, of course, completely run out of fashion. Although Castro wrote two symphonies (the first finished in August, 1883, and the second in 1887) these are even less frequently thought of today in Mexico than is MacDowell's First Indian Suite in the United States.

RELIGIOUS MUSIC IN NINETEENTH CENTURY MEXICO

As Mme. Calderón de la Barca found it, religious music had become syncretized with secular music during the turbulent years just before the mid-century. The popular villancicos and *motetes* which continued to be written during the years of struggle and Reform laws—with necessary changes of title and text—would find a safe and comfortable abiding place beside the P. P. Bliss and Ira D. Sankey specialties that crowded the popular English hymnals of the same epoch. In the popular alabados, villancicos, and motetes, published by Rubén M. Campos as representative music of their epoch, lush thirds and sixths hang with cloying monotony over their tunes; the harmonies are crushingly banal; and their most exalted moments sound like "lifts" from tenth-rate Italian operas. At mid-century when a new high altar in utterly execrable taste was installed in the metropolitan cathedral, music had catapulted to a disastrous low in the cathedral's history. But worthy musicians in priest's orders were not completely lacking; Agustín Caballero, first director of the Conservatorio Nacional (1866), enjoyed the confidence and respect of all informed musicians in the capital; [84] and there were others later such as José G. Velázquez, trained at Ratisbon,[85] and organist at the Shrine of the Virgin of Guadalupe during the '90's, who were respectable musicians.

Some few cathedrals continued to offer a bare pittance to musicians after the sequestration of property unsettled the revenues of the church, though in the main all salaries ceased. Even the Shrine of the Virgin of Guadalupe, which remained affluent during the more unpropitious moments of the century, radically reduced its scale of payments to musicians shortly after mid-century.[86] The Mexican bishop most outspoken in his efforts for the resuscitation of musical standards was Bishop Rafael S. Camacho of Querétaro who during a twenty-year period (1875–95) interested himself in reform. Under his guidance the Querétaro School of Sacred Music was founded with Guadalupe Velázquez as director, in February, 1892. The Caecilian influences transmitted through Velázquez, who never learned to value Solesmes principles until they were forced upon him, procured rather pale results, however. His own compositions, though not operatic, reach an opposite extreme of complete colorlessness.[87] They also notably lack any contrapuntal vitality.

NATIONAL AND REGIONAL DANCES

The jarabe, as we have already shown, suffered the interdict of the church during the late colonial epoch. But with independence gained, it became the most popular of the distinctive national dance types. As conventionally danced, the woman wearing a *china poblana* costume and the man wearing a *charro* suit enacted a game of courtship. The woman, playing the coquette, alternately attracted and repelled her suitor, using small and light rapid tappings of her feet to encourage his suit and then turning away at the crucial moment. Frances Toor describes the conventional ending of the jarabe thus:

> At the end comes "The Dove," during which the man follows his partner as she dances around the broad brim of his sombrero, imitating the courtship of doves. As she stoops to pick up the hat, he passes his right leg over her, and they finish by facing the audience to do "The Diana." [88]

Various regional variants of the dance were to be encountered at the close of the nineteenth century, and the standardization of the jarabe into an urban dance has caused the true jarabe-enthusiast alarm. The traveler in Mexico during recent years has usually seen a jarabe robbed of the spontaneity and freedom of the older jarabes.

It is necessary when speaking of such Mexican dance-types as the jarabe or the huapango or the sandunga, to discriminate between the dances themselves and the dance-music that accompanies them. The usual descriptions of these dances say little or nothing of the music, and a great deal about the costumes, the feet movements, the body positions, and the visual spectacle. The nineteenth century writers on the jarabe were just as prone to omit any specific description of the music [89] as are modern writers. In 1861 a Spaniard traveling in Mexico, Don Niceto de Zamacois, wrote a long panegyric of the national dance, but even he, wordy as he was, said nothing about the actual character of jarabe-music. He apostrophized the beautiful Mexican women, said Adam would return and eat his apple again for the privilege of seeing a jarabe danced, called it a dance to enliven even the cold blood of senators, invited everyone to come hear a Mexican harpist start the jarabe, and declared it a better medicine than any yet known for all the ills of man. [90] But amid all his glittering adjectives, no real description of the music occurred. As with Zamacois, so with the other writers of the century. The reason writers neglected to describe the music perhaps arose from the fact there was really so little to say about it. The music was fast, in ⅜ or ¾ usually, with 16 or 24 measures in each *son*; the *son* was an individual tune, and when the jarabe was danced five or more *sones* were sung in succession. The son with 16 measures was divided into two parts; the first eight measures were instrumental, the last eight vocal with accompaniment. Those with 24 consisted of three groups of eight measures, the first group instrumental, the second vocal, the third instrumental.

Any technical description of the jarabes that were printed would emphasize the following points: *1* The rhythms were always spirited, with an almost equal distribution of accent on all beats of the measure *2* Dotted rhythms and syncopation were frequent *3* Feminine endings were of approximately equal frequency with masculine endings (at cadences) *4* The major mode was almost invariably used *5* Tonic-dominant harmony of the most conventional variety underlay the melodies *6* Harmonization of the melodies in thirds and sixths (especially thirds) was the rule *7* Within each individual *son* no modulations were attempted *8* Simple modulations from tonic to dominant or sub-dominant were frequent between one *son* and the next *9* Keys with only one or two accidentals—at most—were the rule *10* A flourish and climax at the end of the whole series of *sones* was usual. The printed jarabes were almost always for piano solo, but in actual performance a combination of harp, string bass, small guitar, and flute provided the instrumental accompaniment for the dance. Bands comprising such heterogeneous ensembles have commonly been called *sones mariaches*.

The huapango, a dance indigenous to the hot country between Tampico and Veracruz, capriciously alternates rhythms between ¾ in one measure and ⅜ in the next. The rapid gait of the beats and the alternation of accents produces an extremely agitated and nervous dance. The word *huapango* has been variously derived. Some etymologists believe it to be a corruption of the Nahuatl *cuahpanco—cuaitl*, which means a piece of wood, *ipan*, meaning on or over, and *co*, place. Others believe it to be a corruption of *Huaxtecas de Pango* (= Panuco). Whatever derivation be accepted, the dance itself is mestizo, not Indian.[91]

A typical accompanying ensemble would be a violin, two large guitars, and a small guitar. Another rhythmic characteristic to be noted in addition to the shift between ¾ and ⅜ would be the frequent sharp accent on the last eighth note in the measure. A point of harmonic interest is the frequent use of interior tonic pedals. The site for a huapango ordinarily is a wooden platform. Men and women dance as couples; the men sing, the women do not. Frequently all the singing is done by one soloist in a high falsetto. The nearest Spanish analogue of the huapango would be the fandango.

The sandunga, a dance now completely out of fashion, but once popular in the Isthmus and especially around Oaxaca, was a slower dance than jarabe or huapango, resembling most a dreamy waltz. This dance was a couples dance, with men and women facing each other in rows. The word sandunga in Spanish means "fascination, allurement, or gracefulness." The music requires no special remarks; any moderato waltz in the minor mode could be used for a sandunga.

THE NINETEENTH CENTURY IN RÉSUMÉ

Perhaps as desirable a way as any for gaining an overall perspective of nineteenth century musical life in Mexico will be to set down a summary list of weaknesses and then, by way of contrast, a summary list of strengths. The weaknesses were palpable: *1* Italian opera was the consuming passion *2* The piano, while it became a universal household instrument, was not valued for its own sake, but rather because it was a convenient maid-of-all-work *3* Chamber music hardly existed *4* Symphonic music was unknown outside Mexico City *5* Amateurs, rather than professionals, dominated musical circles *6* Music criticism of the type known in the European capitals after 1850 never made any appearance in Mexico until after the end of the Porfirian epoch.

The counterbalancing strengths may now be listed: *1* The Mexican public was avidly musical, in the sense that high and low professed an overwhelming fondness for music *2* There was a large enough public ready to buy piano music—even if of the salon type—to sustain five publishing houses in business [92] *3* As a matter of principle the government accepted music activities as entitled to subsidy *4* A national conservatory offering free instruction was founded *5* Though modeled on Italian lines, a very large number of operas were written by Mexicans *6* The preponderancy of amateurs was desirable while opportunities for a livelihood in serious music remained as scarce as they were during the century *7* Music was regarded as a worthy vocation even among the highest classes, which was not true in the United States 8 Though beginning with the ubiquitous Italians in the saddle, gradually they were pushed out along with other foreigners, so that Mexicans themselves might occupy such prestigious posts as directorships of conservatories, conductorships of orchestras, and so on.

Weighing the weaknesses and then the strengths we feel justified in calling the century one of significant advance, musically speaking. As diverse as were the different colorful political leaders of the century, they all shared one trait in common—a belief that music was important enough in national life to merit government support. The United States has not yet arrived at this cardinal principle. A study of the careers of Santa Anna, Maximilian, and Porfirio Díaz, to name only three diverse political figures of the century, shows that even at critical moments in their administrations they supported—even if very poorly—professional music activities.

Fairly to judge the century one should compare Mexico with other Latin countries of the same epoch; as was pointed out in relation to the dates when first performances of Beethoven symphonies occurred, even in such a favored location as Rome, his works began to be performed only five years or so before their first orchestral presentation in Mexico City.

Finally one ought also to remember that however welcome Díaz made the foreign monarchs of finance, during his régime considerable progress was made in establishing the vital principle that Mexican musical opportunities legitimately belonged to Mexicans themselves. At a time when United States conservatories vied with each other in bidding for foreign directors, the Conservatorio Nacional, and other regional music schools, engaged Mexicans exclusively. By 1900 Mexicans had decided to dominate their own musical life for better or for worse. For worse one might say, looking at the caliber of some of the music performed and composed. But in the minds of many Mexicans today, this "worse" stage was necessary in order that a "better" one might finally arrive.

NOTES

1. Alejo Carpentier, *La música en Cuba* (México: Fondo de Cultura Economica, 1946), pp. 65–71.
2. Juan Bautista Plaza, "Music in Caracas during the Colonial Period," *The Musical Quarterly*, April, 1943, p. 212.
3. Guillermo Furlong, *Músicos Argentinos*, p. 170.

4. José Ignacio Perdomo Escobar, *Historia de la Música en Columbia* (Bogotá: Biblioteca Popular . . . , 1945), p. 33. The printing, however, was to have been done in Spain.

5. The Coliseo Nuevo, opened in 1753, was actually the fourth theater erected in New Spain. See Enrique de Olavarría y Ferrari, *Reseña Histórica del Teatro en México* (México: Imprenta "La Europea," 1895), I, 28–9. During the nineteenth century the Coliseo Nuevo, after refurbishing, became known as the Teatro de México or the Teatro Principal. Late viceregal opera was produced in this playhouse.

6. Mary Neal Hamilton, *Music in Eighteenth Century Spain* (Urbana: University of Illinois Press, 1937), p. 20. Gilbert Chase, however, has referred to *La Selva sin Amor* as a genuine opera (*Musical Quarterly*, July, 1939, p. 300) ; whether or not it was sung throughout or interspersed with spoken dialogue cannot perhaps now be definitely known since the music has long disappeared. At its inception an aristocratic entertainment, the zarzuela became during the eighteenth century distinctly middle-class entertainment.

7. On tonadillas, see Hamilton, *op. cit.*, pp. 47–9, 53–70.

8. Two other types of musical skit that were popular in the late viceregal theaters were the *loa* (a prologue partly sung and partly spoken), and the *entremés* (a burlesque interlude between acts).

9. *Diario de México* (I, 100), October 25, 1805.

10. *Ibid.* (I, 236), November 25, 1805.

11. *Ibid.* (I, 264), December 2, 1805.

12. *Ibid.* (I, 264), December 2, 1805. For the story of *Siana y Silvio* see the *Diario*, November 18, 1806. In an Arcadian setting a lovesick shepherd courted a coy shepherdess; she stoutly resisted him, however, until they both were overtaken by storm. The storm over, she remained in his arms for a happy ending. It seems that in the December, 1805, presentation one of Medina's daughters played the shepherd, and the other the shepherdess.

13. Medina's obituary appeared in the *Diario*, November 18, 1806.

14. Luciano Cortés was *primer galán* of the Companía del Coliseo Nuevo; the members of the troupe with their respective functions are listed in Olavarría y Ferrari, *op. cit.*, I, 177.

15. *Diario de México*, April 14, 1816.

16. *Ibid.*, April 21, 1816; in this issue the salaries of sixteen orchestral players are given "para que el público se entere de los costos de esta empresa."

17. The disturbed political situation in 1816 contributed to the ruin of the Coliseo.

18. The *Gaceta Extraordinaria del Gobierno de México*, November 4, 1817, carried notice of a march by Corral dedicated to Apodaca in the most servile terms. See Olavarría y Ferrari, I, 192–3.

19. Cristiani's "grande ópera en tres actos titulada *El Solitario*, cuyo heroico argumento está sacado de la conocida historia de Carlos el Temerario" was performed December 2, 1824, and repeated later in the same month. See Olavarría y Ferrari, I, 215–6.

20. *Diario de México*, October 24, 1807.

21. *Ibid.*, December 16, 1806.

22. *Ibid.*, November 18, 1806.

23. *Gazeta de México*, July 2, 1793.

24. *Ibid.*, October 21, 1796.

25. *Ibid.*, September 12, 1786.

26. Saldívar, *op. cit.*, p. 193.

27. *Ibid.*, p. 194 (*Gazeta de México*, XII, 200).

28. On the Cuban *contradanza*, see Carpentier, *op. cit.*, pp. 96–107.

29. Guitar melody in numerical cipher; piano accompaniment added.

30. Haydn's *Seven Last Words* long enjoyed tremendous popularity in Spain; in his own piano arrangement (Op. 49) it became a favorite with amateurs. De Falla's first appearance in public was as a performer of this piano version.

31. *Diario de México*, October 24, 1805. "Andrés Madrid, blind, will insert native tunes in the playing rolls of Spanish musical clocks."

32. Saldívar, *op. cit.*, p. 270.

33. *Ibid.*, p. 269.

34. *Ibid.*, p. 276.

35. "Conspiración de Valladolid de 1813," *Boletín del Archivo General de la Nación*, July–August–September, 1932, p. 472.

36. The biographical details in this section are derived from Jesús C. Romero, *José Mariano Elízaga* (México: Ediciones del Palacio de Bellas Artes, 1934).

37. *Diario de México*, July 3, 1809 (article by Renato de Mosvos).

38. Reprinted in Romero, *op. cit.*, pp. 106–7.

39. José Mariano Elízaga, *Elementos de Música* . . . (México: Imprenta del Supremo Gobierno en Palacio, 1823), p. iv.

40. *Ibid.*, p. vi.

41. "Gothic" was a favorite word of execration with Eximeno also.

42. Felipe Pedrell, *P. Antonio Eximeno* (Madrid: Unión Musical Española, 1920).

43. Antonio Eximeno, *Duda de D. Antonio Eximeno sobre El Ensayo Fundamental* . . . (Madrid: Imp. Real, 1797), p. 21.

44. Romero, *op. cit.*, p. 142.

45. Romero, "Historia del Conservatorio," *Nuestra Música*, July, 1946, p. 176.

46. *Ibid.*, p. 175.

47. Rossi, who after his return home became director of the Milan Conservatory, arrived in Mexico in January, 1836. For his Mexican career see Luis Castillo Ledón, "Los Mexicanos Autores de Óperas," *Anales del Museo Nacional de Arqueología, Historia y Etnología*, 1910, p. 327.

48. Bullock, pp. 169–170.

49. Mme. Calderón de la Barca, *Life in Mexico* (Everyman Edition), p. 354.

50. *Ibid.*, p. 338.

51. J. J. von Tschudi, *Travels in Peru* (New York: Wiley & Putnam, 1847), pp. 59–60. Tschudi (p. 71) remarked all the ladies of Lima "are passionately fond of music. Most of them play the piano-forte or the guitar, and also sing; but for want of instruction neither their playing nor their singing is above mediocrity." The curse of mediocre instruction lay over Mexico and Peru alike.

52. Mme. Calderón de la Barca, p. 139.

53. *Ibid.*, p. 137.

54. *Ibid.*, p. 198.

55. *Ibid.*, p. 286.

56. *Ibid.*, p. 156.

57. For biographical details, see Manuel G. Revilla, "Cenobio Paniagua," *Revista Musical Mexicana*, II (1942), 178 ff., 202 ff., 216, 234, 251–2.

58. For biographical details see Ignacio M. Altamirano, "D. Melesio Morales," reprinted in *Revista Musical Mexicana*, III (1943), 10 ff., 35 ff., 63 ff., 110 ff., 180 ff., 206–7, 228 ff.

59. Melesio Morales, *Reseña que Leyo a sus Amigos* (México, 1907), p. 18.

60. The only significant figure unmentioned in Morales's catalogue of students was Gustavo E. Campa, but Morales called him a Judas also.

61. *Anita*, words only, published at Mexico City, Tipografía de "El Tiempo."

62. The vocal score with piano reduction of the orchestra is now in the possession of G. Baqueiro Fóster. I am much indebted to him for his kind permission to study this and other inaccessible scores in his private collection.

63. Gustavo E. Campa, *Críticas Musicales* (Paris, 1911), p. 332.

64. For a convenient summary of biographical details see Otto Mayer-Serra's article, "Peralta," in his encyclopedia, *Música y Músicos de Latino-América*.

65. Olavarría y Ferrari, III, 16.

66. Facsimile opposite p. 140 in Mayer-Serra, *Panorama de la Música Mexicana* . . . (México: El Colegio de México, 1941).

67. Castillo Ledón, *op. cit.*, p. 340.

68. This list is supplied by Romero in "La Ópera en México," *La Ópera en Yucatán* (México: Ediciones "Guión de América," 1947), pp. 52–3.

69. Olavarría y Ferrari, III, 56–7.

70. José G. Montes de Oca in "Retratos Existentes en la Biblioteca Pública de la Ciudad de Guadalajara," 1924 (typewritten essay deposited at the Biblioteca Benjamín Franklin, México, D.F.), lists a Concerto for Piano and Orchestra by Juan A. Aguilar, a "Seven Last Words" by Abel Loreto, and a *Himno Guadalupano* by Tiburcio Saucedo, as examples of the "meatier" compositions by Guadalajara composers in the pre-World War I epoch.

71. Jesús Galindo y Villa, "El Himno Nacional Mexicano," *Anales del Museo Nacional de Arqueología, Historia y Etnografía*, 1927, p. 75.

72. Consult the article "Rosas" in *Música y Músicos de Latino-América* for a convenient summary of biographical details.

73. These pieces are preserved in the Conservatorio Nacional Library.

74. Rubén M. Campos, *El Folklore Musical de las Ciudades* (México: Secretaría de Educación Pública, 1930), p. 183.

75. Melesio Morales, *Reseña* . . . , p. 13. Dr. Durán was the orator of the occasion.

76. Olavarría y Ferrari, III, 11. A four-hand performance of the Pastoral (with Ortega) is also recorded.

77. *Ibid.*, III, 100–1.

78. For Ituarte's biography see Manuel G. Revilla, "D. Julio Ituarte," *Revista Musical Mexicana*, II, 83 ff., 113 ff.

79. *Ibid.*, p. 115.

80. William Berrien, "Latin American Music," *Concerning Latin American Culture* (New York: Columbia University Press, 1940), p. 157. Berrien thought Castro's "Europeanization" was a shallow veneer.

81. For biographical information concerning Castro see Romero, *Durango en la Evolución Musical de México* (México: Ediciones "Guión de América," 1949), pp. 25–30.

82. Quoted in Gustavo E. Campa, *Críticas Musicales*, p. 340 and p. 345.

83. *Ibid.*, p. 348.

84. Guillermo Prieto, *Memorias de Mis Tiempos* (México: Libreria . . . C. Bouret, 1906), I, 101. Prieto echoed the common opinion concerning Caballero's standing as musician.

85. Ezequiel de la Isla, "El Padre J. Guadalupe Velázquez," *Revista Musical Mexicana*, I, 88.

86. The basilica orchestra in 1835 included 8 violinists, 2 clarinetists, a flautist, bassoonist, timpanist, and unspecified numbers of trumpeters, 'cellists, and string bassists; see *Colegiata de Guadalupe: Directorio para el gobierno de los ministros de orquesta aprobado y mandado observar por el muy ilustre cabildo de esta insigne Colegiata de S. M. de Guadalupe* (México: Grabado de la Guadalupana, 1835). When this "lush" organization was in danger of extinction the musicians banded together in a Caecilian Philharmonic Society (1845), attempting to control prices by musicians' union methods. For the activities of this musicians' syndicate organized by José María Bustamente see *El Siglo XIX*, December 3 and 4, 1845. Unfortunately the musicians succeeded only in worsening their economic plight, especially as far as church employment went.

87. An uninteresting and pallid *Ave Maria* is reproduced in *Revista Musical Mexicana*, I, 84–5; also an equally correct but dull *Ave Maris Stella*, p. 86.

88. Frances Toor, "Mexican Folk Dances," *Renascent Mexico* (New York: Covici-Friede, 1935), p. 182.

89. Antonio García Cubas, *El Libro de Mis Recuerdos* (México: Editorial Patria s.a., n.d.), pp. 210–1, and elsewhere, does print the tunes of various jarabes, but without offering any analysis.

90. Gabriel Saldívar, *El Jarabe: Baile Popular Mexicano* (México: Talleres Gráficos de la Nación, 1937), p. 2.

91. Gerónimo Baqueiro Fóster, "El Huapango," *Revista Musical Mexicana* I (1942), 174–83.

92. Baqueiro F., "Aportación Musical de México para formación de la Biblioteca Americana de Caracas: 1882–3," *Revista Musical Mexicana* II (1942), 28. In addition to Rivera hijo y Cía, H. Nagel Sucesores, Wagner y Levien, and D. Carlos Godard, there was another firm, Bizet Hnos., making the five. This list of Mexican piano pieces and songs with piano accompaniment, reaching a total of 391 items, reveals the high concentration of publishing activity during the early years of Porfirio Díaz's presidency (the so-called "Porfirian" period).

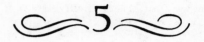

FULFILLMENT DURING THE
TWENTIETH CENTURY

Thoroughly drastic changes overtook every phase of Mexican political, social, and cultural life after the expulsion of the eighty-one-year-old President Porfirio Díaz in 1911. The Mexican historian of our own time, because of these drastic changes, tends to see everything anterior to 1911 as *ancien régime*. The music of the latter Porfirian years, like the painting and architecture, is nowadays brushed aside as pompous, dowdy, and insufferably inflated. Composers, moreover, who attracted President Díaz's favorable attention or who received prizes at the hands of his lieutenants, have all been sentenced to obloquy by the succeeding generation of revolutionary composers for the crime of having won his approval.

Late Porfirian opera has, in particular, supplied an easy target for revolutionary attack. The operas of Castro, Campa, Elorduy, and others, have all been lumped together as "simply entertainment for the effete capitalist classes, largely foreign, who ruled Mexico during Díaz's later years."

Doubtless Gustavo E. Campa's 1901 opera *Le Roi Poète*—dealing as it does with the life of a fifteenth century poet-king, Nezahualcoyotl of Texcuco—does now seem mawkish because of the way it sugar-coated and glamorized the Aztec past. The libretto, in French because Campa adored French music and because no singers were supposed to have wanted to sing so commonplace a language as Spanish, seems a strange anomaly. And doubtless Ricardo Castro's *La Légende de Rudel*, also with a French libretto, but sung at the Teatro Arbeu in Mexico City during October,

1906, in Italian, seems nowadays to have been a too unutterably precious affair.

"LA LÉGENDE DE RUDEL" [2]

By what right, one asks, should a Mexican opera have concerned itself with a twelfth century Provençal troubadour, Rudel? According to the opera, Rudel, already bound in spirit to a distant ideal of perfect womanhood, nevertheless plighted his faith to a French maiden. As Henri Brody (Castro's librettist) wove the story, Rudel after deserting the hapless Ségolaine then took ship for the East. En route, however, the Almighty invoked a terrible storm, and the ship was like to have foundered because of his presence aboard. Less grateful than Jonah, Rudel when cast ashore blasphemed the Eternal Providence. He, however, was picked up and carried into the presence of that paragon of beauty, the Countess of Tripoli. In her presence he sang a golden-throated swan's demise, and forthwith died at her feet. She then summoned her attendants to apostrophize in choral song his departing spirit.

In this opera Castro abandoned act divisions and accepted divisions into episodes instead. Each episode then was subdivided into scenes; the first episode (two scenes) was laid in France, the second (three scenes) aboard ship, and the third (seven scenes) in Tripoli. Rudel's part was written for tenor, Ségolaine's for soprano, the countess's for contralto, the ship's pilot's for baritone, the pilgrim's for baritone, and the messenger's for high baritone. Three choruses, one of pilgrims, one of sailors, and one of the countess's women, also were called for in the score.

Before writing off *La Légende de Rudel*, however, simply as a period piece, one might well for the sake of historical perspective compare it with a famous American opera premiered the same year—Frederick S. Converse's attractive but outmoded *The Pipe of Desire*, first given at Boston on January 31, 1906, and then later heard in New York. This opera, as is well known, had the honor of being the first by an American produced at the Metropolitan. Even though it received this recognition, however, it cannot be said that a careful scene-by-scene comparison of the Converse with the Castro opera reveals the first as in any noticeable way superior to the second. On the contrary, a careful inspection of the two reveals that Castro had quite as much to say musically as Converse, and was technically prepared to say it.

Because Castro dedicated *La Légende* to Don José Ives Limantour, Díaz's minister of finance, who was supposed to have given the country away to foreign financiers, and because moreover Castro was patronized by the "científicos"—a hated political group—Castro's reputation plummeted when a new political party came into power. But even if not again produced after Díaz fell from power, *La Légende* deserves a better judgment than has sometimes been given it. Moments such as Ségolaine's love-duet with Rudel, or the storm scene with its thunderings and lightnings, or the languorous orientale, are flavorful music in the same way Saint-Saëns's *Fifth Piano Concerto* with its trip to the Nile is flavorful music. Even if dated, such music has the virtue of typifying an era.

CAMPA'S INDICTMENT OF THE MASSES

Campa and Castro by no means appealed to the generality of Mexican audiences. They were both distinctly aware of their limited audiences. Campa was moreover so unwise as to set down on paper his unkind opinion of what he was pleased to call the brute Mexican herd. When later the revolution broke, he could not be forgiven for his open-mouthed disdain of the commoners of Mexico. In one of his more forthright essays he wrote as follows concerning the Mexican public-at-large:

> If as a conscientious artist I am obliged to defer and bow before the opinions and the almighty caprice of a heterogeneous mass of people, unequally educated, and many with dubious cultural backgrounds—a mass of people which is called "the public" . . . —then I protest volubly. . . . We talk in high-sounding terms of our appreciation of the classics . . . of Haydn, . . . —but his works are never performed amongst us; of Mozart, . . . who has however never won the approval of Mexican audiences; . . . we speak of Beethoven, . . . but know his symphonies only in the poor four-hand reductions that circulate here; . . . we know nothing of Brahms.
>
> I do not blame anyone for this ignorance; but I do find in this ignorance of truly great masterpieces support for my contention that the public cannot competently decide on the merits of the great masterpieces. . . . The public, in the broadest sense, is after all not the friend of high art in Mexico, and cannot pretend to be. Opera costs three pesos, sometimes four or five. But bullfights cost five to ten pesos, and a box at a bullfight eighty pesos, and days before our bullfights the public in huge numbers

lines up to buy seats. Do they for operas?—hardly. . . . What the
Mexican public really likes is bullfights.[3]

Campa, director of the Conservatorio Nacional at the time he wrote
this indictment, published it along with several other essays on Mexican
music life at the safe distance of Paris (1911), but if he unfavorably
criticized the Mexican "public" for preferring bullfights to operas the
Mexican public reciprocated in disliking him as a puffed-up follower of
foreign music fads.

JULIÁN CARRILLO (1875—)

It is customary in discussing Mexican composers to speak of Melesio
Morales as the "paladin" of the Italian school of composition, of Gustavo
E. Campa as the "paladin" of the French school, and of Julián Carrillo
as the "paladin" of the German school. Although Carrillo was by no
means the first Mexican to write symphonies he was the first to win performances of a symphony of his in Germany, and the first to undertake
an extensive period of training in a German conservatory.

He was born in San Luis Potosí, and early demonstrated talent for the
violin. At twenty he enrolled in the Conservatorio Nacional in the capital,
and studied harmony with Morales. His progress was so rapid in violin-
playing that President Díaz in admiration for his gifts presented him in
1899 with an Amati and nominated him to a prize for foreign study. The
same year Carrillo traveled to Germany and enrolled at the Leipzig
Conservatory; he studied composition with Jadassohn and conducting
with Hans Sitt, and played under Nikisch in the Gewandhaus orchestra.
After completing the Leipzig course in 1902 he transferred to Ghent
Conservatory, where after another two years he won a prize in violin
playing.

He was twenty-seven when his *Symphony No. 1* in D was first conceived and performed (Leipzig), and it may therefore be classed as a
mature work. In it, Carrillo demonstrated a gift for broad, sonorous
orchestral writing in the German romantic vein. As a historical note, Carrillo later appended to the score this bit of fact: "This symphony was the
first written by a Mexican composer that gained a performance in Germany; a German orchestra conducted by a Mexican Indian played it."
A synopsis of thematic material follows:

Dedicated to President Díaz, Carrillo's first symphony was enthusiastically approved at its inaugural performance in Mexico under Carlos
J. Meneses's baton, July 2, 1905. Immediately after the Mexican premiere
of his first symphony Carrillo set to work on a second, which awaited
1912, however, for its first hearing. The second was cast in C major; after
a long slow introduction, longer than that of his first symphony, the
allegro started with this theme:

The year before introducing his second symphony Carrillo was chosen
the Mexican delegate to the International Music Congress, and attended
sessions at Rome and London. Upon his return he occupied for a time a
central position in Mexican musical life. Conductor of what was called a
Beethoven orchestra, he was in the same kind of advantageous limelight
which later surrounded Chávez. Like Chávez he was able to go to New
York and there to divulge his own music, though he did not conduct as
prestigious orchestras as Chávez was later invited to conduct in the United
States. During the 1916–17 season, however, Carrillo was sufficiently
active in and about New York to spread his name in the metropolitan
dailies.

In 1922 he wrote his first five pieces in a new atonal style calling for
microtones. Signaling the advent of a new musical style, Carrillo called
his first piece in microtones, "Prelude to Columbus." Carrillo's name for
his microtone system has been *Sonido Trece*, which means "thirteenth
sound." The significance of Carrillo's name for his new microtone style
is easily explained: twelve chromatic intervals divided the octave in the

old system, but in his new system of smaller divisions, "in-between" notes must be inserted into the conventional chromatic scale. Any "in-between" note inserted between successive notes in the twelve-note chromatic scale is a "thirteenth" sound. Hence the term, *Sonido Trece.*

Alois Hába in Czechoslovakia has been another twentieth century composer who has interested himself in microtones; but since Carrillo feels he pioneered before Hába, and in fact dates the inception of his interest in microtones as early as 1895, he does not wish to be spoken of in the same breath with Hába. The notation of microtones, in particular, Carrillo feels to have been a fresh discovery of his own. He has honestly considered himself an original inventor of a new system of music notation, a system of notation by numbers instead of notes on a five-line staff.

His system of number notation works like this: the note C is represented by the numeral 0; C ♯ or D ♭ by the numeral 8; D by 16; D ♯ or E ♭ by 24; E by 32; F by 40; F ♯ or G ♭ by 48; and so forth on up the chromatic scale. In-between pitches are represented by in-between numerals. Carrillo feels that for practical purposes "sixteenth of tones" represent the ultimate refinement in pitch distinction. The different octaves in which a particular note may be heard are in Carrillo's system indicated by a system of dashes above, below, or through the numeral used to designate the note in question. A red line drawn horizontally across the page in Carrillo's system represents middle C.

As anyone familiar with organ tablatures already knows, the system of using numerals to designate notes is a very old idea; Cabezón and Correa de Arauxo used it. What is new about Carrillo's idea is the potentiality his system affords for writing "in-between" pitches. He feels that the modern development of electronic instruments, where pitches differing by only a single vibration can if desired be produced, opens up new musical vistas. As yet no electronic instrument producing "in-between" pitches (except the theremin) has been widely exploited. But in time, Carrillo has felt, the electronic manufacturers will commercially produce instruments capable of sounding middle C at 256 vibrations per second, a sharper C only a cent of a tone higher, another two cents higher, and so on. When this development occurs, he feels his system of numeral notation will prove indispensable.

Carrillo has elaborately expounded his ideas on notation in a *Teoría Logica,* published by him in a handsome private edition. His disciples in Mexico regard his discoveries with much the same reverence that Schillinger's disciples in the United States regard the Schillinger system. Carrillo's "Sonido 13" music has, moreover, not gone completely unperformed. In 1931 Leopold Stokowski interested himself sufficiently in "Sonido 13" music to program Carrillo's *Preludio á Colón;* again in 1951 Stokowski returned to Carrillo's music, giving a first performance of *Horizontes* in Pittsburgh on November 30. Later in the same season he played *Horizontes* in Baltimore and Washington also; Carrillo came to Washington to acknowledge applause at the latter performance.

While devoting himself to the writing of music in fractional tones, Carrillo has not puristically eschewed other more conventional types of composition. In the Fleisher Collection at the Free Public Library in Philadelphia are deposited scores of Carrillo's tone-poem *Penumbras: En el Paseo de la Reforma* (1930), and *Xochimilco* (1935). *Penumbras* ("Half-shadows along the Reforma boulevard") depicts in impressionist manner a twilight stroll along Mexico City's most famous boulevard. An English horn accompanied by muted strings laced with harp and celeste filigree discloses the ambulatory theme. *Xochimilco* picturizes the famous floating gardens every tourist sees while visiting Mexico. Instead of the whole-tone scale clichés so rampant in impressionist music, Carrillo builds his own arbitrary scales in both these pieces. In *Xochimilco* he exploits a seven-note scale with two augmented seconds. The first theme employs a C-sharp minor scale, but with a flatted fifth degree; the second theme employs an F-minor scale, but also with a flatted fifth degree.

Carrillo, unlike many composers, has had time to devote himself to various successful business enterprises, and therefore has not been reduced to shameful penury in old age. In the 1920's he was able to relinquish his Conservatorio Nacional teaching connection without financial detriment to himself. He has also been able to offer his children exceptional educational advantages. His daughter has been a keyboard exponent of certain microtone pieces and has traveled to Europe twice with her father in order to play his works at various international music congresses.

MANUEL M. PONCE (1882–1948)

Ponce, internationally renowned as the composer of the song, *Estrellita,* like Carrillo also grew to maturity during the Porfirian epoch. His early compositions were as unlike his later ones as Stravinsky's *L'Oiseau de Feu* is unlike *Orpheus.* Ponce's growth was perhaps a more organic growth than Carrillo's, and unlike the latter, he attempted no overthrow of conventional notation procedures.

Since his death in 1948, the Mexican public has increasingly taken Ponce to heart, and at present his "little star" (Estrellita means "little star") has grown into a great one, so that he now shines perhaps as the major star of Mexican music before Chávez. Honoring his memory, a room for chamber concerts in the Mexico City National Palace of Fine Arts has been renamed *Sala Manuel M. Ponce*. Ponce's works, moreover, continue to receive posthumous publication. In the second quarterly issue of *Nuestra Música*, 1950 series, Dr. Jesús Romero, eminent musicographer, devoted almost forty pages to a documentary record of the maestro's private and public life. The authenticity of every document was furthermore checked by submitting the article to Ponce's widow, Señora Clema M. de Ponce, for any necessary corrections. From an inspection of the data assembled by Dr. Romero we can peer into the inner circumstances of Ponce's life; the following summary is an attempt at abridging Romero's forty-page article.

Ponce's father, Felipe de Jesús Ponce, had been a Maximilianist, and therefore was in temporary exile from his home city when his famous-to-be son, a twelfth child, was born at Fresnillo, Zacatecas, December 8, 1882. The following year, however, the family was able to return to Aguascalientes, a town some three hundred miles northwest of the capital, which for Ponce, despite his later international wanderings, always remained "home." At the age of nine the child composed his first piece, *La Marcha del Sarampión* ("The March of Measles"), written during an attack of the childhood disease. At ten he started singing in a boy choir at San Diego Church in Aguascalientes, where his brother (the third child) was priest. At thirteen he became assistant organist, and at fifteen organist in the same church. At eighteen he came to Mexico City and spent a year studying at the Conservatorio Nacional, but was dissatisfied with the instruction he received. He returned to Aguascalientes, and at twenty began teaching solfège in the local conservatory ("academy of music"). The principal event in 1903 was a December concert in his home town during which he performed various Bagatelles he had written before a group of visiting notables from the capital.

At twenty-two he began his wider wanderings. He played in 1904 in Guadalajara, San Luis Potosí, and St. Louis, Missouri; and then took ship at New York in November of that year bound for Europe. When in Italy he applied to Marco Enrico Bossi for tuition, but Bossi refused him, saying: "Your style is too old-fashioned; your music would have been up-to-date in 1830 but not in 1905. You have talent but have been improperly trained." Ponce then studied with Luigi Torchi in the Liceo Musicale at Bologna. After a year in Italy he went on to Germany, and in 1906 played the Bach D major Partita in a June 18 recital at the Beethoven Hall in Berlin. At the end of 1906 he was ready to return to Mexico; but his German friends who delighted in German folk-song insisted he waste no further time in bringing to light the folk-music treasures of Mexico, urging him not too exclusively to devote himself to the "European classics."

Back in Aguascalientes he set up a private studio, but in July, 1908, was called to fill a temporary teaching position in the Conservatorio Nacional at Mexico City. During 1909 he toured with the Saloma Quartet, alternating his piano solos with their string quartets, or cooperating in such a number as the Dvořák Quintet. In January, 1910, he founded a piano studio in Mexico City. Among his first pupils was Carlos Chávez, who was eleven in 1910. Chávez studied piano four years with Ponce, and preserved a filial affection for him throughout life. Ponce pioneered in teaching Debussy in Mexico, and the first all-Debussy program was given by Ponce's pupils on June 24, 1912. Chávez, now thirteen, opened the program with *Clair de lune*.

The first large work of Ponce was his Piano Concerto, which he premiered on July 7, 1912, at the opening concert of the Orquesta Beethoven series in the Teatro Arbeu, Julián Carrillo conducting. Two days later at an all-Ponce concert in the same Teatro Arbeu the concerto was repeated with Ponce again at the piano, and Carrillo conducting. During 1912 and '13 Ponce was busy composing his inimitable *canciones mexicanas; Marchita el Alma* appeared in December, 1913, and the group from which *Estrellita* is extracted in February, 1914. During these revolutionary years Ponce tried his hand not only at folk-song arrangements, but also at essays in behalf of a native folk-music development. In one essay he wrote:

Our salons welcomed only foreign music in 1910, such as Italianate romanzas and operatic arias transcribed for piano. Their doors remained resolutely closed to the *canción mexicana* until at last revolutionary cannon in the north announced the imminent destruction of the old order. . . . Amid the smoke and blood of battle were born the stirring revolutionary

songs soon to be carried throughout the length and breadth of the land.
Adelita, Valentina, and *La Cucaracha,* were typical revolutionary songs
soon popularized throughout the republic. Nationalism captured music at
last. Old songs, almost forgotten, but truly reflecting the national spirit,
were revived, and new melodies for new corridos were composed. Singers
traveling about through the republic spread far and wide the new nationalist song; everywhere the idea gained impetus that the republic should have
its own musical art faithfully mirroring its òwn soul.[4]

Ponce went to Cuba in March, 1915, and remained there until June,
1917; occasional interruptions included a trip to New York where he
gave an Aeolian Hall recital of his own works on March 27, 1916. As
usually occurs in New York when a previously unknown person attempts
a program of original works, scant attention was paid Ponce's Aeolian
Hall concert. For one or another reasons Ponce in later life regretted his
United States associations. His Aeolian program occurred in March, and
the next June (1916) he offered his services to the Mexican consul in
Havana at the time partial mobilization was effected (in consequence of
the Columbus, New Mexico, incident). He was not accepted for duty,
however, because it was felt his artistic services were potentially more
valuable than his military services. He visited his Aguascalientes home
at the end of 1916, and definitely moved back to Mexico in July, 1917,
when he established his own studio ("Academia Beethoven") in Mexico
City. In September, 1917, he married Clema Maurel in the Church of
Our Lady of Lourdes. In December he conducted the Orquesta Sinfónica
Nacional. The next year he brought out his piano and orchestra *Balada
Mexicana.* In 1919 he edited (at first in association with Rubén M.
Campos) twelve numbers of the *Revista Musical de México.*

Ponce in 1925 was named "Professor de perfeccionamiento de piano"
in the Conservatorio Nacional, but soon after his nomination he set out for
another extended European trip. He avidly interested himself in the
latest trends abroad and settled in Paris where he consulted regularly
with Paul Dukas. Marc Pincherle has written charmingly of the impressions Ponce left on his numerous friends in the French capital during the
seven years Ponce remained there before returning to Mexico. During
this second extended European trip—Ponce's first having been made,
as we saw, during 1905-7—his musical style became immeasurably more
contrapuntal and his rhythms tauter. When he returned to Mexico in

1932 he came as an established European celebrity. He was immediately named an interim Director of the Conservatorio Nacional, and the sheaf of orchestral compositions he brought back from his European sojourn strikingly advanced his musical reputation in the home country. On November 20, 1934, Stokowski played a symphonic triptych, *Chapultepec*, in Carnegie Hall, New York, after having premiered it four days earlier in Philadelphia. In 1939 Chávez revived Ponce's 1912 Piano Concerto. In 1941 Ponce visited South America for the first time, and was fêted at Montevideo and Santiago de Chile. At Montevideo Ponce conducted the first performance of a newly composed work, his *Concierto del Sur*.

After another one of the many hiatuses that marked Ponce's association with the Conservatorio Nacional he resumed teaching there in 1942. On August 20, 1943, his masterly Violin Concerto was premiered under Chávez's baton with Henry Szering fulfilling the soloist's role. Again in 1943 Ponce withdrew from the Conservatorio Nacional and occupied the chair of folklore in the rival Escuela Universitaría de Música. In 1947 (July 4) Chávez presented a Ponce festival concert at the Palacio de Bellas Artes, with the famous Spanish guitarrist, Andrés Segovia, interpreting Ponce's *Concierto del Sur*. On April 24, 1948, Ponce at the age of sixty-five died from uremic poisoning.

The most important of his orchestral works were *Chapultepec, Suite en estilo antiguo, Poema elegiaco, Ferial (divertimento)*, and *Cantos y Danzas de los Antiguos Mexicanos*. For solo instrument with orchestra he wrote a piano and a violin concerto. His published works, issued by seven houses, included over 150 separate works. His publishers were F. Boungiovanni (Bologna), Giralt y Anselmo López (Havana), Wagner y Levien, Enrique Munguía, and Otto y Arzoz (these three of Mexico City), Schott (Mainz), and Senart (Paris).

He had a unique ability to speak directly to the masses, and yet also to speak, when he so desired, in a sophisticated idiom appealing to the most advanced musical mind. Accused by Bossi in 1905 of writing in an 1830 style, Ponce in the 1930's was an avant-garde. He was able to change with the times. His conversion to newer ways of thinking was, moreover, sincerely felt, and unlike others whose modernisms were an unconvincing veneer, he spoke as urgently in his later style as in his earlier. The completeness of his change in style may be gauged from the following excerpts. The first is his 1912 manner; the second is his 1943 manner:

It should be understood that the orchestral integument in the Violin Concerto is composed of highly dissonant contrapuntal lines, whereas that in the Piano Concerto is composed of lush "Rachmaninoffian" chords.

Not only did Ponce show an extraordinary ability to enlarge his musical vocabulary, but also he shifted his "subject-matter." In his 1938 *Música Yaqui* (the second of his *Instantaneas Mexicanas*) he affixed a pentatonic melody of Yaqui origin over a spare bass with an aural result so diverse from that of his mestizo *canciones mexicanas* that no one unacquainted with the amazing growth of Ponce would believe it possible the composer of *Estrellita* could so have changed his stance. Ponce insisted the melodies given below were original Yaqui music:

Yaqui Music

But his handling of Indian materials in this particular "snapshot" of Yaqui life, and also in such a number as the *Danse des anciens mexicains* (premiered under Revueltas's baton, October 13, 1933), showed imaginative insight few other transcribers of Indian music have yet brought to the treatment of non-Western folk-music.

CARLOS CHÁVEZ (1899—)

Chávez, deservedly the best known of Mexican musicians, combines a truly amazing range of abilities. A conductor, a composer, a pianist, a musical scholar of rare ability, an executive director of a national bureau of fine arts—he has distinguished himself in every department of endeavor open to a musician.[5]

His two principal teachers during adolescence were Ponce and Pedro Luis Ogazón. The latter was a devotee of the Virgil Clavier method, and if from Ponce Chávez gained a romantic warmth, from Ogazón he acquired a wholly admirable precision of finger technique. Because he started at the age of twelve with Ponce and continued with so superior a pedagogue as Ogazón, Chávez was spared the necessity of unlearning what he gained during the crucial years of adolescence.

He began to publish in his early twenties. Still in print are such early songs as *Ecstasy* (strongly reminiscent of Henri Duparc), and his arrangements of various songs of the 1910 revolution (including *La Cucaracha*). The words for *Ecstasy* derive from Victor Hugo's 1828 *Les Orientales;* the general thought of Hugo's poem is "The heavens declare the glory of God and the firmament showeth forth His handiwork," and Chávez, who dedicated his song-setting to his sister, Estefanía, headed the poem with a quotation from the Apocalypse of St. John.

In 1921, the year in which *Paginas Sencillas, Cuatro Valsas,* and other works, began to appear in print, Ponce wrote an interesting appraisal of his erstwhile pupil, which he published in the *Revista* of the Unión Filarmónica de México. Ponce, unlike certain other teachers, never succumbed to petty fears of his former pupil's success, but on the contrary welcomed his progress with a cheer. In his 1921 article Ponce referred to his pupil as Carlos Chávez Ramírez, the latter name being that of Chávez's mother, which in accordance with common practice in Mexico was used concurrently with his father's:

> Carlos Chávez Ramírez is a rare example of ability conjoined with industry . . . and he entirely eschews the "dolce far niente" attitude so dear to many of us here. . . . The first thing one notices in his compositions is a desire to be original, which by all rights he should be. Who does not wish to be original nowadays? Debussy with his intensely personal mannerisms indubitably fascinates our young composers whose aspirations go far beyond a mere imitation of the classics and romantics. . . . Is the Debussy reflection so strong in Chávez Ramírez that one can call him an imitator? We do not believe so. . . . There are obviously certain procedures in his music characteristic of the composer of *Pelléas,* but beneath them there is discernible a latent streak of romanticism and a lyric strain

that the immoderate use of dissonances and the persistent rhythmic intricacies cannot hide. . . .

Carlos Chávez Ramírez is very young, although he gives the appearance of being older—of being a serious man, in fact, and a trifle on the melancholy side. He has talent, and must be watched. The question is: since he shows influences of Schumann and Chopin, and yet on the other hand of modernism with its sparkling novelties and exoticisms also, will he choose the one or the other path—that of the romanticists or that of the modernists? Here is a difficult question, and the answering of it involves the whole future of the young composer. . . .

The same year during which several sheaves of songs and piano works were published (by Wagner and Levien, with G. Schirmer affiliation), Chávez with the encouragement and blessing of the dynamic Secretary of Public Education, José Vasconcelos, set about writing *El Fuego Nuevo* —"The New Fire"—which was to be a Mexican ballet. When he had finished it Chávez with score under arm and a recommendation from Vasconcelos set about persuading Julián Carrillo to give it a trial reading with his Orquesta Sinfónica. For one reason or another, Carrillo balked at giving the young composer a chance to hear his score. This rebuff was not lightly forgotten by Chávez. Later when he was in a similar position of orchestral authority he tried to set a pattern of receptivity to new scores. But Carrillo perhaps was busy with other matters at the moment and did not realize he was rejecting the work of a genius.

In 1922 Chávez married Otilia Ortiz, a woman of the most extraordinary musical perceptivity. Soon after marrying, he set out on a trip to New York, and then went to Europe where he visited the principal continental centers. Ignaz Friedman, aboard the vessel on which Chávez sailed, took an interest in him and helped him secure publication of his Second Piano Sonata with the German firm, Bote and Bock. Upon his return from Europe he stayed two years in New York, where he made invaluable music contacts. Meanwhile J. J. Tablada, writer for *El Universal,* Mexico City newspaper, reported Chávez's musical activities so he would not be completely forgotten at home.

During 1925–6 Chávez was a theater organist in the Teatro Olimpia at Mexico City. He impressed the orchestra men who cooperated with him in supplying background music for films, and later when a rift between *académicos* and *jazzistas* in the musicians' union orchestra developed, his Teatro Olimpia colleagues were strong backers of his candidacy for the post of conductor. Only he, they felt, could supply strong enough musical leadership to overcome the bickering between "academic" and "jazzist" factions in the union orchestra. In the fall of 1928 Chávez as a youth of twenty-nine stepped into the conductorship of the Sindicato de Filarmónicos orchestra, and during the next twenty years this orchestra from modest beginnings grew to be one of the most important in the New World.

The strength of Chávez's leadership resided not only in his inherent musicality, but perhaps equally in his sound business sense and in his flair for "creating" news. As an example of his superb ability to capitalize upon the newsworthy, the story is told of his second concert with the musicians' union orchestra during his first season as conductor. At that concert he programmed a suite which in October, 1928, still had the appeal of an exciting novelty—John Alden Carpenter's *Skyscraper Suite*. Great was the indignation that so strident and mechanistic a work should have intruded itself into a Mexican orchestral concert. During the remainder of the month, the newspapers were filled with animated criticisms. In a few weeks the excitement ran itself out, but meantime the lively discussion "gave him fortuitously and unexpectedly the opportunity for which he had vainly fought throughout his youth—that is, to be suddenly projected into the limelight of public interest." Otto Mayer-Serra, who has chronicled Chávez's life, remarks further of this incident that "with his extraordinary political instinct, and with the courage of a fighter" Chávez knew how to turn this Teatro Iris incident, and other later incidents of the same kind, into maximum advantage. Later in the same first season, Chávez again programmed the *Skyscraper Suite*, but this time "by popular request." Needless to say, all the publicity of the first hearing stimulated interest in a second hearing; and the house was full.

Chávez's business sense was of paramount value in the building of the orchestra. He knew from the start how to converse with government officials, with prominent diplomats, and with financiers. Although the national conservatory had been supported by government stipend since the administration of Juárez, none of the various orchestras playing in the national capital had been so subsidized. Chávez succeeded in building the first stable orchestra in Mexico in large measure because he knew how to win government as well as private support for the enterprise. He from the very start showed his disposition to make his orchestra a national institution; unlike other conductors, he played all the orchestral works of young Mexican composers he could lay hands on. He furthermore gave Mexican performing artists ample opportunities to be heard.

His appointment as Director of the Conservatorio Nacional followed shortly upon his appointment to the orchestral conductorship. From December, 1928, until March, 1933, and again for eight months during 1934, he occupied the conservatory directorship, and in that educational post exerted himself to the utmost for a renascence of national art. As an educator as well as in the role of conductor, his energy was a dominant characteristic.

Meanwhile Chávez kept himself abreast every new development in the United States. The International Composers' Guild in New York began including his works. At first Paul Rosenfeld remarked upon Chávez's music "lightly recalling not only French impressionism but German romanticism as well." Ponce in 1921 had remarked on the same double strain of influence. Rosenfeld in his 1928 *By Way of Art* went on to speak of Chávez's *El Fuego Nuevo*—the music of which Carrillo would not play—as "the very early, still very dainty and Debussian forerunner of *Los Cuatro Soles*." But Chávez had composed *El Fuego Nuevo* before traveling abroad anywhere, and when he returned to Mexico after each of his many United States trips, he always returned with a better understanding of the international rise and fall of musical temperature. Paul Rosenfeld as late as 1936, the year before Chávez conducted the New York Philharmonic, still could say: "Chávez is not a Mexican so much as a North American composer." But steadily Chávez proceeded to emphasize more and more the Aztec in himself—the Indian in his heritage—with a resultant strengthening of international sentiment in behalf of his music. It is significant that his most "Indian" composition, the *Sinfonía India,* was composed not in Mexico, but in the United States.

His command of the English language, his intimate acquaintance with all the musical great of this nation, and especially with vanguardist composers, his oft-expressed appreciation for the achievements of the United States—all these assets have been of inestimable advantage to him. So ardently a friend of United States music that in the very moment of a budding orchestral career he was willing to risk a performance of the then-revolutionary *Skyscraper Suite,* he has never lacked warm friends from that moment in the cities of skyscrapers. Because United States visitors in

Mexico have felt him to be "truly a kindred spirit," he has continued throughout his career to draw American tributes.

The first "big-league" performance of a Chávez work in this country occurred March 31, 1932, when Leopold Stokowski conducted Chávez's ballet with designs by Diego Rivera, *H.P.* Discussing the premiere in *The New York Times*, John Martin stressed the next day that *H.P.* ("Horse-power") entirely lacked plot, and added "It perhaps seems less vital today than it did in 1926, when the composer first conceived it." He spoke also of the music as being "endlessly contrapuntal," and complained that machinery dances had already "been done to death." But regardless of the somewhat captious comments made concerning the music, Chávez's name had been brought to the attention of the influential Eastern public, and thus an auspicious beginning had been made.

The publicity before Chávez's first appearance in New York as orchestra conductor stressed his friendship with Diego Rivera, and his desire to do for music what Rivera had done for painting. His services as an educator were also stressed. In the report of an interview (*New York Times*, January 16, 1936) he was quoted as saying Mexican music has been "in a sad way up to about a decade ago"—that is until about the time he took over the reins of the Conservatorio Nacional. In his New York publicity Chávez around 1936 also began to talk lengthily about Indian music. Aztec music he said for publication "was a very strong music —imperative—contemplative at times, but not romantic and never plaintive. It was music characteristic of a stoic, combative race." Exactly the "strong," "imperative" note was that which Chávez's music was intended to sound, as it evoked the memory of a glorious past.

At the Philadelphia premiere of the *Sinfonia de Antígona*, an eleven-minute one-movement piece which today stands as one of the twin pillars upholding Chavez's reputation as a composer, the *Inquirer* critic called it "too astringent to be intriguing," but asserted "it has definite character." On April 10, 1936, Olin Downes heard Chávez in his Boston debut with the Boston Orchestra. Downes remarked that Stravinsky had undoubtedly been "useful" to Chávez. Downes compared the music with "savage wood carvings," and said the music was "racial." This report of a racial quality was, of course, extremely welcome.

As Chávez's debut with the New York Philharmonic came closer, his activities in Mexico drew more and more attention. One writer noted "a fifth of the audience was made up of Americans" when Chávez conducted in Mexico City. *New York Times* readers learned on November 8, 1936, that "Mexican music has been, until recently, without creative impulse." On February 11, 1937, occurred at long last the great event that had been so long heralded: Chávez's debut with the Philharmonic. Downes unqualifiedly praised his conducting. "So far as euphony and technical finish are concerned," Downes said, "the orchestra surpassed any accomplishment since the days of Toscanini." The *Daphnis and Chloe* performance was called superior to anything in its line attempted that season in New York. But the *Sinfonía de Antígona* was less warmly received. "The music has a certain bareness. . . . At a second hearing . . . the work does not impress as much as it did in Boston last April 10. Powerful, elemental things in it seem impeded rather than aided in expression."

The second week of Chávez's appearances brought similar notices. Again it was agreed his handling of Debussy and Ravel was magnificent. But in his review, Downes (who was followed by the other critics) devoted only minimal attention to a work which assuredly deserved more than the one slim paragraph out of a total of twelve paragraphs in the review. The *Sinfonía India* received its New York premiere that second week of Chávez's appearances, but Downes thought it comparatively unimportant, and relegated it to the last of his twelve-paragraphed review. He praised it as "redolent of the soil," but said it "would profitably be cut in certain places." The *Sinfonía India* is a twelve-minute composition. Downes also spoke of its "harshness of harmonic setting and barbaric rhythms," but the adjective *barbaric* was, of course, an open sesame to avant-garde approval.

Again in 1942 when Dmitri Mitropoulos conducted the New York premiere of Chávez's Piano Concerto (Eugene List, soloist), the music was called "powerful, primitive, and barbaric." Noel Straus said, "Indian music harking back to a remote past obviously forms the basic material of the composition." He also wrote of the "unrelieved, acute dissonances in every measure" hammered out with an insistence that "might be called an obsession." He decided it was consistently cacophonous, but was impressed "by its elemental strength and originality.'" He noted "strange, brash outbursts of sound, primeval in effect."

During the latter years of the war Chávez received frequent tributes from composers in such allied nations as Britain and Russia. But during those same years he began to hear louder and louder protests from musicians in his own nation calling him a "musical dictator." The force of these protests finally caused him to relinquish his conductorship of the great Orquesta Sinfónica de México that he had so painstakingly built over a space of twenty-odd years. On March 11, 1949, Chávez's resignation was regretfully accepted by the civil association charged with backing the orchestra. At the moment of his resignation, however, Mexican music did not entirely lose his dynamic and driving leadership. He continued as Chief of the Department of Fine Arts, a government bureau charged with the fomenting of all artistic activities in Mexico.

In March, 1951, he returned to the podium in Mexico City and was clamorously greeted. After a magisterial performance of the Beethoven Ninth Symphony the public accorded him an ovation. When he resigned in 1949, he stepped aside so that younger men might have an opportunity to make their mark. It has always been his intention to promote Mexican music, and not simply that segment of it represented by himself. By relinquishing authority for a space of two years, he allowed any other contenders to enter the field. Since, however, none of equal stature presented himself, his services upon his return to the podium were doubly welcomed.

CHÁVEZ'S MUSICAL STYLE

It is possible to generalize concerning a particular epoch in Chávez's creative career, but not perhaps concerning the whole of it. His early pieces may, if one wishes, be discarded as "juvenilia" but since there is so large a quantity of these pieces written at around the age of twenty, to discard them all tremendously reduces the catalogue of his works. If they are dismissed because they seem derivative, it should nevertheless be remembered that his "juvenilia" are peculiarly Mexican in that they were written before he traveled abroad.

The pieces written during his first years abroad bear abstract titles such as "Polygons," "Hexagons," "36," "Energy." In the catalogue of his mature works it is possible to draw a distinction between "extramural works" and "intramural works." To the former class belong his works with abstract titles, and the two or three orchestral works which are now internationally known (especially the *Sinfonía de Antígona* and the *Sinfonía India*). To the latter class belong such works as *Obertura Republicana* and *Llamadas;* these latter evince his interest in the political questions, and often give the impression of being "made-to-order" music.

In his mature style Chávez wrote linear music. His melodies have predominantly been diatonic; and they have for the most part been melodies on what would correspond to white notes of the piano. Only Chávez could have written twenty pages of piano preludes without a single note other than those that occur in the scale of C. As far as rhythms are concerned, his pieces set a certain basic unit and stick to it. If the basic unit is an eighth, running eighths will continue throughout the entire piece or section of a piece. If the basic unit is sixteenths, running sixteenths will continue throughout the entire piece or section of a piece. His rhythms thus exhibit the kind of incessant drive which one finds in Bach's Brandenburg Concertos, for instance. The uninterrupted eighth, or sixteenth, or quarter flow may quite conceivably be handled as Bach handled such uninterrupted flow—by transferring the movement from voice to voice. But the incessant flow of baroque rhythms is a recognizable trait in many of Chávez's most dissonant compositions.

A distinctive feature of his instrumentation is the heavy battery of percussion he customarily includes. Whenever his scores call for indigenous instruments, such as teponaztlis, however, he usually provides a cued-in part for modern analogues, such as the xylophone in the case of the teponaztli. Although the percussion adds shimmer and brilliancy, his orchestral palette also includes bright brass and woodwind thrusts. His strings are rarely treated *divisi,* and the most unthinkable effect in a Chávez orchestration would be the voluptuous languor of a *divisi* chord from such a composition as R. Vaughan Williams's *Fantasia on a Theme of Thomas Tallis.* Chávez's most incisive departure from standardized custom in the treatment of the string choir is his constantly independent treatment of the string basses. The basses, as a matter of fact, are often treated as melody-producing instruments that have no need of 'cello reinforcement in order to sing in warm, human tones. Were a further generalization in order, we might say that Chávez's string parts seem to offer fewer challenges—as far as notes are concerned—than do either his woodwind or brass parts. A very extended search would be necessary in order to find passages demanding the digital dexterity that any of the Strauss tone-poems exact.

Since Chávez alone among Mexican composers has found a United States publisher—G. Schirmer—for an important segment of his creative output, analysis of his piano and also of his orchestral style can easily be undertaken independently by any interested person. The added avail-

From *Sinfonia de Antigona* by Carlos Chávez. Copyright 1948 by G. Schirmer, Inc. Used by permission.

ability of records for the two fundamental orchestral works—the two
sinfonías—gives an arm-chair analyst an easy opportunity with the scores
open before him to dissect the works. In order to assist the reader in this
exercise, an analysis of the first of these two symphonies is offered below.

The *Sinfonía de Antígona*, written at Mexico City in 1933, is a one-
movement symphony. Though its structure was not dictated by any stereo-
typed conception of "sonata-allegro" form, the overall form of the movement
may best be understood as a modified sonata-allegro preceded by a slow introduction. The *calmo* introduction explores two themes, the first of which is
repeated seven times by the first bassoon; this laconic three-note theme is then
transferred successively to the first harp and to the first violins, the latter playing it four times at their extreme upper limit (in what would be the top octave
of the piano).

The second theme in the introduction is allotted first to English Horn and
Viola in unison: it begins with a drop of a fourth.

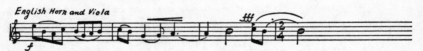

These two themes, one chromatic and the other disjunctly diatonic, are heard
in combination first at letter *1* and then again at letter *3*. Transcribed below in
short score is the passage beginning three bars before letter *3*.

The first group may be thought of as comprising the whole section in ⅝ time beginning at letter *6* and closing at *9*. An oboe melody so constructed as to emphasize the recurring skip of a fourth is the leading theme in this *tempo moderato* section:

Seven bars of transition lead into the second group commencing at letter *10*. The hecklephone doubled at the octave by a piccolo enunciates the following melody, which because it again emphasizes skips of a fourth bears a certain family likeness to the oboe melody heard at letter *6*.

The section lasting from *16* to *18* may be thought of as a closing group, and *18* to *27* may be regarded as fulfilling the function of a development section, reaching its sonorous climax two bars before letter *27*. At *27* occurs a short recapitulation of the thematic material heard in the first group, but with changed instrumentation so that what was heard as an oboe melody at letter *6* now is transferred to Violins I and II and Viola in a three-octave doubling. The coda extends from letter *32* to the end.

The movement is obviously a highly concentrated one. At the time the sinfonía was conceived, Chávez was concurrently creating incidental music for Jean Cocteau's "contraction" of the Sophocles drama, *Antigone*. Although incidental music and sinfonía were independently gestated, nevertheless there was a considerable sharing of thematic material and of general mood in the two. Ultimately it might therefore be said that the highly concentrated energy and tautness of the Cocteau "contraction" of the drama found its way into Chávez's "Antigone symphony."

The musical means whereby Chávez has in this sinfonía reconstructed the mood of the Greek drama may be briefly listed: (1) He has selected as a prevailing tonality the two E-octave species known in Greek theory as dorian and hypodorian, these two being the octave species whose *ethos* would, according to the definitions of Plato, best express the Antigone's two opposing calls of duty. (2) The E-octave species with an f♮ (Greek dorian) has been used for thematic material expressing one kind of duty—that of obligation to the gods;

the other E-octave species using f♯ (Greek hypodorian) has been used for thematic material expressing the other type of duty—that of obligation to the state.
(3) Were a programme worked out for the sinfonía the introduction with its
pitting of f♯ and f♮ against the e-fundamental could be construed as a weighing
of both kinds of duty conjointly, religious and civic; the first group as the appeal
of conscience, the second group as the at first coaxing and finally brutal call of
civic duty; and the recapitulation and coda as Antigone's appeal again to
conscience as the only safe guide. (4) The sections in the E-f♮ octave-species
(Greek dorian), which bear construction as Antigone's meditation on her duty
to the gods (conscience), are cast in ⅝ rhythm, quintuple meter being known
as that favored in such hymns as the two authentic Delphic Hymns preserved
from Greek antiquity.

A psychological conflict of the kind Antigone faced can therefore without
too gross a distortion be read in the musical symbols Chávez has selected. At
the time he was composing this work he was already engrossed in the problems
of Aztec music. With more positive information available on the characteristics of Greek music than Aztec, he set himself the task of reconstruction.
Again he returned to another essay in the re-creation of a "Greek mood" in
his 1947 suite, "The Daughter of Colchis." In this latter work, although he
did not literally transcribe, nevertheless conspicuous likenesses can be discerned
between two of Chávez's themes and two surviving Greek fragments. If it is
impossible to say how systematically Chávez has studied Aristoxenos or Aris-
teides it is at least certain he has more successfully than any composer of our
time essayed in the *Sinfonía de Antígona* and *La Hija de Cólquide* a reconstruction of Greek themes.

Chávez's essential greatness is not, however, to be measured simply in
terms of his success in evoking the Greek past, the Indian past, or any other
past. He is emphatically a composer of our time, and when he has ex-
plored antique themes his purpose has always been that of adding to
present-day musical resources rather than that of divorcing himself from
the immediately contemporary. In order properly to evalue his contribution to twentieth century music it is moreover necessary to examine his
whole output. His *Concerto for Piano and Orchestra* as revealed in
Claudio Arrau's interpretation is one of the two or three most vital of
our epoch; his *Concerto for Four Horns* is another strangely powerful
work; his *Second String Quartet* as played by the Roth Quartet is scarcely
less impressive than Bartók's Second. Judged in totality, then, Chávez's
creative achievement is seen not only as a Mexican achievement of the

very first rank, but also as an achievement not behind any thus far brought to the attention of the public by any New World composer.

SILVESTRE REVUELTAS (1899–1940) [6]

Revueltas was the product of a small-town environment. He was born in a town of three thousand inhabitants some hundred miles northwest of Durango, and spent his childhood there. Almost before he could talk a violin was tucked under his chin. The father owned a store, but was by no means affluent. Report has it that when he was seven Silvestre organized an orchestra among his own playmates, who were paid in lumps of candy from father Revueltas's store. At the age of fourteen Revueltas went from Durango to Mexico City, where he studied violin with the distinguished artist, José Rocabruna, and composition with Rafael J. Tello.

From 1916 until 1918 he studied at St. Edward College, a school in Austin, Texas. He there acquired fluency in English and proceeded thence to Chicago, enrolling in Chicago Musical College under Sametini in violin and Borowski in composition. After two years he interrupted his Chicago studies for an extended Mexican visit, but returned in 1922 to finish the four-year course of study. During his second Chicago period he made distinguished headway as a violinist under Vaslav Kochanski's and Otokar Ševčik's tuition. During the 1924 and 1925 seasons he was therefore sufficiently perfected a performer to cooperate on equal terms with Carlos Chávez, the pair giving notable first performances of hitherto unknown European works in the Mexican capital during those two years.

The years 1926 and '28 were spent at San Antonio, Texas, and Mobile, Alabama, in which cities Revueltas served as theater violinist and orchestra conductor. Chávez called him back to Mexico in 1929 to become sub-director of the Orquesta Sinfónica de México. After five years in this capacity Revueltas added a teaching responsibility (in chamber music) at the Conservatorio Nacional. Meanwhile with Chávez's encouragement he began to compose a series of lastingly important orchestral works. The first of these was a musical picturization of the well-known resort town, Cuernavaca, with the title, *Cuauhnáhuac* (1930). Successive works followed with such titles as "Corners" (1930), "Windows" (1931), "Penny-

Banks" (1932), "Bright Colors" (1932), "Plains" (1934), all of which titles, according to Revueltas himself, were only suggestive aids for un-tutored listeners. A 1933 piece bore the enigmatic title *8xRadio;* with this title as with several others, Revueltas intended nothing very profound. *8xRadio* meant simply "eight minutes of radio music," [7] and was a piece commissioned for radio performance lasting exactly that length of time. In 1935 Revueltas wrote music for a famous film, *Redes;* much of his creative energy during the final five years of his life was consumed in writing movie music, some of which is strikingly good in the same way Prokofieff's movie music is.

Revueltas like many another financially straitened Mexican musician overburdened himself with a plethora of activities in his mature years. He tried to teach at the conservatory, direct the students' orchestra there, conduct a loose organization known as the Orquesta Sinfónica Nacional, compose film music, assist Chávez in the OSM, act as secretary for LEAR (League of Revolutionary Artists and Writers), besides doing some violin playing from time to time. All this busy round of activity was not made easier by his devotion to the interests of the Spanish Loyalists; in 1937–8 he visited Spain, appearing as conductor of his own works at Madrid, Barcelona, and Valencia. The strain told on his health, and instead of resting he simply pushed himself more fiercely. Revueltas died prematurely, with infinite loss to Mexican music, October 5, 1940. At the moment of his death he was engaged on a ballet, *La Coronela* ("The Colonel's Wife"); Blas Galindo finished it, and Candelario Huízar or-chestrated it.

Perhaps the most frequently played piece of his in this country has been his symphonic poem, *Janitzio,* in which he pictorialized the resort island in the middle of Lake Patzcuaro (premiered by the OSM at Teatro Hidalgo, Revueltas conducting, December 8, 1933). The astounding gift for melody Revueltas possessed was perhaps his greatest single asset. His melodies are instinct with life, vibrant with energy. Unlike Chávez, Revueltas never self-denyingly reduced his melodic material to an all-prevailing diatonicism. Aaron Copland compared Revueltas's spontaneity with Schubert's,[8] and remarked that "he composes organically tunes which are almost indistinguishable from the original folk material itself"—the original folk material being mestizo melody of the kind heard everywhere along the highways and byways of Mexico. His spontaneity and his easy assimilation of the prevailing popular styles enabled him to achieve in his picturization of such resorts as Cuernavaca and Janitzio peculiar authenticity.

Copland rightly commended Revueltas's music for its gaiety, its wistfulness. He said its flavor reminded him of highly spiced Mexican food. Revueltas's typical mood is that of a gaudy fiesta. From the *Toccata for Violin and Small Orchestra,* the initial violin passage is extracted below as an example of the intense rhythmic energy which Revueltas knew how to infuse into even his single lines.

But he could also be as tender as a nurse for a sick child. His *Canción de Cuna* with text by the famous Spanish poet, García Lorca, breathes peace, serenity, and through its tears speaks of profound things. The *Homenaje a García Lorca* for small orchestra (1935) is a miracle of wistful beauty. Revueltas was not only authentically Mexican; he was one of the musical seers of our generation.

CANDELARIO HUÍZAR (1888—) [9]

Huízar, like Revueltas, originated in a small provinical town: in his case, Jerez in the state of Zacatecas. Son of a blacksmith, he assisted his father at the forge. But he resented the necessity of exactly following the paternal trade, and while still in early adolescence apprenticed himself to a silversmith. At seventeen he commenced study of the alto saxhorn and joined the village band. A year later he moved to Zacatecas so he could combine study of the horn with silversmithing. At nineteen he married a hometown girl from Jerez. How with no money, family responsibilities, and the background of modest beginnings which was his, he could have later achieved such preeminence that he was called Mexico's best orchestrator and teacher of orchestration is a marvel. In 1918 (at the age of thirty) he at last got to Mexico City, there to enroll in Gustavo E. Campa's composition class. Ten years later after spending the intervening time as a bandsman, he became a hornist under Chávez. The contact with Chávez, like a catalyst, finally brought to pass a chemical reaction that resulted in Huízar's series of four symphonies, his tone-poem *Pueblerinas*, and his string quartet.

The typical problem Huízar posed himself in his symphonies was the integration of pentatonic Indian material within the larger framework of the classical sonata form. His only two works in which he avoided the formalistic problem of the classical sonata were his two symphonic poems, *Imagenes* (1929) and *Surco* (1935). Certain pentatonic themes, such as the principal ones in the first movement of *Symphony No. 4* (1942), were literal quotations from Cora and Huichol melodies; but in *Oxpaniztli* (1936), despite the Aztecan title, the melodies were of synthetic facture.

Huízar has won hearty respect because he triumphed over seemingly insuperable odds. Starting with no advantages, he showed what a Mexican pulling himself up by his own bootstraps could do. *Pueblerinas* ("Village Girls"), a fresh-sounding noisy piece composed in 1931, seems to be the piece of his which will continue to be played oftenest, but his Fourth Symphony is a greater work.

BLAS GALINDO (1910—) [10]

Like Huízar, Galindo was late in arriving at a music vocation. Moreover he too came from a provincial town, whose musical atmosphere he later categorized as viceregal. His father, a prosperous merchant, lost heavily during the revolutionary disturbances attendant upon the long struggles initiated by Madero. The state of Jalisco was like other parts of Mexico torn by strife all through the early 'twenties, and Blas, quitting school in his natal village of San Gabriel, Jalisco, took to the mountains, where he lived a wandering life as a guerrillist. With a gun slung under one arm and a guitar under the other, he was welcome in any band of Indian fighters. His sympathies were, of course, with his own people, since he himself is a full-blooded Huichol.

At nineteen he returned home, and began his first systematic study of music rudiments. The San Gabriel village priest invited him to play the church organ, which he started doing, finding his way over the keys, however, entirely by ear. He also started playing a clarinet in the village band when he was twenty, and because of his native musical aptitude was soon given an opportunity to conduct it. Within about a year's time he learned to read music.

One day in May, 1931, he left home with the vague idea of studying to be a lawyer at Mexico City. He hoped that as a lawyer he could work for social justice. But when he reached the capital, almost penniless, he happened to hear Revueltas conduct a nationalist composition at a Conservatorio rehearsal, and decided music should be his life work. He enrolled, and beginning at the bottom studied twelve years, at last graduating with the highest certificate offered by the conservatory, "Maestro en composición"—awarded him in December, 1944. He was fortunate in arriving at a moment when Chávez was in the act of regenerating the conservatory, and therefore came immediately under the master's tutelage.

Chávez in his celebrated class in "musical creation" taught composition directly, without requiring long preliminary studies in the conventional propaedeutics, harmony and counterpoint. Chávez's method started the students with melody-creation. Simple melodies were succeeded by complex melodies; diatonic by twelve-tone melodies. Instrumentalists were procured to play the single-line melodies, so students might immediately hear their creations. Composition thus became a unitary experience, with the fundaments of instrumentation proceeding bilaterally with melody-creation. After extensive experience in writing and hearing melodies sung and played, the students then proceeded to multiple-voice creation. The linear concept was thus paramount from the start, rather than the vertical which conventional harmony induces. Two melodies were combined, with instrumentalists or singers realizing at sight the students' creations. Then three melodies were combined, and later four. Never was the practical subordinated to any merely theoretical concept of music creation. Although counterpoint was thus taught, no recourse was had to conventional Fuxian principles. Believing that all music creation should be relevant to the present, Chávez never had recourse to disciplines which only prepared students to write in a dead style.

Galindo, when he himself came to be head of the conservatory, remembered all that Chávez had imparted. Under Chávez's own dynamic leadership, a group of several composers—including besides Galindo, Daniel Ayala (1908—), Jose Pablo Moncayo (1912—), Salvador Contreras, and others—developed vigorously. Whether without his own personality, his method would work as well yet remains to be demonstrated. Much of the renown Galindo, Ayala, Moncayo, and the rest, have achieved also stems from the fact Chávez as director of the OSM welcomed their endeavors and programmed them repeatedly long after they had ceased being his personal pupils.

Blas Galindo became acquainted with international renown entirely through the efforts of his mentor. When preparing his Museum of Modern Art concerts Chávez invited Galindo to prepare an orchestral synthesis of several popular songs; the resultant *Sones Mariachi,* made up of the "thirds-ian" music sung and played by strolling bands re-set for symphony orchestra, put Galindo's name in the Columbia Record catalogue. Later Chávez's good offices resulted in Galindo's appointment to summer scholarships at Tanglewood, where he studied with Copland and secured a commission from the Koussevitzky Foundation. A succession of desirable events in Mexico was also procured through Chávez's interest. Galindo's 1944–5 *Cinco Preludios* (piano) were published in 1946 by Ediciones Mexicanas de Música. This was but the first of several issues by the same press. Galindo was also elevated to the directorship of the Conservatorio only four years after receiving the certificate, "Maestro en composición." Each new work of Galindo in the meantime has been played either at the Conciertos de los Lunes, or by the OSM, or given a hearing in some other auspicious forum.

As would be but natural, Galindo has shown influences. Any interested observer can detect likenesses between Galindo's Preludes (Ediciones Mexicanas) and Chavez's Preludes (G. Schirmer). The insistence upon white notes, white notes, and nothing but white notes in Galindo's Prelude No. 1 cannot but remind us of the same insistence in Chávez's Prelude No. 1. On the whole, however, Galindo is nowhere near Chávez in astringency. Galindo had grown to maturity during an epoch when Herod had already been out-Heroded, and nothing the younger men could do would sound more *outré* than what their predecessors had done. Wisely, because he could not hope to be more daring than the nihilists of the 'twenties, Galindo has contented himself with a less acrid style than would have been internationally acceptable a decade earlier.

He has demonstrated an almost French concern for precision of form. Both his *Sonata para violin y piano* (1945) and *Sonata para violoncello y piano* (1948) are major works in his catalogue, and both are highly polished structurally. The 'Cello Sonata (dedicated to the memory of Natalie Koussevitzky) may here be briefly analyzed as a working model of his procedures. There are three movements in this ten-minute work, labeled: I Allegro, II Lento, III Allegro vivace. The tonics in each of the three movements fall back progressively in the circle of fifths to the lower fifth; that is to say, the first movement has A for its tonic, the second (governed by a phrygian cadence) has D for its tonic, the third has G for its tonic. The first movement deploys its first and second subjects interestingly; at the recapitulation everything goes by reverse—the second subject comes first, the first second. Whereas the 'cello had the second subject in the exposition, at the recapitulation the piano has it; similarly with the first subject—at the recapitulation roles of the 'cello and piano are reversed.

The facets of Galindo's style which shine in this 'Cello Sonata are the same facets which shine in his other works. Listing the features of his style, we note *1* rhythmic vivacity is secured by frequent interpolation of figures which run counter to the meter, as for instance ♫♫ ♫♫ in ¾, ♫ ♫. ♫. in ⁶⁄₈, ♫♫ ♫♫ ♫ in ¼; also by the interpolation of occasional measures of ⅞ and ⅝. *2* Melodies proceed twice as often by scale-step as by skip; skips of fourths, fifths, sevenths, ninths, are used more often than skips of thirds, sixths. *3* Novel melodic lines are frequently created by distorting simple scale passages; *e. g.*

(at Letter ④ *)*   *(penultimate measure of First Movement)*

4 Within a given section, accidentals occur extremely rarely, and chromaticisms almost never. *5* Pan-diatonic harmony prevails. *6* Abrupt and rather remote changes of key-signature occur, such as from four sharps to three flats, or four flats to no accidentals. *7* Parallelisms of sevenths, fifths, and seconds occur as freely as parallelisms of thirds. *8* Level planes of emotion, with terraced changes in mood, are the rule.

Certain features in Galindo's music do seem Mexican enough; anyone who has seen the terraced farms in the high mountainous regions of Mexico will find the abrupt changes of signature, the abrupt changes of mood in the music, and the abrupt changes of pace in the rhythmic flow, reminiscent of the step-like cultivated hillsides. But there is in reality little that is obviously regional in most of Galindo's music. It is therefore to be anticipated that his music will not draw to itself the attention it might otherwise receive. The *Sones Mariachi* sounded enough like a curio shop to attract listeners, as did also *Arroyos* (premiered at the Berkshire Festival, August 17, 1942), but his 1942 Piano Concerto and his 1945 *Nocturno* for orchestra sounded no distinctly regional notes. His is a vital message even in his most abstract moments, however, and it is much to be hoped that recitalists in this country will discover his piano preludes, his violin and his 'cello sonatas.

EL GRUPO DE LOS CUATRO [11]

During 1935, while Galindo was filling a temporary music teaching post at a rural normal school (state of Hidalgo), one of his former fellow-classmates from the conservatory urged him to return to the capital and help stage a composition concert. Salvador Contreras was the initiator of what soon came to be called *El Grupo de los Cuatro*—"the group of four." Contreras suggested that he, Galindo, Moncayo, and Ayala, present a program showing what the four of them had done since Chávez had stopped teaching his class in "music-creation" (which all four had attended together). The uniting of their forces in a November, 1935, concert at the *Teatro Orientación* proved a happy idea; a newspaper critic fathered the phrase *Grupo de los Cuatro*, and the four found attention as a group which might have been denied them had they sought individual recognition.

The Russian Five and the French Six were groups fresh in the memory of all students of music history. Why not a Mexican Four? The first concert in which they consciously appealed to the public as "the Four" occurred in May, 1936. The idea of "the Four" grew apace. Pictures of the four together were widely distributed for publicity purposes. The idea that from such a group would come the music of the future was further advanced in newspaper and magazine articles. Nicolas Slonimsky in his *Music of Latin America* (published in 1945) introduced English readers to "the Four," and in various other publications in the United States during the subsequent decade the group was referred to as an earnest of Mexico's musical renascence.

Ayala, oldest of the group, is a Yucatecan. He often has called himself an autodidact. In 1938 he published an astounding article in which he announced Mexico had no authentic teachers of conducting or performance. For his denial of any personal indebtednesses to teachers and for his sweeping condemnation of the music teaching profession in Mexico he was not thanked. Soon after publishing this article he removed to Morelia; after two or three years there he returned home to Mérida, Yucatan. Having at last arrived home, he came into his own. He was appointed director of the Mérida Conservatory, conductor of the Mérida Orchestra, and conductor of the Yucatecan Band. During 1940 he visited Dallas, Texas, where he conducted an orchestra. His impressions of the United States were later crystallized in a symphonic poem entitled "My Trip to the United States," premiered at Mérida in 1947.

Ayala's musical style is eclectic. At one moment he re-echoes the strains he played during his several years as violinist in a cabaret orchestra. At another he evokes the primitive Maya past, using only pentatonic scales. His better known works are *Tribu* ("Tribe"), premiered by Chávez with the Orquesta Sinfónica de México October 18, 1935; *Paisaje* ("Landscape"), an orchestral suite in three parts written in 1935; *Panoramas de México,* an orchestral suite in three parts ("Sonora," "Veracruz," "Yucatan") written in 1936; *Los Yaquis y Los Seris,* two suites employing Indian percussion instruments (1938); and *El Hombre Maya,* a ballet suite. Regional patriotism is strongly developed in Yucatan, and the Yucatecan wishes his region to shine musically. Ayala since his return home has therefore been enthusiastically supported.

Contreras, like Ayala, has been diverted from his single-minded devotion to composition. His 1940 *Música para Orquesta Sinfónica,* a twelve-minute piece, was premiered by Chávez; the OSM also played the first performance of Contreras's *Suite* (1947). His other principal works include: a String Quartet, a Violin and 'Cello Sonata, and *Obertura en forma de danza.*

José Pablo Moncayo, born in Guadalajara, has distinguished himself as conductor, pianist, and composer. His catalogue of original works includes *Tres piezas para piano solo* (published by Ediciones Mexicanas de Música), a 1944 Sinfonietta, a 1947 triptych for symphonic orchestra entitled *Tres piezas,* an *Homenaje a Cervantes* ("Tribute to Cervantes"), a *Huapango,* and music for a one-act opera, in three scenes, *La Mulata de Córdoba* (1948).

The story of the mulatto enchantress who lived shortly before independence in Córdoba, the half-way town between Puebla and Veracruz, has taken on almost the quality of the legendary in Mexican story-telling. Because she lived alone, had no visible sources of income, and yet never lacked for anything and was in fact even able out of her largesse to supply the wants of the poor, she earned the reputation of being a sorceress. She was haled before the tribunal of the Inquisition at Mexico City, but never admitted her guilt. When the Holy Office pronounced she was in league with the devil, she eluded their condign punishment. She mysteriously vanished like a puff of smoke, leaving behind only a cryptic word on her cell-wall. This legend supplied the two librettists, Agustín Lazo and Xavier Villaurrutia, with material first for a ballet-scenario, utilized by Blas Galindo; later they re-worked the material into a one-act opera libretto for Moncayo's use.[12]

Moncayo's creative output has not been as profuse as many of his friends had anticipated when he first began to write. The obvious reason is the multiplicity of other money-making activities in which he has of necessity engaged. His problem, like that of most other Mexican composers of this century, has been that of the free-lance. His piece most frequently played, the *Huapango,* is without doubt one of the most brilliant in the entire Mexican repertory. If he can somehow find time to add other compositions of similar pith to his catalogue, his promise will be justified. But up to the present he seems destined to be like Dukas a one-piece composer with all repeat performances listing the same title.

LUIS SANDI (1905—) [13]

At the same 1948 festival during which Moncayo's one-act opera was presented, another one-act opera entitled *Carlota* was produced. Music for the latter was written by Luis Sandi, who at the time he wrote it was Music Chief within the Department of Fine Arts, a government bureau. (He resigned this post in the fall of 1951.) His services to Mexican music have thus been dual in character—he has been a creator and at the same time a coordinator of educational activities in the republic. His success in doing both is proved by his ability to do two such diverse things in the same year as finish an opera and simultaneously complete a new edition of a music history school text.

As an educator he deserves unstinted praise. He has prepared not one but a series of graded texts for teaching music history and theory. These texts emphasize the role Mexico has played in the history of the art. Secondary students using his texts have learned the names of Mexico's chief musicians not only of the embalmed past but also of dynamic present. In his *Introducción al Estudio de la Música*, 1948 edition, Sandi presented music theory and history as a synchronized study. It is his belief that "appreciation" courses for secondary students should teach the rudiments of music theory first. The first eight units in his 29-unit text deal with what we usually in the United States call "fundamentals of theory." The tenth and eleventh units deal with pre-Columbian music in Mexico and Peru respectively. The last two units deal with colonial and republican music in Mexico.

An analysis of the music examples in Sandi's texts proves illuminating. Side by side with excerpts from Bach, Mozart, Mendelssohn, and Mussorgsky, are contemporary examples from Revueltas and Stravinsky. A Mexican corrido shares a place with the sequence, *Victimae Paschali*. *Marchita el Alma*, the *canción mexicana* published in Ponce's arrangement during 1913, appears side by side with an Alfonso the Wise *cantiga*. The obvious advantages of Sandi's treatment are many: students do not find the music of their own country neglected; students do not find their own national music branded as essentially inferior; students cover the whole sweep of Mexican music history, devoting as much attention to the present era as they do to past centuries.

It has long been known by educators in the United States that American composers are slighted in music appreciation courses. At least theoretically, Sandi's distribution has much to commend it to authors this side of the Rio Grande. His other educational theories deserve mention. He believes strongly all primary and secondary emphasis should be placed on singing, not playing of instruments. Elementary emphasis on instruments, he feels, may yield good results in a country such as the United States where schools can rent or lend instruments to children, but Mexico is not able to render school children such free or near-free services involving expensive outlays yet. He strongly hopes to decentralize music advantages so that children in outlying districts will share those children now possess only at Mexico City. He points to the number of important modern composers who have originated in remote towns and villages as one reason Mexico must spread its advantages, since talent has a way of springing up everywhere, not just in the Federal District. He believes in stimulating as much original composition among elementary and secondary students as possible, and to this end has organized frequent school contests for creative work.

In 1938 he organized at the capital the *Coro de Madrigalistas*, a choral group singing principally a cappella music. This society has won accolades of praise for its singing of Guerrero and Victoria, but true to his convictions concerning living music, he has conducted his singers in equally telling performances of such modern Mexican works as Rafael J. Tello's short requiem, *Pequeña Misa Funebre*. Sandi's madrigalists are without doubt one of the foremost a cappella organizations in Latin America today.

His own compositions include a *Concertino para Flauta y orquesta*, a *La Hoja de Plata Suite* ("Silverplate Suite"), *Norte* for small orchestra, and *Feria* ("The Fair") for orchestra with additional Indian instruments. His was the arrangement of *Yaqui Music* Chávez played in his May, 1940, concerts in New York.

MIGUEL BERNAL JIMÉNEZ (1910—)

Bernal Jiménez sang in the Morelia Cathedral choir as a child, and studied in what is now the Escuela Superior Oficial de Música Sagrada in Morelia. The founder of that school, José M. Villaseñor, divined Bernal's potentialities in Catholic music, and sponsored his trip to Rome. From 1928 until 1933 Bernal studied at the Pontifical Institute of Sacred Music, where he became a polished organist and an expert in Gregorian music. In 1936 Bernal was appointed director of the Morelia school where he himself had started.

His compositions since his return home have reflected the local scene. His *Michoacán*, a symphonic suite written in 1940, contains three movements, *Alborada* ("Daybreak"), *Canción*, and *Corrido*. Scored for large orchestra (eleven woodwind players, four trumpeters, harp *and* piano, in addition to other standard components), this suite shows Bernal a complete master of orchestration. His melodies, prevailingly diatonic, are draped oftenest in a resplendent gown of chromatic harmony. With

Respighian opulence the *Alborada* in the *Michoacán* Suite develops a final fortissimo climax in an A major section marked "Grandioso." The *Canción* contains a throbbing melody sung by all the strings, except basses; the woodwind repartee accompanying this lush melody adds suitable shimmer to the total sound. The *Corrido* explores a combination of ⅔'s and ¾'s. Three variations on the corrido theme are followed by a fugue (also with alternating ⅔ and ¾ measures). During the fugue exposition a liberal use of accented "wrong notes" in the counterpoints, of doubled leading tones, of fifths on successive beats in two-part passages, exhibit Bernal in one of his rare, wryly humorous, veins. After a fugue development à la Weinberger, Bernal pushes forward to a frenetic climax. At the very end of the whole affair, the orchestral players are instructed to shout, "Viva Michoacán!"

In 1941 Bernal's *Noche en Morelia* ("Night in Morelia") added to his growing reputation as a composer. Chávez's playing of this "nightpiece" in an Orquesta Sinfónica de México concert provided an occasion for rapturous applause. On September 12, 1941, Bernal's opera, *Tata Vasco*, which dealt with the Vasco de Quiroga, first bishop of Michoacán, was premiered at Morelia; immediately there was agitation for its presentation at the Palacio de Bellas Artes in Mexico City. Plans for its presentation in the capital were at the last moment frustrated, however, since it was felt the opera might stir religious conflict. Unlike Verdi, who could change the locale of *Rigoletto* so as not to offend the Austrians, Bernal could not change the locale of *Tata Vasco*. The presentation of *Noche en Morelia* soon after the *Tata Vasco* incident showed, however, that Chávez was friendly enough to Bernal's non-religious music.

Bernal's *Tata Vasco*, despite the difference in religious tradition from which it springs, shows certain striking similarities to another religious opera of our time, Vaughan Williams's *The Pilgrim's Progress*, first presented in 1951. Both are essentially pageants; in both great crowds of people are handled with the result that choral singing plays a dominant role. The plot interest in both lags, possibly because mundane interests such as the love of man and woman, or the desire to achieve power, are eliminated. The principal characters seem more symbolic than actual in both: the bishop, shown as a great friend and protector of the Indians, seems superpersonal because of his virtue; the pilgrim because exclusively concerned with spiritual interests seems also to live always in a transcendent world.

In both, musical fragments several centuries old are blended with the composers' own material. Vaughan Williams used the hymn tune, "York," and Bernal fragments of Gregorian chant for analogous purposes. The extraneous fragments Vaughan Williams used were, however, better integrated into the total score than were those Bernal used. The eclecticism of the latter's style offends many who have heard his opera, though others consider it dramatically justifiable. The Tarascans sing neo-Indian melodies, the clergy Gregorian chant, and the conquistadores *romances*. Even if the music sounds "pasted together," the close juxtaposition of opposed styles must be admitted a useful means of inducing tension in an otherwise static score.

Bernal's ballet, *Tingambato*, also with a religious theme, was presented at the Palacio de Bellas Artes in August, 1943. The ballet-plot has to do with the Virgin's displeasure at the constant internecine warfare of the Spanish conquering population during the seventeenth century.

Bernal does not see "Indianism" as Mexico's only musical salvation. In a 1941 article he asked rhetorically: "Must we elevate to a dogma everything done by indigenous and mestizo music?" [14] He went on to say that popular art, simply because intuitive, was not therefore beyond improvement. At heart he would seem to favor the Pedro de Gante approach to the Indian, the attitude of *noblesse oblige*.

During the 1945–6 season he toured the United States as organist. In June, 1948, *Tata Vasco* reduced to oratorio form was presented at Madrid during a visit sponsored by the Franco regime.[15] The Spanish Orquesta Nacional played several of his pieces during the same month. The Spanish newspapers gave him much favorable publicity, and though his visit was not comparable with that of Revueltas's 1937–8 visit in a political sense, it nevertheless could be said that no Mexican since Revueltas had been so fêted in the Spanish capital.

SCHOLA CANTORUM; NUESTRA MÚSICA; MÉXICO EN EL ARTE

Bernal's services to musical scholarship include not only his reports on conservatories in eighteenth century Mexico and on orchestral music in his native Morelia, but also his editorship of the monthly magazine, *Schola Cantorum*. His intention in this monthly is twofold, practical and scholarly. He prints historical documents pertaining to sacred music in Hispanic America, and at the same time includes practical suggestions for present-day choirmasters throughout Latin America. Though some-what neglected in United States libraries, the magazine in nearly every issue contains at least one article of lasting worth.

Another music periodical which from time to time has included articles of extraordinary value is the quarterly published at Mexico City under Rodolfo Halffter's editorship entitled *Nuestra Música*. A typical issue of this latter magazine includes one article having to do with the history of music in Mexico, a second with music today in Mexico, a third having to do with music in another Latin American republic, and a fourth dealing with music in the United States or Europe. The editorial board includes Jesús Bal y Gay, Carlos Chávez, Blas Galindo, J. Pablo Moncayo, Adolfo Salazar, and Luis Sandi. *México en el Arte*, a periodical devoted to the several fine arts in Mexico (published by the Departamento de Bellas Artes), almost invariably includes one article on Mexican music. Both these latter magazines are handsomely produced.

OTHER COMPOSERS

The vitality of modern Mexican music is perhaps nowhere better illustrated than in the profusion of composers with sufficient merit to win mention in such reference manuals as Slonimsky's 1945 *Music of Latin America*.[16] And it is probably true that where one such composer as José F. Vásquez has engaged the attention of a visiting celebrity such as Stokowski, or Iturbi, or Slonimsky, ten other Mexican composers have failed to make such contacts, and therefore are not listed in any catalogue of names. Vásquez, for instance, showed his piano concerto to Iturbi, who wrote across the face of the score: "My impression of this work is a very favorable one; the balance between piano and orchestra seems especially well handled. I add my note of personal admiration for Mr. Vásquez." But others have not had the good fortune of personal contact with Iturbi.

The Fleisher Collection in the Free Public Library of Philadelphia contains thousands of pages of twentieth century Mexican orchestral works. Most of these were obtained in photographic reproduction by Slonimsky during his "fishing expedition" in Latin American musical waters. Lincoln Igou made this contemporary Mexican orchestral music in the Fleisher Collection the subject of his Ph. D. dissertation offered in 1946 to Northwestern University at Evanston with the title, "Contemporary Symphonic Activity in Mexico." Even after writing over 400 pages of analyses Dr. Igou did not, however, feel he had exhaustively investigated the Mexican scores in the Fleisher Collection. If after his lengthy coverage he did not exhaust the resources of the Fleisher Collection, which is at best a representative rather than a complete gathering of modern Mexican scores, he could not have treated the whole of the contemporary Mexican symphonic repertory without extending his dissertation to several volumes. That which he did investigate was of sufficient magnitude to convince him the modern Mexican repertory is one of the most considerable national repertories of our time.

POPULAR MUSIC IN MEXICO TODAY

The symphonic repertory because of its greater artistic pretension naturally attracts the attention of scholars. But the "commercial" music produced in Mexico today, though by its very nature ephemeral, deserves at least passing attention. Certainly today in Mexico the broad populace knows the music of Agustín Lara, Mexico's Irving Berlin, far better than the music of any symphonic composer thus far named in this chapter. Lara, born at Tlacotalpan in the state of Veracruz in 1900, has made tremendous sums of money from his commercial songs. He has been married to Mexico's Hedy Lamarr; he has drawn full houses night after night when he has left off radio work for awhile in order to act in plays; he has achieved renown throughout the entire Latin world with his records.

Alberto Domínguez's *Frenesí* ("Madness"), Consuelo Velásquez's *Bésame Mucho* ("Kiss Me a Lot"), and Lara's *Cada Noche un Amor* ("Love Every Night") have made their composers internationally famous, in the same sense that Hoagy Carmichael (composer of "Stardust") is famous. Nothing peculiarly Mexican is to be encountered in these commercial songs. Cuban, Argentinian, and Brazilian rhythmic elements intermesh; the cosmopolitan musical atmosphere guarantees these "hits" wider audiences than the mere Republic of Mexico could ever provide Lara, Domínguez, Prado, or Velásquez.[17] The words are often extremely suggestive, and love, kisses, the moon above, flowers, and love again, are the topics treated. The music adheres to the basic tonic-dominant patterns, and the melodies are rarely individualized.

FOREIGN CONTRIBUTORS TO MEXICAN MUSICAL LIFE

Just as the various waves of European unrest have brought to the United States certain distinguished scholars and composers during recent years, so waves of unrest in Europe have brought notable musical personalities to Mexico. Chiefly these immigrants in Mexico have come from Spain. At various stages in our recital of events we have mentioned Jesús Bal y Gay; Bal y Gay through the intermediacy of Professor J. B. Trend at Cambridge University made certain English connections before coming to Mexico. He is a composer, musicologist, and music critic. His *Serenade for Strings*, published by Ediciones Mexicanas, has frequently been played by the Orquesta Sinfónica de México. His own music, like his scholarly writing, is formally impeccable. His melodic lines are always beautifully contrived, and though never lush his string writing is always smoothly sonorous. Arthur Foote's *Suite for Strings in E* and Bal y Gay's *Serenade* are compositions with similar virtues.

Rodolfo Halffter, not perhaps as well known in Spain as was his brother, Ernesto, nevertheless occupied a position in the forefront of Spanish life. He has been editor of the Ediciones Mexicanas de Música, editor-in-chief of *Nuestra Música*, and yet has found time to continue an active career as composer since arriving in Mexico. Adolfo Salazar, one of the most distinguished music historians of our epoch, has been music critic for *Novedades*, a daily, and has continued a fecund scholar during his Mexican residency.

The proportion of foreigners contributing to Mexican music life is distinctly smaller than the proportion contributing to United States music life. Each person who has come to Mexico has been handled as an individual, and the guiding principle has been: no one shall be invited whose presence here will displace a Mexican. Persons who have come have uniformly been expected to cooperate rather than dominate, and immigrants without prior knowledge of the language have been rigorously excluded.

OUTLOOK FOR THE FUTURE

Despite the presence of a minute number of immigrant musicians, it is nevertheless obvious that the achievements of the century have been the doing not of these immigrants but of the Mexicans themselves. With a population vastly inferior in numbers to that of the United States— something less than a sixth—Mexican creative accomplishment has yet kept pace with that of her more populous northern neighbor. If during our generation she cannot boast of Stravinsky, Schoenberg, and Hindemith as new-found "Mexicans," at least her indigenous school can at every point be compared favorably with the American indigenous school. Her achievement of the immediate past is, moreover, the best guaranty of her continued progress.

CONCLUSION

Mexico is a land with a dynamic, living music. But the reconstruction of the past makes it ever clearer that Mexico not only now, but through the long sweep of four centuries has been a country whose total musical contribution places her in the forefront of Western Hemisphere republics. As more and more documents bearing on Mexico's musical history come to light, her neighbors on either side can confidently anticipate ever securer reason to congratulate her on the achievement of the past, as well as the promise of the future.

NOTES

1. Porfirio Díaz, from whose first name the adjective Porfirian is taken, ruled Mexico from 1876–1911. Nominally he was president.
2. *La Légende de Rudel: Poème lyrique en trois parties*, Op. 27 (Leipzig: Friedrich Hofmeister, 1906), was Castro's second opera, the first having been *Atzimba: Drama lírico en tres Actos* (México: Nagel, Sucs., 1900). The Mexican press notices for *La Légende* were not uniformly favorable. In Campa's opinion (*Críticas Musicales*, pp. 311–2) it was, however, Castro's best work. "I do not know another Mexican lyric work so replete with poetic sentiment, depth of feeling, so competently written, and so continuously inspired," Campa asserted.
3. Gustavo E. Campa, *op. cit.*, pp. 170–4.
4. Manuel M. Ponce, *Nuevos Escritos Musicales* (México: Editorial Stylo, 1948), p. 25.
5. A complete Chávez bibliography was published by the Pan American Union (Music Series, No. 10) in 1944: *Carlos Chávez: Catalog of his Works, with a Preface by Herbert Weinstock*. In dealing with Chávez's career we have had recourse to certain supplementary materials such as Otto Mayer-Serra's "Carlos Chávez: Una Monografía Crítica," *Revista Musical Mexicana* I (1942), 5 ff., 35 ff., 61 ff., and 75 ff.

A classified catalogue of Chávez's composition will be found in the 1944 Pan American Union brochure, pp. 1–10. To this 1944 list may be added the following compositions:

DATE	TITLE	MEDIUM	PUBLISHER OR MS	PLACE AND DATE OF PUBLICATION
1943	Concerto de Vivaldi en Sol menor	Orchestra	MS	
1943–4	Cuarteto Doble, Ballet for "The Daughter of Colchis"	Wind and String Quartet	MS	
1943–4	Third String Quartet	String Quartet	MS	
1946	Canto a la Tierra	Chorus and Piano	Ediciones Mexicanas de Música	México 1946
1947	Suite: "La Hija de Cólquide"	Orchestra	Ediciones Mexicanas de Música	México 1951
1947	Toccata for Orchestra	Orchestra	MS	
1948	Fuga	Piano	MS	
1949	Homenaje a Chopin (Etude)	Piano	Ediciones Mexicanas de Música	México 1949
1948–50	Concerto for Violin and Orchestra	Violin and Orchestra	MS	
1950	Homenaje a Chopin (Three additional Etudes)	Piano	MS	

6. For a bibliography of Revueltas's works and for additional musical analysis of his style see O. Mayer-Serra, "Silvestre Revueltas and Musical Nationalism in Mexico," *Musical Quarterly*, April, 1941.

7. Nicolas Slonimsky in *Music of Latin America* (New York: Thomas Y. Crowell, 1945), p. 249, says the title means that eight performers are required for rendition of it. Both interpretations of the title have been advanced, but in neither case is the significance of the title profound.

8. A. Copland, "Mexican Composer," *New York Times*, May 9, 1937.

9. For complete biography see Blas Galindo, "C. Huízar," *Nuestra Música*, May, 1946 (bibliography of his works appears on p. 64).

10. For further biographical details see Francisco Agea, "Blas Galindo," *México en el Arte*, November, 1948 (bibliography of his works on last four unnumbered pages).

11. For a detailed study see B. Galindo, "Compositores de mi Generación," *Nuestra Música*, April, 1948.

12. Complete text of libretto in *México en el Arte*, August, 1948. The significance of *La Mulata* is discussed in Luis Herrera de la Fuente, "La Ópera de Bellas Artes," *México en el Arte*, September, 1948.

13. For a more extended survey of Sandi's works see C. Chávez, "Luis Sandi," *Nuestra Música*, July, 1949.

14. O. Mayer-Serra, "Tata Vasco," *Commonweal*, September 12, 1941, p. 487.

15. *Schola Cantorum* (Morelia, Michoacán), June, 1948, p. 90.

16. Slonimsky in his chapter, "Mexico," *op. cit.*, listed twenty-eight contemporary Mexican composers whom he thought worthy of biographical treatment. Of those he listed but whose works we have not selected for extended analysis the following three are perhaps the most important:

Eduardo Hernández Moncada (1899—), conductor and composer; Carlos Jiménez Mabarak (*c.* 1912—), pianist and composer; and José Rolón (1883–1945), symphonic composer.

The names of the nine others listed in his book were Rafael Adame (1906—), Alfonso de Elias (1902—), Juan B. Fuentes (1869—), Juan León Mariscal (1899—), Mejía Estanislao (1882—), Miguel C. Meza (1903—), Pedro Michaca (1897—), Arnulfo Miramontes (1882—), and José Pomar (1880—). Time has yet to prove the worth of all Slonimsky listed, but at least their profusion is a happy augury. Since his survey other new talents have appeared in Mexico, among them José Yves Limantour, brilliant organizer and conductor of the Jalapa orchestra, and Jesús Ferrer, promising young composer.

The new composer who excited perhaps the most attention during 1952 was Luis Herrera de la Fuente, a talent who, like Chávez, combines rare conducting ability with true creative instinct. After visiting Mexico in the autumn of 1952, Luigi Dallapiccola, famous Italian composer, stated that the number of promising creative talents in Mexico today exceeds that in most European nations which he has visited.

17. O. Mayer-Serra, *El Estado Presente de la Musica en Mexico* (Washington: Pan American Union, 1946), p. 22.

BIBLIOGRAPHY

Since information on music in Mexico is at present widely dispersed, it has seemed useful to list below certain sources which contain only passing references to music. We have chosen to list such works because we have ourselves repeatedly quarried rich metal from books and articles which at first glance seemed highly unlikely ground over which to prospect.

Gilbert Chase in the section on "Mexico," pp. 157–201, of his *A Guide to Latin American Music* (Washington: U.S. Government Printing Office, 1945) amassed almost six hundred titles of articles and books dealing with music in Mexico. His bibliography included titles of works in Spanish, English, French, German, and Portuguese; the usefulness of his list was further enhanced by the brief annotations he supplied. Because of the easy availability of his list, we have chosen not to duplicate it, except insofar as it contains titles of works which have been found positively helpful in the writing of our own book. But we have listed a large number of titles not given in his bibliography. Our additions fall within the two following classes: works published since 1945; or works with unpromising titles which Chase did not examine, but which have proved unexpectedly useful. Nearly all titles in our bibliography represent works from which we have actually quoted either in our text or notes.

Titles of musical compositions have been excluded. In 1947 the Conservatorio Nacional at Mexico City issued a 35-page checklist of Mexican compositions shelved in its library. It has been found impracticable to reprint that list here, but the conservatory librarian is prepared to supply it upon payment of a fee. Additional lists of Mexican compositions may be obtained from the following representative music publishers: A. Wagner y Levien Sucs., and Ediciones Mexicanas de Música, both of México, D.F.

Abreu Gómez, E. *Sor Juana Inés de la Cruz: Bibliografía y Biblioteca* (México: Monografías Bibliográficas, 1934).

Acosta, José de. *Historia Natural y Moral de las Indias* (Seville: Imp. en casa de Iuan de Leon, 1590). Reprinted by The Hakluyt Society, 1880, in English translation.

Agea, Francisco. "Blas Galindo," *México en el Arte*, November, 1948.

―――. *Orquesta Sinfónica de México: Notas*, 1936 (I, V), 1937 (II, VII, X, XI), 1938 (VI), 1939 (V, X), 1942 (III, IV, V, VII, VIII, IX, XII, XIII).

Aguirre Beltrán, Gonzales. "The Slave Trade in Mexico," *Hispanic American Historical Review*, August, 1944.

Alcázar Molina, Cayetano. *Los Virreinatos en el Siglo XVIII* (Barcelona-Buenos Aires: Salvat editores, s.a., 1945).

Altamirano, Ignacio. *Discursos de Ignacio M. Altamirano (1834–93)* (México: Secretaría de Educación Pública, 1934).

―――. "D. Melesio Morales," *Revista Musical Mexicana*, Jan. 7, Feb. 7, Mar. 7, and May 7, 1943.

Andrade, Vicente de P. *Ensayo bibliográfico mexicano del siglo XVII* (México: Imp. del Museo Nacional, 1899).

Anglés, Higinio. *La Música en la Corte de Carlos V* (Barcelona: Instituto Español de Musicología, 1944).

―――. *La Música Española* . . . (Barcelona: Biblioteca Central, 1941).

Arco y Garay, Ricardo del. *La Sociedad Española en las Obras Dramáticas de Lope de Vega* (Madrid: Escelicer, s.l., 1942).

Ayesterán, Lauro. *Zipoli, el gran compositor y organista romano del 1700 en el Rio de La Plata* (Montevideo: Imp. Uruguaya, s.a., 1941).

Baker, Theodor. *Über die Musik der Nordamerikanischen Wilden* (Leipzig: Breitkopf und Härtel, 1882).

Baqueiro Fóster, Gerónimo. "Aportación musical de México para la formación de la biblioteca americana de Caracas, 1882–1883," *Revista Musical Mexicana*, July 21, 1942.

―――. "El secreto armónico y modal de un antiguo aire maya," *Revista Musical Mexicana*, January 7, 1942.

―――. "Hernández Moncada, el compositor," *Revista Musical Mexicana*, August 21, 1942.

―――. "El Huapango," *Revista Musical Mexicana*, April 21, 1942.

Barrio Lorenzot, Juan Francisco del. *Ordenanzas de gremios de la Nueva España* (México: Dirección de Talleres Gráficos, 1920).

Barwick, Steven. "Sacred Vocal Polyphony in Early Colonial Mexico," *Harvard University Ph.D. Diss.*, 1949.

Basalenque, Diego. *Historia de la provincia . . . de Michoacán, del orden de N.P.S. Agustín* (México: Tip. Barbedillo y comp., 1886).

Bautista Plaza, Juan. "Music in Caracas during the Colonial Period," *Musical Quarterly*, April, 1943.

Beristaín y Souza, José Mariano. *Biblioteca Hispano Americana Setentrional* (Amecameca: Colegio Católico, 1883).

Bermúdez Plata, Cristóbal (ed.). *Catálogo de Pasajeros a Indias . . .* (Seville: Imp. de la Gavidia, 1946).

Bermudo, Juan. *Declaración de instrumentos* (Osuna, Juan de Leon, 1555).

―――. *El arte tripharia* (Osuna, Juan de Leon, 1550).

Bernal Jiménez, Miguel. *El archivo musical del Colegio de Santa Rosa de Santa María de Valladolid siglo XVIII, Morelia Colonial* (Morelia: Ediciones de la Universidad Michoacana de San Nicolás, 1939).

———. "La Música en Valladolid de Michoacán" *Nuestra Música,* 3er Trimestre, 1951.

Berrien, William. "Latin American Music," *Concerning Latin American Culture* (New York: Columbia University Press, 1940).

Blankenburg Angela. "German Missionary Writers in Paraguay," *Mid-America* (Chicago), January, 1947.

Blumenfeld, Harold (trans.). *Michael Praetorius: Syntagma Musicum, Vol. II* (New Haven, 1949).

Bonniwell, William R. *A History of the Dominican Liturgy 1215–1945* (New York: Joseph F. Wagner, 1945).

Boturini Benaduci, Lorenzo. *Idea de una nueva Historia General de la America Septentrional* (Madrid: Imp. de J. de Zuñiga, 1746).

Bowles, Paul. "On Mexico's Popular Music," *Modern Music*, May–June, 1941.

Braden, Charles S. *Religious Aspects of the Conquest of Mexico* (Durham: Duke University Press, 1930).

Brasseur de Bourbourg, Charles Étienne. *Histoire des nations civilisées du Mexique et de l'Amérique-centrale* (Paris: Arthur Bertrand, 1857).

Bretón Fontecilla, Cecilia. "Una obra musical de Fray Juan Navarro," *Schola Cantorum*, August, 1942.

Brinton, Daniel G. *Ancient Nahuatl Poetry* (Philadelphia, 1887).

———. *The Güegüence, A Comedy-Ballet* (Philadelphia, 1883).

Bullock, William. *Six Months' Residence and Travels in Mexico* (London: J. Murray, 1824).

Burgoa, Francisco de. *Geográphica Descripción de la Parte Septentrional, del Polo Artico de la América* (México: Publicaciones del Archivo General de la Nación, 1934).

Calderón de la Barca, Frances Erskine. *Life in Mexico during a residence of two years in that country* (New York: E. P. Dutton, 1931).

Campa, Arthur L. *Spanish Folk-Poetry in New Mexico* (Albuquerque: University of New Mexico Press, 1946).

Campa, Gustavo E. *Críticas Musicales* (Paris: Librería Paul Ollendorff, 1911).

Campos, Rubén M. *El folklore musical de las ciudades* (México: Secretaría de Educación Pública, 1930).

———. *El folklore y la música mexicana* (México: Secretaría de Educación Pública, 1928).

Carpentier, Alejo. *La música en Cuba* (México: Fondo de Cultura Económica, 1946).

Carrillo, Julián. *Pláticas musicales* (México, 1923).

———. *Teoría lógica de la música* (México: E. Pardo e hijos, 1938).

Castañeda, Daniel. "La música y la revolución mexicana," *Boletin Latino-Americano de Música*, October, 1941.

Castañeda, Daniel. "Una flauta de la cultura tarasca," *Revista Musical Mexicana*, March 7, 1942.

Castañeda, Daniel and Mendoza, Vicente T. "Los Teponaztlis . . . ," "Los Percutores Precortesianos," "Los Huehuetls," *Anales del Museo Nacional de Arqueología, Historia y Etnografía, cuarta época, VIII* (1933).

——. *Instrumental precortesiano: Instrumentos de percusión* (México: Imp. del Museo Nacional, 1933).

Castillo Ledón, Luís. "Los mexicanos autores de óperas," *Anales del Museo Nacional de Arqueología, Historia y Etnología*, November, 1910–January, 1911.

Cervantes de Salazar, Francisco. *Crónica de la Nueva España (1560)* (Madrid: Hauser y Menet, 1914).

——. *México en 1554* (México: Universidad Nacional Autónoma, 1939).

——. *Tumulo Imperial dela grand ciudad de México* (México: Antonio de Espinosa, 1560).

Chase, Gilbert. *A Guide to Latin American Music* (Washington: U.S. Govt. Printing Off., 1945).

——. *The Music of Spain* (New York: W. W. Norton, 1941).

——. "Origins of the Lyric Theater in Spain," *Musical Quarterly*, July, 1939.

Chávez, Carlos. "La Música," *México y la Cultura* (México: Secretaría de Educación Pública, 1946).

——. "The Music of Mexico," *American Composers on American Music*, ed. Henry Cowell (Stanford, 1933).

——. "Luís Sandi," *Nuestra Música*, July, 1949.

——. *Toward a New Music: Music and Electricity* (New York: W. W. Norton, 1937).

Chávez, Ezequiel A. *El primero de los grandes educadores de la América* (México: Editorial Jus, 1943).

Ciudad-Real, Antonio de. *Relación breve y verdadera de algunas cosas . . .* (Madrid: Coll. Doc. Ined. Hist. de España, 1872–3).

Clavijero, Francisco. *Storia antica del Messico* (Cesena: G. Biasini, 1780–1).

Colegiata de Guadalupe. *Directorio para el gobierno de los ministros de orquesta aprobado y mandado observar por el muy ilustre cabildo de este insigne Colegiata de S. M. de Guadalupe* (México: Grabado de la Guadalupana, 1835).

Collet, Henri. *Le Mysticisme Musical Espagnol* (Paris: Librairie Félix Alcan, 1913).

Copland, Aaron. "Mexican Composer," *New York Times*, May 9, 1937.

——. "Composer from Mexico: Carlos Chávez," *Our New Music* (New York: Whittlesey House, 1941).

Cresson, H. T. "Aztec Music," *Proceedings of the Academy of Natural Sciences of Philadelphia, 1883* (1884).

Cuevas, Mariano. *Documentos Inéditos del Siglo XVI* (México: Talleres Gráficos del Museo Nacional de Arqueología . . . , 1914).

——. *Historia de la Iglesia en México* (El Paso, Texas: Editorial "Revista Católica," 1928).

Densmore, Frances. *Papago Music* (Washington: U.S. Govt. Print. Off., 1929).

——. *Yuman and Yaqui Music* (Washington: U.S. Govt. Print. Off., 1932).

Diario de México. Oct. 24, Oct. 25, Nov. 25, Dec. 2, 1805; Nov. 18, Dec. 16, 1806; Oct. 24, 1807; July 3, 1809; Apr. 14, 1816.

Díaz del Castillo, Bernal. *Historia verdadera de la conquista de la Nueva-España* (Madrid: Imp. del Reyno, 1632). Issued by The Hakluyt Society in English translation (Maudslay), 1908–16.

Durán, Diego. *Historia de las Indias de Nueva España* (México: Imp. de J. M. Andrade y I. Escalante, 1867–80).

Elízaga, José Mariano. *Elementos de Música* (México: Imp. del Supremo Gobierno en Palacio, 1823).

——. *Principios de la Armonia y de la Melodía* (México, 1835).

Escobar, José Ignacio P. *Historia de la música en Columbia* (Bogotá: Biblioteca Popular, 1945).

Eslava, Hilarion. *Música Religiosa en España* (Madrid, 1860).

Esteva, Guillermo A. *La música Oaxaqueña* (Oaxaca: Talleres tipográficos del Gobierno, 1931).

Estrada, Jesús. "Clásicos de Neuva España: Ensayo histórico sobre los Maestros de Capilla de la Catedral de México," *Schola Cantorum,* June, July, 1945.

Eximeno, Antonio. *Duda de D. Antonio Eximeno sobre el Ensayo fundamental practico de contrapunto del M. R. P. M. Fr. Juan Bautista Martini* (Madrid: Imp. Real, 1797).

Fernández de Oviedo y Valdés, Gonzalo. *Historia General y Natural de las Indias* (Madrid: Imp. de la Real Academia de la Historia, 1851–5).

Florimo, Francesco. *La Scuola Musicale di Napoli e i suoi Conservatorii* (Naples: Vinc. Morano, 1881).

Foster, E. A. *Motolinia's History of the Indians of New Spain* (Berkeley: The Cortés Society, 1950).

Furlong, Guillermo. *Músicos Argentinos* (Buenos Aires: Editorial Huarpes, 1945).

Gaceta Extraordinaria del Gobierno de México. November 4, 1817.

Galindo, Blas. "C. Huízar," *Nuestra Música,* May, 1946.

——. "Compositores de mi Generación," *Nuestra Música,* April, 1948.

Galindo, Miguel. *Nociones de Historia de la Música Mejicana I* (Colima: Tip. de "El Dragón," 1933).

Galindo y Villa, Jesús. "El Himno Nacional Mexicano," *Anales del Museo Nacional de Arqueología, Historia y Etnografía,* 1927.

Gallop, Rodney. "The Music of Indian Mexico," *Musical Quarterly,* April, 1937.

——. "Otomí Indian Music from Mexico," *Musical Quarterly,* January, 1940.

Galpin, F. W. "Aztec Influence on American Indian Instruments," *Sammelbände der internationalen Musikgesellschaft* (Leipzig, 1903).

García, Genaro. *El Clero de México durante la dominación española* (México: Doc. Inéd. ó muy Raros, 1907).

García Cubas, Antonio. *El Libro de Mis Recuerdos* (México: Imp. Manuel León Sánchez, 1934).

——. *Escritos Diversos del 1870 a 1874* (México: I. Escalante, 1874).

García Icazbalceta, Joaquín. *Bibliografía Mexicana del Siglo XVI* (México: Librería de Andrade, 1886).

——. *Colección de Documentos para la Historia de México*, Vol. I (México: Librería de J. M. Andrade, 1858).

——. *Don fray Juan de Zumárraga* (México: Andrade y Morales, 1881).

——. *Nueva Colección de Documentos para la Historia de México*, Vol. II (México: Imp. de Francisco Díaz de León, 1889).

——. *Obras*, Vol. III (México: Imp. de V. Agüeros, 1896).

Gazeta de México. Sept. 12, 1786; July 2, 1793; Oct. 21, 1796.

Génin, Auguste. "Notes on the Dances, Music, and Songs of the Ancient and Modern Mexicans," *Annual Report of The Smithsonian Institute*, 1920.

González Obregón, Luís. *Croniquillas de la Nueva España* (México: Ed. Botas, 1936).

——. *México Viejo y Anecdótico* (México: Vda. de C. Bouret, 1909).

——. *La Vida de México en 1810* (Paris-México: C. Bouret, 1911).

Green, Samuel A. *A Second Supplementary List of Early American Imprints* (Cambridge, Mass.: University Press, 1899).

Hamilton, Mary Neal. *Music in Eighteenth Century Spain* (Urbana: University of Illinois Press, 1937).

Hannas, Ruth. "Cerone's Approach to the Teaching of Counterpoint," *Papers of the American Musicological Society*, 1937.

Herrera y Ogazón, Alba. *El Arte Musical en México* (México: Dirección General de las Bellas Artes, 1917).

Herrera y Tordesillas, Antonio de. *Historia general de los hechos de los Castellanos en las islas i tierra firma del mar oceano* (Madrid: Imp. real, 1726).

Herring, Hubert and Weinstock, Herbert. *Renascent Mexico* (New York: Covici-Friede, 1935).

Hewes, Harry L. "The Mexican Ballet-Symphony 'H.P.'," *Bulletin of the Pan American Union*, June, 1932.

Igou, Lincoln. "Current Symphonic Activity in Mexico," *Northwestern Univ. Ph.D. Diss.*, 1946.

Iguíniz, Juan B. "La Biblioteca Palafoxiana de Puebla," *Anales del Museo Nacional de Arqueología, Historia y Etnología*, 1913.

Illing, Carl Heinz. *Zur Technik der Magnificat-Komposition des 16. Jahrhunderts* (Wolfenbüttel: Georg Kallmeyer Verlag, 1936).

Isla, Ezequiel de la. "El Padre J. Guadalupe Velázquez," *Revista Musical Mexicana*, February 21, 1942.

Juana Inés de la Cruz, Sor. *Poemas de la Unica Poetisa Americana, Musa Dezima* (Madrid: Juan García Infançon, 1690).

Kastner, Santiago (ed.). *Francisco Correa de Arauxo: Libro de tientos . . .* (Barcelona: Instituto Español de Musicología, 1948).

Kelemen, Pál. "Church Organs in Colonial Mexico," *Bulletin of the Pan American Union*, March, 1942.

Kollmann, J. "Flöten und pfeifen aus Alt-Mexiko," *Festschrift für Adolf Bastien* (Berlin: D. Reimer, 1896).

Lach, Robert. "Die musikalischen konstruktionsprinzipien der altmexikanischen tempelgesänge," *Festschrift für Johannes Wolf* (Berlin, 1929).

Landa, Diego de. *Relación de las cosas de Yucatán* (México: Editorial P. Robredo, 1938).

León, Nicolás. *Bibliografía Mexicana del Siglo XVIII* (México: Imp. de F. Díaz de León, 1902–8).

Leonard, Irving A. *Don Carlos de Sigüenza y Góngora: A Mexican Savant of the Seventeenth Century* (Berkeley: University of California Press, 1929).

————. "On the Mexican Book Trade, 1683," *Hispanic American Historical Review*, August, 1947.

López de Elizalde, Mariano. *Tratado de Música y Lecciones de Clave* (Guadalajara, 1821).

López de Gómara, Francisco. *Historia de México, con el descubrimiento dela Nueva España* (Antwerp: Juan Steelsio, 1554). Various modern reprints.

Lorenzana, Francisco Antonio. *Concilium Mexicanum Provinciale* (México: Typ. Josephi Antonii de Hogal, 1770).

————. *Missa Gothica seu Mozarabica et Officium itidem Gothicum* (Puebla: Typis Seminarii Palafoxiani, 1770).

Lumholtz, Carl. *Unknown Mexico* (New York: Charles Scribner's Sons, 1902).

Maldeghem, R. J. van. *Trésor Musical* (Brussels: C. Muquardt, 1893).

Marino, Gio. Battista. *L'Adone* (Turin: G. B. Paravia & Co., 1922).

Martens, Frederick H. "Music in the Life of the Aztecs," *Musical Quarterly*, July, 1928.

Mayer-Serra, Otto. "Carlos Chávez: Una Monografía Crítica," *Revista Musical Mexicana*, Jan. 7, Jan. 21, Feb. 7, and Feb. 21, 1942.

————. *El Estado Presente de La Música en México* (Washington: Pan American Union, 1946).

————. *Música y Músicos de Latino-América* (México: Editorial Atlante, s.a., 1947).

————. *Panorama de la Música Mexicana desde la independencia hasta la actualidad* (México: El Colegio de México, 1941).

————. "Silvestre Revueltas and Musical Nationalism in Mexico," *Musical Quarterly*, April, 1941.

————. "Tata Vasco," *Commonweal*, September 12, 1941.

Medina, José Toribio. *La Imprenta en Puebla* (Santiago de Chile: Imp. Cervantes, 1908).

————. *Biblioteca hispano-americana* (Santiago de Chile: 1898–1907).

Méndez Plancarte, Gabriel. *Poetas Novohispanos: Segundo Siglo, Parte Segunda* (México: Universidad Nacional Autónoma, 1945).

Mendieta, Gerónimo de. *Historia Eclesiástica Indiana* (México: Antigua Librería, 1870).

Mendoza, Vicente T. *El Romance Español y El Corrido Mexicana* (México: Eds. de la Universidad Nacional Autónoma, 1939).

————. "Música Precolombina de América," *Boletín Latino-Americano de Música*, 1938.

Mendoza, Vicente T. "Música Indigena de México," *México en el Arte, IX,* 1950.

Merklin, Albert. *Aus Spaniens altem Orgelbau* (Mainz: Rheingold-Verlag, 1939).

México. *Archivo General de la Nación.* "Conspiración de Valladolid de 1813," *Boletín del Archivo General de la Nación,* July–August–September, 1932.

————. "Solicitud para la reapertura del Colegio de Santiago Tlatelolco," *Boletín del Archivo General,* Jan.–Feb., 1935.

————. *Libros y Libreros en el Siglo XVI* (México: Publicaciones del Archivo General de la Nación, 1914).

————. *Arzobispado.* "Carta Pastoral: Música Sagrada," *Schola Cantorum,* June, 1945.

————. *Constituciones del arçobispado . . . de Tenuxtitlan Mexico* (México: Juan Pablos, 1556).

————. *Conservatorio Nacional.* "Obras de Compositores Mexicanos que se guardan en el Conservatorio Nacional de Música: Inventario hecho en 1947 por la sección de investigaciones musicales del Instituto Nacional de Bellas Artes." Typewritten list.

————. *Departamento de Bellas Artes. La Catedral y el Sagrario de México* (México: Departamento Editorial de la Dirección General de las Bellas Artes, 1917).

Michaca, Pedro. *El nacionalismo musical mexicano* (México: Universidad Nacional de México, 1931).

Mitjana y Gordón, Rafael. *Estudios sobre algunos músicos españoles* (Madrid: Sucs. de Hernando, 1918).

————. *Francisco Guerrero (1528–1599)* (Madrid: Talleres poligráficos, 1922).

Molina, Alonso de. *Vocabulario en lengua castellana y mexicana* (México: Antonio de Spinosa, 1571).

Molina Solís, J. F. *Historia del descubrimiento y conquista de Yucatán* (Mérida: Imp. R. Caballero, 1896).

Montanos, Francisco de. *Arte de canto llano* (Zaragoza, I. de Ibar, 1670).

Montejano y Aguíñaga, Rafael. "La conversión de los indios por medio de la música," *Schola Cantorum,* September, 1947.

Montes de Oca, José G. "Retratos Existentes en la Biblioteca Pública de la Ciudad de Guadalajara," 1924. Typewritten essay deposited at the Biblioteca Benjamin Franklin, México, D.F.

Montúfar, Alonso de. "Carta del Arzobispo de México al Consejo de Indios," *Anales del Museo Nacional de Arqueología, Historia y Etnografía,* 1934.

Morales, Melesio. *Reseña que leyo a sus amigos en la celebración de sus bodas de oro y del cuadragesimo aniversario de la fundación del conservatorio de música* (México, 1907).

Morley, Sylvanus G. *The Ancient Maya* (Stanford: Stanford University Press, 1946).

Motolinía, Toribio de. *Memoriales* (Mejico: García Pimentel, 1903).

Muñoz Camargo, Diego. *Historia de Tlaxcala* (México: Oficina tip. de la Secretaría de fomento, 1892).

Navarro, Juan. *Liber in quo Quatuor Passiones Christi Domini continentur* (México: Didacus López Davalos, 1604).

Olavarría y Ferrari, Enrique de. *Reseña Histórica del Teatro en México* (México: Imp. "La Europea," 1895).

Palafox y Mendoza, Juan de. *Reglas, y ordenanzas del choro de esta santa Iglesia Catedral de la Puebla de los Angeles (1648)* (Puebla: Joseph Pérez, 1711).

Pan American Union. *Carlos Chávez: Catalog of his Works, with a Preface by Herbert Weinstock* (Washington, 1944).

Pedrell, Felipe. *P. Antonio Eximeno* (Madrid: Unión Musical Española, 1920).

Peers, E. Allison. *A Critical Anthology of Spanish Verse* (University of California Press, 1949).

Peñafiel, Antonio (ed.). Cantares en Idioma Mexicano (México: Secretaría de Fomento, 1899).

Philadelphia, Pennsylvania. *The Edwin A. Fleisher Collection of Orchestral Music in the Free Library of Philadelphia: A Descriptive Catalogue*, Vol. II (Philadelphia, 1945).

Ponce, Manuel M. "El folklore musical mexicano," *Revista Musical de México*, September 15, 1919.

———. "La canción mexicana," *Revista de Revistas*, December 21, 1913.

———. "Nuestros Músicos: Gustavo E. Campa," *México Musical*, March, 1932.

———. *Nuevos Escritos Musicales* (México: Editorial Stylo, 1948).

Pope, Isabel. "Documentos Relacionados con la Historia de la Música en México," *Nuestra Música*, 1er Trimestre, 1951.

———. "The Musical Development and Form of the Spanish Villancico," *Papers of the American Musicological Society* (1940).

Preuss, Konrad Theodor. *Die Nayarit-expedition* (Leipzig: B. G. Teubner, 1912).

Prieto, Guillermo. *Memorias de Mis Tiempos* (México, Librería . . . C. Bouret, 1906).

Puebla Cathedral, Puebla, Pue. *Compendio de las Reglas esenciales del Arte del Canto llano para instrucción de los infantes del Coro de la Santa Iglesia Cathedral de la Puebla de los Angeles* (México: Imp. del Gobierno Imperial, 1822).

Ray, Alice. "Mexico City Addresses for Music Information, 1949." Typewritten list deposited at Biblioteca B. Franklin, México, D.F.

Redfield, Robert. *Tepoztlán, a Mexican village; a study of folklife* (Chicago: University of Chicago Press, 1930).

Revilla, Manuel G. "Cenobio Paniagua," *Revista Musical Mexicana*, Oct. 21, Nov. 7, Nov. 21, Dec. 7, Dec. 21, 1942.

———. "D. Julio Ituarte," *Revista Musical Mexicana*, Aug. 21, Sept. 7, 1942.

Riaño, Juan F. *Critical and Bibliographical Notes on Early Spanish Music* (London: Bernard Quaritch, 1887).

Ricard, Robert. *La Conquête Spirituelle du Mexique* (Paris: Institut d'Ethnologie, 1933).

Rincón, Antonio del. *Arte Mexicana* (Mexico: Pedro Balli, 1595).

Rivera Cambas, H. *México: Leyendas y Costumbres* (México: Editorial Layac, 1945).

Robelo, Cecilio A. "Diccionario de Mitología Nahoa," *Anales de Museo Nacional*, Segunda epoca, 1905–8.

Rolón, José. "La música autóctona mexicana y la técnica moderna," *Música*, Aug. 15, 1930.

———."Organización musical de México," *Boletín Latino-Americano de Música*, April, 1937.

Romero, Jesús C. *Durango en la Evolución Musical de México* (México: Ediciones "Guión de América," 1949).

———. "Historia del Conservatorio," *Nuestra Música*, July, 1946.

———. *José Mariano Elízaga* (México: Ediciones del Palacio de Bellas Artes, 1934).

———. "La Ópera en México," *La Ópera en Yucatán* (México: Ediciones "Guión de América," 1947).

———. *Música Precortesiana* (México: Talleres Gráficos . . . Editorial Stylo, 1947).

Romero Flores, Jesús. *Iconografía Colonial* (Mexico: Museo Nacional, 1940).

Sachs, Curt. *World History of the Dance* (New York: W. W. Norton, 1937).

Sahagún, Bernardino de. *Historia General de las Cosas de Nueva España* (México: Imp. del ciudadano A. Valdés, 1829–30).

———. *Psalmodia Christiana . . . Ordenada en cantares ó Psalmos: paraque canten los Indios en los areytos, que hazen en las Iglesias* (México: Pedro Ocharte, 1583).

Salazar, Adolfo. "El Caso de Domenico Zipoli," *Nuestra Música*, May, 1946.

Saldívar, Gabriel. *Historia de la Música en México: Epocas Precortesiana y Colonial* (México: Editorial "Cultura," 1934).

———. *El Jarabe, baile popular mexicano* (México: Talleres gráficos de la nación, 1937).

Sánchez, Manuel. *Regla de N.P.S. Francisco y breve declaración de sus preceptos para su mejor observancia . . . y breve explicación del canto llano con advertencias* (México: Bernardo de Hogal, 1725).

Sartorius, Christian Carl. "Musikalische leichenfeier und tänze der Mexiko-Indianer," *Caecilia*, Vol. VIII (Mainz, 1828).

Saville, Marshall H. *The Wood-Carver's Art in Ancient Mexico* (New York: Museum of the American Indian, 1925).

———. "A primitive Maya musical instrument," *American Anthropologist*, Vol. X (1897).

Schmeckebier, Laurence E. *Modern Mexican Art* (Minneapolis: The University of Minnesota Press, 1939).

Sedano, Francisco. *Noticias de México desde el año 1756 . . . en 1800* (México, 1880).

Seeger, Charles (and others). "Music," *Handbook of Latin American Studies* (Cambridge: Harvard University Press, 1936—).

Seler, Eduard. *Collected Works: Englished under the editorial supervision of J. E. S. Thompson for the Peabody Museum* (Cambridge, Mass.: 1939).

Sigüenza y Góngora, Carlos de. *Glorias de Querétaro* (México: Vda. de B. Calderón, 1680).

Slonimsky, Nicolas. *Music of Latin America* (New York: Thomas Y. Crowell, 1945).

Sosa, Francisco. *Biografías de mexicanos distinguidos* (México: Ed. de la sección de fomento mexicano, 1884).

Spain. *Archivo de Indias. Colección de Documentos Inéditos . . . del Archivo de Indias*, Vol. XIII (Madrid, 1870).

Spain. *Ministerio de Fomento. Cartas de Indias* (Madrid: Ministerio de Fomento, 1877).

Spell, Lota M. "Music in the Cathedral of Mexico in the Sixteenth Century," *Hispanic American Historical Review*, August, 1945.

———. "Music and instruments of the Aztecs: the beginning of musical education in North America," *Papers and Proceedings of the Music Teachers' National Association*, 1926.

———. "The first teacher of European music in America," *Catholic Historical Review*, October, 1922.

———. "The First Music-Books Printed in America," *Musical Quarterly*, January, 1929.

Steck, Francis Borgia. *Motolinia's History of the Indians of New Spain* (Washington, D.C.: Academy of American Franciscan History, 1951).

Suárez de Peralta, Juan. *Noticias históricas de la Nueva España* (Madrid: Imp. de M. G. Hernández, 1878).

Tamariz de Carmona, Antonio. *Relación y descripción del Templo Real de la ciudad de la Puebla de los Angeles en la Nueva España, y su Catedral* (Puebla, 1649).

Toor, Frances. "Mexican Folk Dances," *Renascent Mexico* (New York: Covici-Friede, 1935).

Torquemada, Juan de. *Veinte i un libros rituales i Monarquía Indiana* (Madrid: N. Rodríguez Franco, 1723).

Tozzer, Alfred M. (ed.) *Landa's Relación de las Cosas de Yucatán* (Cambridge: The Peabody Museum, 1941).

Trend, J. B. *The Music of Spanish History to 1600* (Oxford, 1926).

Tschudi, J. J. von. *Travels in Peru during the years 1838–42* (New York: Wiley and Putnam, 1847).

Vaillant, George C. *Aztecs of Mexico* (Garden City: Doubleday, Doran & Co., 1941).

Valtón, Emilio. *Impresos Mexicanos del Siglo XVI* (*Incunables Americanos*) (México: Imp. Universitaria, 1935).

Vázquez Santa Ana, Higinio. *Historia de la Canción Mexicana* (México: Talleres gráficos de la nación, 1931).

Wagner, Henry R. *Nueva Bibliografía Mexicana del Siglo XVI* (México: Editorial Polis, 1940).

———. *The Rise of Fernando Cortés* (Berkeley: The Cortés Society, 1944).

Weinstock, Herbert. *Mexican Music* (New York: Museum of Modern Art, 1940).

Wilson, Charles M. "Open Sesame to the Maya," *Bulletin of the Pan American Union*, July, 1948.

Yurchenco, Henrietta. "Grabación de Música Indigena," *Nuestra Música*, May, 1946.

INDEX

Names and places are indexed. For a summary of topics see the table of contents.